# To Conserve a Legacy

American Art from Historically

Black Colleges and Universities

American Art from

Historically Black Colleges and

Universities

# To Conserve a Legacy

Richard J. Powell

Jock Reynolds

with an Introduction by

Kinshasha Holman Conwill

**Addison Gallery of American Art**
Phillips Academy, Andover, Massachusetts
and
**The Studio Museum in Harlem**
New York, New York

Distributed by
The MIT Press, Massachusetts Institute of Technology, Cambridge, Massachusetts

# A T & T

We at AT&T have long held that communication is the beginning of understanding. For more than a century, AT&T has concentrated on building a comprehensive telecommunications network, and has set great store by the creativity and diversity of our employees to imagine new solutions for changing communication needs. And since the 1940s, AT&T has supported artistic expression as one of the most profound forms of communication and has helped to bring a diverse array of contemporary artists to a wider public.

We are particularly pleased to play a role in supporting *To Conserve a Legacy: American Art from Historically Black Colleges and Universities.* The impressive exhibition is the most public piece of a multiyear initiative that has integrated scholarship, heritage, history, art conservation, and mentoring with the appreciation of important works of art, both familiar and rediscovered. The qualities of innovation, teamwork, respect for individuals, and the highest integrity characterize the *Legacy* project and are the cornerstones of AT&T's corporate philosophy.

The close collaboration of dozens of people representing two major museums—The Studio Museum in Harlem and the Addison Gallery of American Art; six historically black colleges and universities —Howard, Fisk, Clark Atlanta, North Carolina Central, Tuskegee, and Hampton; with Duke University and the Williamstown Art Conservation Center, has constituted a network of cultural institutions that has been working together for more than three years to realize this historic project in eight cities. This network becomes even larger with the involvement of the many presenting museums in those cities. We applaud this extended partnership.

In its commitment to the arts, AT&T has been associated with the world of ideas that shapes people's sense of the possibilities of life. In supporting *To Conserve a Legacy*, AT&T is deeply privileged to celebrate the visionaries of African American contemporary art and the seminal institutions that have conserved and promoted their vision for future generations.

C. Michael Armstrong
Chief Executive Officer

# Ford Motor Company

Ford Motor Company is pleased to support *To Conserve a Legacy: American Art from Historically Black Colleges and Universities*. We salute the Addison Gallery of American Art and The Studio Museum in Harlem for organizing this outstanding collaborative project, including the internship program, conservation of important art works, exhibition, and scholarly catalogue.

Over the next three years, these masterpieces of American art from historically black colleges and universities will be seen—many for the first time—by the general public in eight cities. Through these paintings, audiences around the country will experience impressions of the black community—its vitality, its strong cultural identity, and its visions. The images will speak to all Americans.

Ford has a long tradition of supporting the arts. We believe they enrich our lives and our communities, and help to promote mutual understanding. It is our hope that these art works increase that understanding, and be a source of inspiration and enjoyment for all who see them.

William C. Ford, Jr.
Chairman

This exhibition was organized by the
Addison Gallery of American Art,
Phillips Academy, Andover, Massachusetts,
and The Studio Museum in Harlem,
New York

In association with
the Williamstown Art Conservation Center
and Participating Institutions:

Clark Atlanta University Art Galleries,
Clark Atlanta University, Atlanta, Georgia

Fisk University Art Galleries,
Fisk University, Nashville, Tennessee

Hampton University Museum,
Hampton University, Hampton, Virginia

Howard University Gallery of Art,
Howard University, Washington, D.C.

North Carolina Central University Art
Museum, North Carolina Central University
Durham, North Carolina

Tuskegee University, Tuskegee, Alabama


The exhibition and its national tour
are made possible by
AT&T and
Ford Motor Company.
Both companies have also provided support
for the conservation programs and the
catalogue.

Additional support has been generously
provided by
the Henry Luce Foundation,
the John S. and James L. Knight Foundation,
the National Endowment for the Arts,
a federal agency,
the LEF Foundation,
the Greentree Foundation,
the Joseph Harrison Jackson Foundation,
and the Trellis Fund.

Exhibition Dates

The Studio Museum in Harlem, New York
March 17–July 11, 1999

Addison Gallery of American Art, Phillips Academy, Andover, Massachusetts
August 31–October 31, 1999

The Corcoran Gallery of Art, Washington, D.C.
November 20, 1999–January 31, 2000*

The Art Institute of Chicago
February 19–April 30, 2000

Clark Atlanta University Art Galleries
with The High Museum of Art, Atlanta, Georgia
June 6–September 25, 2000

North Carolina Central University Art Museum
with Duke University Art Museum and the Center for Documentary Studies,
Durham, North Carolina
October 15–December 1, 2000

Fisk University with Tennessee State Museum, Nashville, Tennessee
January 2–March 31, 2001

Hampton University Museum, Hampton University, Hampton, Virginia
with the Chrysler Museum, Norfolk, Virginia
April 22–July 29, 2001

*Howard University Gallery of Art, Howard University, Washington, D.C., will present an
ancillary exhibition of works from the permanent collection

Editor: Louise Stone
Design and typesetting: Katy Homans
Printing: Meridian Printing, East Greenwich, Rhode Island

Published by the Addison Gallery of American Art, a department of Phillips Academy,
Andover, Massachusetts, and The Studio Museum in Harlem, New York.

front cover/jacket: Frederick C. Flemister, *Man with a Brush*, 1940: checklist 91
back cover/jacket: Charles S. Livingston, *George Washington Carver*, n.d.: checklist 165
frontispiece: Jacob Lawrence, *Palm Sunday*, 1956: checklist 155

Library of Congress Cataloging in Publication Data

Powell, Richard J., 1953–
    To conserve a legacy : American art from historically Black colleges and universities / Richard
Powell and Jock Reynolds ; with an introduction by Kinshasha Holman Conwill.
        p.  cm.
    Catalog of a traveling exhibition held at The Studio Museum in Harlem, Mar. 17–July 11, 1999
and the Addison Gallery of American Art, Aug.–Oct., 1999 and other institutions.
        ISBN 0-262-16186-9 (hc : alk. paper). — ISBN 0-262-66151-9 (pbk. : alk. paper).
    1. Afro-American art—Exhibitions.    2. Afro-American universities and colleges—Art collec-
tions—Exhibitions.    3. Art—Private collections—Southern States—Exhibitions.    I. Reynolds,
Jock.    II. Studio Museum in Harlem.    III. Addison Gallery of American Art.    IV. Title.
N6538.N5P68   1999
704.03'96073'0074—dc21                                                                98-50539
                                                                                        CIP

# Contents

*To Conserve a Legacy: American Art from Historically Black Colleges and Universities* is dedicated to the memory of Felrath Hines, artist and conservator, a man who spent a lifetime caring for the works of other artists while also contributing his own creative expressions to the growing legacy of American Art.

N. Jay Jaffee (b. 1921)
*Felrath Hines, I.R.T. BKLYN,* 1946
Gelatin silver print
Collection of Dorothy C. Fisher

# Acknowledgments

BJ Larson
Project Manager
Addison Gallery of American Art

A complex project on the scale of *To Conserve a Legacy: American Art from Historically Black Colleges and Universities* would not be possible without the dedication, talent, and support of numerous individuals and organizations. On behalf of the consortium, I offer our deepest appreciation to everyone who contributed to aspects of the project: conservation treatment, intern training program, exhibition, and publication.

We are grateful to Suzanne Sato, Director of the Arts & Culture Program at the AT&T Foundation, and Mabel Cabot, Director of Corporate Programming at Ford Motor Company for their enthusiastic involvement with and support of the project. AT&T and Ford Motor Company provided the major grants that made *To Conserve a Legacy* possible. Additional funds were generously provided by a host of organizations, and we want to especially thank Ellen Holtzman, Program Director for the arts at the Henry Luce Foundation; Gary Burger, Program Director of the Arts & Culture Program at the John S. and James L. Knight Foundation; Jennifer Dowley, Director of Museums and Visual Arts at the National Endowment for the Arts, a federal agency; John Payson, President of the Greentree Foundation; Dr. Kenny Jackson Williams, Secretary-Treasurer, the Joseph Harrison Jackson Foundation; Marina Drummer, Executive Director, and Lyda Kuth, Associate Director, at the LEF Foundation; and Betsy Frampton, President of the Trellis Fund.

The co-organizers of the project, the Addison Gallery of American Art and The Studio Museum in Harlem, oversaw myriad tasks including fiscal management, fundraising, catalogue production, exhibition preparation and tour. At the Addison Gallery, Susan Faxon, Interim Director, directed the Internship Training Program with the assistance of Denise Johnson, Registrar; Allison Kemmerer, Associate Curator; Leslie Maloney, Brian Coleman, and John Sirois, Preparators; and Julie Bernson, Education Coordinator. The Addison's curatorial staff offered valuable editorial advice and organizational assistance to the project catalogue. We would especially like to thank Juliann McDonough, Curatorial Assistant, for her prodigious and tireless work on this project—from tracking art work in the early stages of the project, to collecting information to form the checklist, to coordinating every aspect of the catalogue production—and Alison Cleveland, Administrative Assistant, for organizing logistics and travel for the curators, interns, and consortium group members.

The Studio Museum in Harlem also devoted enormous time and energy to the project. Director Kinshasha Holman Conwill gave generously of her energy, experience, and advice to oversee a talented staff who contributed to every aspect of the project. Valerie Mercer, Senior Curator; Miescha Hardison and Sara Marion, Curatorial Assistants; Pam Ford and Pedra Chaffers, education staff; Brett Crenshaw, Project Assistant; Patricia Cruz, former Deputy Director of Programs; Clare Savard, Registrar; and Wendell Walker, Exhibition Designer, have our deepest gratitude.

The Williamstown Art Conservation Center provided conservation evaluations and treatments for the majority of the art works seen in the exhibition as well as for additional works from the collections of the participating universities. Our thanks to Thomas J. Branchick, Director and Conservator of Paintings, for his organization, expert advice, and good humor throughout the project. We would also like to thank Leslie Paisley, Conservator of Paper; Hugh Glover, Conservator of Furniture and Wooden Objects; Katherine Holbrow, Conservator of Objects; Michael Heslip, Associate Conservator of Paintings; Montserrat Le Mense, Assistant Conservator of Paintings; Cynthia Luk, Associate Conservator of Paintings; James Squires, Intern in Paintings, 1998–99; Sandra Webber, Conservator of Paintings; Kirsten Younger, Advanced Intern in Paintings 1997–98; Rebecca Johnston, Assistant Conservator on Paper; Valinda Carroll, Intern in Paper, 1998–99; Alexander M. Carlisle, Assistant Conservator of Furniture and Wooden Objects; Monica Berry, Assistant Conservator of Objects; MK Lalor, Apprentice in Conservation; Barbara Lemmen, Conservator of Photographs; James S. Martin, Director of Analytical Services and Research;

Nicholas W. Zammuto, Intern in Analytical Services and Research; Kathy Tremblay, Office Manager; and Teresa Beer, Accounts Manager.

Encouragement and support were graciously given to the consortium by the leaders of each of the participating universities. Among the enthusiastic advocates for this project are: Dr. Thomas W. Cole, Jr., President of Clark Atlanta University; Charles W. Johnson, President of Fisk University; Dr. William R. Harvey, President of Hampton University; H. Patrick Swygert, President of Howard University; Julius L. Chambers, Chancellor of North Carolina Central University; and Dr. Benjamin Franklyn Payton, President of Tuskegee University.

The following museum directors, curators, and staff members of the consortium organizations were invaluable to the realization of this project: Tina Dunkley, Director of the Clark Atlanta University Art Galleries; Kevin Grogan, Director of the Fisk University Art Collections; Jeanne Zeidler, Director, and Mary Lou Hultgren, Curator of Collections at the Hampton University Museum; Dr. Tritobia Hayes Benjamin, Director, Scott W. Baker, Assistant Director, and Eileen Johnston, Registrar of the Howard University Gallery of Art; Kenneth Rodgers, Director, Norman Pendergraft, former Director, and Pat Jones, Registrar of the North Carolina Central University Art Museum; Daniel T. Williams, Archivist, Cynthia Beavers Wilson, Assistant Archivist, and Uthman Abdur Rathman, Associate Professor, Fine and Performing Arts Department at Tuskegee University.

The project was enriched by the talented and dedicated students who participated in the Internship Training Program: Jonique Gilliam and Elee Elijah Stewart, Clark Atlanta University; Kelli Hall and Hollie Hollowell, Fisk University; Tamara D. Holmes and Ahmad Ward, Hampton University; Carol R. Cooper and James R. Herring, Howard University; Rodney Bennett and Julian Weaver, North Carolina Central University; Pierre Blackman and Rayna Gardner, Tuskegee University.

We are indebted to Katy Homans for the beautiful design of this publication and to Jock Reynolds for his assistance with image sequencing. Special thanks go to Greg Heins, the principal project photographer, as well as contributing photographers, Michael Agee, Merry Armata, Art Evans, Frank Graham, and Robert Lawson. Our thanks also to PhotoArc for creating the cyanotype surrogates. We appreciate the diligent work of research assistants Kathryn Dungy, Rache! Frew, and Lynn Igoe as well as the editorial assistance of Suzanne Hellmuth and Antoinette C. Brown. Our sincere gratitude to Louise Stone, who served as Catalogue Editor; Geri Thomas, Thomas & Hirsch Fine Arts, who served as Project Registrar; and Resnicow Schroeder, the project's public relations firm, for their extraordinary commitment to excellence in their key roles in *To Conserve a Legacy*.

This project owes its existence to the perception and dedication of the exhibition curators, Dr. Richard J. Powell, Chair of the Department of Art and Art History at Duke University, and Jock Reynolds, Director of the Yale University Art Gallery and former director of the Addison Gallery of American Art, whose vision, knowledge, and determination have brought *To Conserve a Legacy: American Art from Historically Black Colleges and Universities* to life.

# Introduction

Kinshasha Holman Conwill
Director, The Studio Museum in
Harlem

For more than one hundred years, historically black colleges and universities (HBCUs) have been in the forefront of the preservation of African American history and culture. Much as the Civil Rights movement of the late 1950s and the 1960s launched major museums dedicated to African American culture and history, the post Civil War era signaled the rise of a host of institutions of higher learning founded specifically for former slaves and free blacks. In the period following the Emancipation Proclamation in 1863, many black colleges and universities were created. Some of the earliest of those institutions began to assemble important collections of African American art and artifacts as well as significant holdings in European and American modernism, African, and Native American art. *To Conserve a Legacy: American Art from Historically Black Colleges and Universities* is an acknowledgment and affirmation of the singular stewardship of these invaluable treasures. The collections of the six institutions that are featured in the exhibition—Clark Atlanta University, Fisk University, Hampton University, Howard University, North Carolina Central University, and Tuskegee University—represent some of the most significant examples of an indispensable heritage.

The first major, publicly accessible collection of African American art was probably housed at the Hampton Institute Museum, now the Hampton University Museum, in Hampton, Virginia. Hampton's museum was founded in 1868 and for almost forty years it held sway as the only such repository until the opening of the art gallery at Howard University in 1928. The establishment of the Schomburg Collection as part of the New York Public Library in the 1920s was a vital addition to the body of institutions dedicated to black culture that predates collections at some HBCUs. Collecting at historically black colleges and universities often preceded the formal creation of museums and galleries, with schools including Fisk and Spelman College acquiring works in the 1930s. The postwar period saw the founding of museums or galleries at Fisk University in 1949, Morgan State College in 1957, and North Carolina Central University in 1972.

In addition to their collecting activities, these institutions also provided the primary training for African American artists, art historians, professors, and curators. The roster of artists and educators associated with HBCUs is long and distinguished. Artists associated with Hampton University include John Biggers, who spent his formative early college years studying at Hampton, Elizabeth Catlett, who graduated from Howard and taught at Hampton, where she was one of Biggers's teachers, and Samella Lewis, who also studied with Elizabeth Catlett at Dillard. Fisk's notable artist-educators include Aaron Douglas, founding chairman of Fisk's art department, and his successor David C. Driskell, whose seminal exhibitions and publications on African American art, *Two Centuries of Black American Art* (1976) and *Hidden Heritage* (1985), include a number of works from HBCUs and are required reading for students of the subject. Howard University was a center of black intellectual life during the years surrounding the development of its collection. James V. Herring, founding chairman of Howard's art department, his successor James A. Porter, and Alain Locke, the seminal intellectual of the New Negro movement, were just a few of the leaders of the university's art programs. Loïs Mailou Jones and James Lesesne Wells also taught at Howard while Elizabeth Catlett was a student there. Henry O. Tanner taught at Clark College and Hale Woodruff taught at Atlanta University in the years before Clark and Atlanta University were merged. The continuity of role models in the ranks of artists and administrators of HBCUs is in itself an immeasurable asset. A student at Fisk in the 1960s might study with Aaron Douglas, a key figure of the Harlem Renaissance, and experience his works and that of leading African American and American modernists. As late as the 1980s, Loïs Mailou Jones regaled her students with stories of life in Paris in the 1930s and acted as a living witness to major shifts and styles in her own work and that of her peers of seven decades.

Indeed, the overall contributions of graduates of historically black colleges and universities is hard to overestimate. According to the College Fund, currently eighty percent of all black federal judges, sixty percent of all African Americans holding a law degree, and fifty percent of black Americans teaching in the public schools did their undergraduate work at HBCUs. A sampling of the illustrious alumni of HBCUs in other fields includes David N. Dinkins, the first African American mayor of New York City, Nobel Laureate Dr. Martin Luther King, Jr., opera diva Jessye Norman, and Kwame Nkrumah, the first president of Ghana. The legendary educator Booker T. Washington—a towering figure of the late nineteenth and early twentieth centuries—was both the founder of Tuskegee Institute and an alumnus of Hampton. Washington's major rival for intellectual and political hegemony W.E.B. Du Bois was a graduate of Fisk and a seminal figure at Atlanta University before joining the staff of the NAACP in 1910, the year after its inception, and subsequently editing its journal, *The Crisis*. Aaron Douglas provided a number of illustrations for *The Crisis*, and his singular style became identified with some of the leading publications and the ideas they espoused in the 1920s and 1930s. Entire groups of outstanding individuals identified with their educational institutions have produced achievements that resonate across the decades, from the first Fisk Jubilee Singers of the 1870s to the Tuskegee Airmen of World War II. The crucial role of historically black colleges and universities persists today. Although HBCUs are three percent of the colleges in the United States, they graduate almost thirty percent of black degree-recipients.

The work of historically black colleges and universities in building important collections was strengthened and augmented by other efforts as well. A number of large-scale private and public initiatives, beginning with the Harlem Renaissance period of the 1920s through the period of the Works Progress Administration/ Federal Art Project (WPA/FAP) in the 1930s, also provided institutional and individual support to black art and artists. Established in 1922 by real estate developer William Harmon, the Harmon Foundation provided unprecedented support of black artists through its annual awards and exhibitions from 1928 to 1933. Harmon Foundation prizewinners included: William Artis, Palmer Hayden, Malvin Gray Johnson, Sargent Johnson, William H. Johnson, Loïs Mailou Jones, Archibald Motley, James A. Porter, Elizabeth Prophet, William Edouard Scott, James Lesesne Wells, and Hale Woodruff. All but Hayden, Sargent Johnson, and Prophet are represented in *To Conserve a Legacy*. Many Harmon Foundation awardees were also graduates of black colleges and universities. The dispersal of the foundation's holdings in 1967 greatly benefited the collections of traditionally black colleges and universities, including Clark Atlanta, Fisk, Hampton, and Howard, and general art museums such as the National Museum of American Art and the National Portrait Gallery.

In 1942 artist and educator Hale Woodruff began the Atlanta University Art Annuals, a national competitive exhibition of the works of black American artists. Woodruff created the art department at Atlanta. The Annuals had initial support from the trustees of Atlanta University (now Clark Atlanta University) and a special grant from the Harmon Foundation to fund the exhibition's top prize, the John Hope Award, named for the university's president. By the time the Atlanta University Annuals ended in 1970, the university had acquired nearly 300 works for its collection by some of the country's most prominent African American artists. Recipients of Atlanta University Annual Art Exhibition purchase prize awards represented in *To Conserve a Legacy* include William Artis, Elizabeth Catlett, Roy DeCarava, Frederick Flemister, Loïs Mailou Jones, Samella Lewis, and Charles White.

In his essay for the catalogue of the exhibition *Revisiting American Art: Works from the Collections of Historically Black Colleges and Universities*, Edmund Barry Gaither, director of the Museum of the National Center of Afro-American Artists, writes: "Ignored as significant repositories of art and marginalized as critical centers of discussion, HBCUs have been undervalued in the history of art and art production in our nation." The dual roles of repositories of art and centers of discussion played by these institutions have been inestimable. Viewed in the historical context of schools that came into existence in the shadow of the Civil War and that maintained the highest standards of excellence in the face of daunting legal, social, and political obstacles, the steadfastness of their commitment is exemplary. The exhibition, publication, conservation, conservation training, and public programs that comprise the *To Conserve a Legacy* project constitute an attempt to address Gaither's eloquent lament. Indeed, this project builds on his earlier efforts and those of scholars, directors, and curators at both the participating institutions and the other fine HBCUs that are not a part of the project. They are also doing extraordinary work to preserve, interpret, and present the profoundly rich collections that are their, and America's, inheritance.

The scope of the exhibition is intended to convey the richness of that heritage. *To Conserve a Legacy* covers over a century of American art in over two hundred works by close to one hundred artists. From central nineteenth-century figures, such as sculptor Edmonia Lewis and painter Robert S. Duncanson, to innovators of the 1970s, such as Sam Gilliam and William T. Williams, the artists in the exhibition exemplify key movements and ideas in the evolution of American artistic production. The inclusion of major artists who are not black provides an essential opportunity to see the work of African American artists in the context of the work of their other American peers. Aaron Douglas is thus seen alongside Georgia O'Keeffe, while the work of Charles Demuth informs the viewer's appreciation of Archibald J. Motley, Jr. The postwar period of American art, central to understanding the African American contribution, is generously represented by key works by leading figures such as Romare Bearden, Elizabeth Catlett, Jacob Lawrence, Alma Thomas, John Wilson, and Hale Woodruff. In the words of co-curator Richard J. Powell: "What is of particular importance to the conceptual framework behind *To Conserve a Legacy* is that the cultural criteria for this exhibition—each art work's intrinsic place within a set of American themes and/or viewpoints—is commensurate with other art historical examinations of American culture."

Certainly this exhibition makes manifest the irreplaceable legacy of historically black colleges and universities in the narrative of American art. Yet, it would be misleading to suggest that the contributions of these institutions are all in the past. As the principal caretakers of late nineteenth-century to late twentieth-century African American art, traditionally black colleges and universities hold incomparable objects and an unsurpassed record of educating artists and scholars of American art. They are not by any means, however, ready or willing to rest on their past accomplishments. The collections at these institutions are growing in depth, in attention to collections care and management, in accessibility to their university and larger communities, in scholarship and loan activity, and in conservation. The leaders of the HBCUs included in *To Conserve a Legacy,* from the college presidents to the museum and gallery directors, curators, and staff, have made impressive and increased commitments to their holdings with new and renovated buildings and galleries and an investment in human and physical resources designed to ensure the future. While much has been done, much remains to be done. The collaborative spirit that made this project possible, what co-curator Jock Reynolds calls "the enduring connections that exist between generations and that bind us all," must be joined by others. The alumni of historically black colleges and universities represent a resource of enormous potential. As the exhibition travels throughout the country, we, the partners in this exceptional undertaking, will be calling upon the beneficiaries of these institutions to help guarantee that the legacy begun a century ago is secured into the next millennium.

Arthur P. Bedou
*Booker T. Washington in New Orleans*, n.d.
Digital reproduction from original gelatin silver
print, 4½ x 6½ in. (image); 7 x 5⅟₁₆ in. (sheet)
Collection of Tuskegee University
checklist 33

Prentiss H. "P.H." Polk
*George Washington Carver*, before 1943
Gelatin silver print
9¹⁄₂ x 7¹⁄₈ in. (image); 10 x 8¹⁄₈ in. (sheet)
Collection of Tuskegee University
checklist 197

Frances Benjamin Johnston
*The Hampton Albums: Football-Team,* 1899–1900
Platinum print
7¹⁄₂ x 9³⁄₈ in. (image); 9¹⁄₂ x 11¹⁄₂ in. (sheet)
Collection of Hampton University Archives
checklist 140

Frances Benjamin Johnston
*The Hampton Albums: Watercolor. Studying the butterfly,* 1899–1900
Platinum print
7½ x 9⅜ in. (image); 9½ x 11½ in. (sheet)
Collection of Hampton University Archives
checklist 149

# Clark Atlanta University Art Galleries

Tina Dunkley, Director

Clark Atlanta University (CAU)[1] possesses a permanent collection of some 640 works of art in three major categories: contemporary American, specifically African American, and African. The three collections include paintings, murals, sculpture, works on paper, ethnographical artifacts acquired through annual purchase, and donations.

Of the three collection categories, the largest and most historically significant is the African American. It comprises some 376 works of art spanning seven decades (1914–1997). The renowned collection is rivaled only by the art collections at Hampton University and Howard University. Significant works in the collection include *Disciples Healing the Sick* by Henry O. Tanner, *Snow Morning* by Romare Bearden, *Brownstones* by Jacob Lawrence, and the *Art of the Negro* mural series by Hale Woodruff.

CAU's tradition in fostering the arts began in 1942 when exhibition opportunities for artists of color were limited due to segregation. Under the guidance of celebrated artist and teacher Hale Woodruff, Atlanta University inaugurated the annual "Exhibition of Paintings, Prints and Sculpture by Negro Artists of America" to provide black artists a national forum to exhibit their work. Over the course of three decades the juried exhibitions presented to the American public over 900 artists from across the country. Each year approximately twelve pieces were purchased for the university collection. In this way, works by artists who were virtually unknown to the mainstream art world, but later hailed as masters (e.g., Jacob Lawrence, Elizabeth Catlett, Charles White, John Biggers, Löis Mailou Jones, and Roy DeCarava), entered the university collection. By the close of the annuals in 1970, the university had acquired 291 pieces by 155 artists.

Interested in broadening the scope of the fledgling collection of American art, University Trustee Chauncey Waddell and his wife Catherine donated eighty-one works by other American artists such as Edwin Dickinson, Werner Drewes, Isabel Bishop, John Marin, Romare Bearden, and Irene Rice Pereira. Through gifts from the estates of Judge Irvin C. Mollison, Judge Samuel Rosenman, James Baldwin, and Lucy Rucker Aiken, the collection continues to grow. Other benefactors have contributed over 150 artifacts from Africa including masks, ceremonial figures, and utilitarian objects.

In light of the recent controversy over the resurrection of negative racial stereotypes of African Americans, the core of the Clark Atlanta University Art Galleries collections serves as a retrospective beacon of a time when black artists were committed to "undoing the stereotype." Alain Locke, well-known spokesman of the New Negro

Reading Room in Trevor Arnett Hall, Former Library of Atlanta University, Georgia.

movement, remarked at the first annual in 1942 that the Atlanta University annuals represented "one of the ultimate goals of the whole art movement among Negroes . . . *to encourage a healthy and representational art of the people with its roots in its own soil.*" (italics added)

In stark contrast to the abstract expressionist movement of the forties, black artists's favorite subjects and themes in the annuals concerned Negroes and racial consciousness.[2] These black artists were responding to a different reality largely propelled by the social and political machinery of Jim Crow.[3] The CAU collections of American art (specifically the 291 works acquired through the annuals) are an antidote to the derogatory stereotypes generated by the media and commercially manufactured products of the late nineteenth and early twentieth centuries. It is an introspective examination and reflection of the black American psyche.

The preponderance of portraits and themes of self-examination in the CAU collection of African American art declares a cultural identity carved from experience within a callous society—ironically, a society descending from liberated colonists, whose artistic legacy began in the seventeenth century with comparable preponderance of individual and family portraits.

In spite of being an adjunct chapter to American art history, the CAU collection exemplifies Locke's notion of the need for "a racially representative tradition," and of Woodruff's success in providing a platform of visual discourse for black artists. Ultimately, the collection bears witness to the contributions of African American artists to the developing art scene.

Clark Atlanta University Art Galleries, 1998.

1. Clark Atlanta University, established in 1988 by the consolidation of Atlanta University, founded in 1865 by the American Missionary Association, and Clark College, founded in 1869 by the Freedmen's Aid Society, is the largest of the United Negro College Fund institutions. It is accredited by the Commission on Colleges of the Southern Association of Colleges and Schools to award the bachelor's, master's, specialist, and doctoral degrees through its schools of Arts and Sciences, Business Administration, Education, International Affairs and Development, Library and Information Studies, and Social Work. The university has a faculty and staff of 1,300 and an enrollment of more than 5,000 students from forty-five states and forty-seven countries. With an enriching curriculum and ever-advancing facilities, Clark Atlanta University is gaining national preeminence as a teaching, research, and service university, and has an excellent record in producing graduates in fields where minorities typically have been inadequately represented.

2. *Time*, 9 April 1945, p. 65.

3. Jim Crow is historically classified as the period of racial segregation legislated by laws that prohibited black Americans from entering public places (1877–1950s).

# Fisk University Galleries and Collections

Kevin Grogan, Director

The founding of Fisk University in 1866 was the direct outgrowth of the work of American missionaries, mainly Congregationalists, who went to Africa following the Amistad Incident in 1839 to set up schools to provide a "meaningful Christian education" for Mende men, women, and children. Some of those missionaries returned to the United States bearing glowing reports of the success of their schools in West Africa. They reasoned that similar schools could be set up in the South to educate the newly freed slaves and to aid them in their attempt to become self-sufficient. When such schools as Fisk, Howard, Talladega, and Tougaloo were founded in the 1860s, their hopes and dreams were realized. Today, Fisk remains one of the great symbols of that age of charity and enlightenment. Most notable among the programs of excellence in all areas of liberal studies for which Fisk has achieved its well-founded fame are those in the fine arts.

The arts have traditionally played a central role in the life of Fisk University. From the early 1870s, when the original Jubilee Singers ensured Fisk's very existence, to the present, the arts have been a vital part of the educational program. And it is interesting to note that even at a time when Fisk's fame resulted directly from the tours of the Jubilee Singers, the university had already become a noted

The Fisk Memorial Chapel. Constructed in 1882 and in continuous use since, the Chapel was made possible by a gift of the widow of General Clinton B. Fisk, the head of the Freedmen's Bureau in post-Civil War Nashville and one of the founders of the "free school" that came to bear his name.

collector of visual art and artifacts. As early as 1876, *Harper's Weekly* reported on the collection of African and Native American art that was then housed in the basement of the theology building on the Fisk campus. The writer noted that many missionaries returning from Africa had given fine examples of "ethnographic" pieces to the collection. The tradition of collecting art that provided a cultural link with black America's heritage in Africa has continued to this day. In many ways the African American collection at Fisk is an affirmation of the spirit that the early founders and collectors imbued in those who followed in the traditions of Fisk University.

The Fisk University Collection of African American Art has played a very important role in the educational plan of the university since the 1930s. The first work by an African American artist to enter the collection was *The Symbolic Negro History Series*, murals by Aaron Douglas who painted them (with the assistance of Edwin Harleston) in three areas on the second floor of the Erastus Milo Cravath Library (now the university's administration building). Douglas, the artist most associated with the Harlem Renaissance, was a pioneer Africanist and a critical contributor to the New Negro movement. His murals, created at the invitation of Charles Spurgeon Johnson, one-time editor of *Opportunity* magazine and Fisk's first black president, ultimately led to Douglas's appointment as chairman of the Fisk art department, a post he held with distinction until his retirement in 1966. Douglas's presence on campus and the success with which he led the art department attracted the attention of other African American artists and the loyal, generous support of the Harmon Foundation.

Douglas was succeeded by David C. Driskell who held a joint appointment as chairman of the art department and director of the university galleries. Driskell brought a very cosmopolitan world view to his new post, as well as a determination to expand public awareness of the achievements of African Americans in the visual arts. Largely through his efforts, the African American collection grew dramatically, as did the schedule of exhibitions and programs. Also during

Driskell's tenure, the university received a gift of hundreds of works of art by African and African American artists through the Harmon Foundation when it ceased operations in 1967.

Perhaps the best known of Fisk University's holdings, however, is the Alfred Stieglitz Collection of Modern Art, which was given to Fisk in 1949 by Stieglitz's widow, the renowned painter Georgia O'Keeffe. In 1948 O'Keeffe contacted Fisk's president, Charles S. Johnson, through their mutual friend, the writer and photographer Carl Van Vechten. She offered Fisk a gift of 101 works of art from her late husband's collection. President Johnson eagerly accepted the offer and immediately set about the conversion of a Victorian building (used as the university gymnasium since 1888) into a suitable home for the Stieglitz Collection.

Jubilee Hall. Constructed in 1873, it is the first facility built for the purpose of providing education to African Americans. Its construction was made possible by the successful tours of the Fisk Jubilee Singers whose efforts as performers raised the necessary funds to purchase the Fisk campus and to build the building.

O'Keeffe, who, as a young woman, had taught in the Texas panhandle, South Carolina, and Virginia, was sensitive to the absence of modern art in the South but sought to place the Stieglitz Collection in a Southern institution that, unlike most of the region's public institutions in the late 1940s, would be accessible to all people. Moreover, she was eager to find a single institution where it would be possible, through the adroit selection of work, to represent the whole of the collection that her late husband had assembled over a period of nearly fifty years. Her other gifts from the Stieglitz Collection (to the Metropolitan Museum of Art, the Art Institute of Chicago, the Philadelphia Museum of Art, and the National Gallery of Art) were intended to address the needs and interests of those institutions. O'Keeffe personally supervised the lighting, painting of the gallery (now named for her friend and Fisk supporter Carl Van Vechten), and the installation of the collection.

The Stieglitz collection remains one of the most important collections of art in the South and a testament to the farsightedness of the donor, as well as to the unique place in American culture occupied by Fisk. Other noteworthy collections at Fisk include more than four hundred of Van Vechten's own portrait photographs; hundreds of drawings by Cyrus Baldridge, which were originally produced for use as illustrations in his book *White Africans and Black*, and a large group of portraits of black Americans created by the noted artist/designer Winold Reiss and donated by him to Fisk in honor of his most famous pupil Aaron Douglas.

The Fisk University Collections are housed and displayed in the freestanding Carl Van Vechten Gallery building, the Aaron Douglas Gallery (which occupies space on the third floor of the university library), and the Appleton Room of historic Jubilee Hall. They remain central to the curricular efforts of Fisk and to the cultural aspirations of Nashville.

# Hampton University Museum

Jeanne Zeidler, Director

Hampton Normal and Agricultural Institute, 1902.

In August 1868 General Samuel Chapman Armstrong, the founder of Hampton University, took the initial step to establish a museum at the young school. Writing to his mother, Armstrong outlined his goal: "I mean to make and to have here the finest collection in the U.S. . . . I think that by taking pains I can beat the other collections in this country." Armstrong was twenty-nine years old when he opened Hampton Normal and Agricultural Institute to fifteen Negro students in April 1868. The school had few resources and no endowment, yet he was determined to build an institution that would be second to none. An important part of this vision was the development of a museum.

Born and raised in Hawaii, Armstrong sought help from his mother in obtaining "specimens of coral, lava, and curiosities of all kinds found in the Pacific." He wrote, "I would prefer that you send what you have to send not in money, but in rare specimens of all kinds . . . the gifts will be very instructive." His purpose was to promote "teaching by the most practical method." Through objects, students learning agriculture, trades, and domestic sciences could absorb technical details and artistic traditions while instruction in geography, world cultures, and history could be made concretely. The collection quickly expanded beyond the Pacific to encompass cultural materials and natural history specimens from around the world.

Interest in African peoples and cultures was apparent at Hampton from the school's founding. By the 1870s, there was an African studies program and the first African pieces were acquired for the museum. Dozens of African pieces from various cultures were registered into the collection over the following three decades. Then in 1911 Hampton acquired the William H. Sheppard Collection of African Art—over four hundred superb pieces gathered by Hampton alumnus William Sheppard between 1890 and 1910 in what is today the Democratic Republic of Congo.

In 1878 Hampton embarked upon a pioneering experiment in American Indian education. More than 1,300 students from sixty-five different tribes attended Hampton over the forty-five-year life of this program. In this context, the school began collecting Native American art. Although assimilation, citizenship, and "civilization" were goals, a central principle of the school's philosophy was that students should know and take pride in their heritage. Armstrong believed that "the Indian will not respect our civilization the more for being taught to despise his own."

The impact of the African and Native American collections on Hampton students was documented in the early years by museum curator Cora Mae Folsom. In 1917 she wrote, "African and Indian collections should and do have a large mission in stimulating race pride." Earlier, in 1911, Folsom reported that the students "like to observe that while the Indian was making a sinewed bow and feathered arrows on this side of the world, the African was making identically the same on his and that the Bakuba woman's loom is just as ingenious as the Navajo and her palm cloth quite as artistic as the wool blanket."

Hampton's museum was recognized by the school as being important beyond the campus. It was a community resource and, according to a 1920 curator's report, the only museum in the South open to African Americans. That year Folsom articulated the value of the collections when she wrote that the African collection is "inspiring—helpful not only at Hampton, but to students of African ethnology in other places, and to artists in search of the new designs and suggestions."

In 1894, with the African and the American Indian collections well established, Hampton turned to another collecting area. That year, with the acquisition of two paintings by Henry O. Tanner, Hampton became the first institution to establish a collection of black art which grew slowly during the first half of this century; a few dozen pieces were acquired, including five additional works by Tanner. In the late 1950s the collection growth accelerated through an evolving relationship with the Harmon Foundation.

From 1967 to 1968 hundreds of works—paintings, works on paper, and sculpture —were acquired from the Harmon Foundation. The acquisition included pieces by Hale Woodruff, Palmer Hayden, Archibald Motley, Jr., William H. Johnson, Sargent Johnson, Claude Clark, Malvin Gray Johnson, Aaron Douglas, two early series by Jacob Lawrence, works by pioneers of contemporary African art such as Ben Enwonwu, and many others, providing a strong core of works created in the 1920s through the mid 1960s.

Over five hundred significant pieces have been added to the fine art collection since 1978. Hampton sought to further enhance the depth and the breadth of the Harlem Renaissance-related materials with the addition of works by such artists as Löis Mailou Jones and Walter Ellison. Another goal was to acquire works by major African American artists of the nineteenth century. The university has purchased works by Tanner as well as Joshua Johnson, Robert S. Duncanson, Edward Mitchell Bannister, James Ethan Porter, and Grafton Tyler Brown in the last decade.

Hampton Normal and Agricultural Institute Museum, c. 1905.

Important for Hampton University is the collection of works by artists trained at, or associated with, the school, including over one hundred pieces from John Biggers, a large group from Samella S. Lewis, and over one hundred works on paper by Elizabeth Catlett. Moe Brooker, Raymond Saunders, David MacDonald, Ron Adams, Greg Henry, Sonya Clark, and Kwabena Ampofo-Anti are among the many contemporary artists whose works have been recently acquired.

The collection of Hampton University Museum numbers over nine thousand objects and continues to be strengthened and enriched. Its growth, by over one-third since 1978, and the expansion of the museum program and facility, were made possible by the vision of the university's president William R. Harvey. He provided visibility and acquisition monies, funded an artist-in-residence program, commissioned major works of public art for the campus, and set an example as a collector. These activities have served to achieve the goal that he stated in the late 1980s: "To create an environment on the Hampton University campus where the arts can flourish."

# Howard University Gallery of Art

Tritobia Hayes Benjamin, Director

The Howard University Gallery of Art was established in 1928 by action of the board of trustees in response to an offer of funds made by a philanthropic couple[1] of Washington, D.C. for the renovation of an existing university facility. The primary purpose was to make revolving exhibitions of contemporary arts and crafts available for immediate visitation and appreciational study by students of the university. This goal was rapidly expanded to include loan exhibitions of different periods, cultures, and countries.

The lower floor of the Andrew Rankin Memorial Chapel was selected and the new facility formally opened with a loan exhibition on April 7, 1930, which suggests that the university collection at that time did not have works of gallery caliber. After the success of the first loan exhibition, a policy and program leading to the development of a permanent collection was adopted as follows: to make good works of art available on a permanent basis to the university community; to establish, at least, the nucleus of a loan collection to be made available for use by reputable cultural and university centers; and to gather into the collection, whenever possible, significant works by contemporary artists without reference to the race, color, or creed of the individual artist.

The first director, Professor James Vernon Herring, (who also founded the department of art in 1921) relied upon the generous help of alumni and friends of the university who donated works of art or made extended loans to the gallery to meet the museum's first objective. Throughout the years, the same relationship of dependence on interested alumni and friends proved fruitful. The first work to enter the collection with funds contributed by friends and alumni and some public organizations, for example, was Henry O. Tanner's *Return from the Crucifixion*, an oil-tempera painting which was the

Opening of Art Gallery, ribbon cutting ceremony with Dr. James A. Porter, Mrs. Nabrit, Dr. James M. Nabrit, Jr., and Mrs. Dorothy Porter, April 2, 1961. Opening exhibition: "New Vistas in American Art."

last completed work prior to his death in 1937. Over the years the collection has grown due to the largess of private collectors, art foundations, various branches of the federal government, and friends of the gallery.

The liquidation of certain army posts throughout the country in the 1940s, Fort Huachuca in Arizona in particular, precipitated the allocation of federally owned works of art, that were given to art centers throughout the country. The Fort Huachuca collection was allocated to Howard University, thereby greatly increasing the paintings and prints in the gallery collection. The transference of works of art from other departments of the government to Howard University accounts for further augmentation of the collection.

In 1941 the gallery was relocated to the east wing, ground floor of Founders Library. The gallery continued its policy of loan exhibitions, and for a decade this site was the venue for many important traveling exhibitions, as well as exhibitions by faculty and students.

The estate of Dr. Alain Leroy Locke, who died in 1954, was received into the collection in 1955. Locke, professor of philosophy and the first African American Rhodes Scholar, bequeathed all of his paintings, books, sculpture, and memorabilia to Howard. Approximately three hundred pieces of African sculpture and handicrafts, including gold weights, served as the core of the collection—which over the years has been augmented by substantial donations. The Locke bequest included an abundance of works by African American artists and increased representation by artists active during the 1930s and 1940s. In 1990, 121 works from Mrs. Beatrice Cummings Mayer of Chicago were donated to the collection in memory of her late husband, Robert B. Mayer. This gift expanded the holdings to include works from Central and South Africa.

The gift of a "study collection" of twelve renaissance and baroque paintings and one renaissance sculpture was received from the Samuel W. Kress Foundation in 1961—one of a number of such donations by the Kress Foundation to art centers and university galleries throughout the country where the teaching of art history was offered as a major discipline. The Irving Gumbel Collection of prints by European etchers, engravers, mezzotinters, and wood-engravers of the sixteenth to nineteenth centuries was donated in 1963. This collection, approximately 350 works on paper, contains prints by Rembrandt, Jacques Callot, Wenceslaus Hollar, and engravers such as Heinrich Goltzius, Lucas van Leyden, the German "Little Masters," and many others.

Polish Art exhibition, Howard University Gallery of Art, c. 1940s.

In 1961 the Fine Arts complex, Cramton Auditorium, Ira Aldridge Theatre, and the Lulu Vere Childers Hall (the College of Fine Arts), opened to the public. Located in Childers Hall, the gallery's spacious new quarters consisted of three interconnecting galleries. The inaugural exhibition, *New Vistas in American Art*, was a resounding success. Several works by black and white artists in this exhibition were acquired with a grant from the Eugene and Agnes Meyer Foundation. That same year, the IBM Corporation donated a group of seven paintings and four sculptures to the gallery.

While it is not possible to mention every donor or gift in this brief profile, in its seven decades of service to the university community and the metropolitan area, the Howard University Gallery of Art, still housed in Childers Hall, has fulfilled its original mission. The collection has grown to over 4,500 pieces, and as it aggressively seeks a new home, the permanent collection will become more accessible to students, scholars, the university community, and the American public.

This essay was prepared with the assistance of an undated and unpublished manuscript written by James A. Porter, "The History of the Galleries of Art at Howard University," The Howard University Gallery of Art archives, Washington, D.C.

1. Mr. and Mrs. Avery Coonley made funds available for the renovation of the Andrew Rankin Chapel which housed the first Gallery of Art.

# North Carolina Central University Art Museum

Kenneth G. Rodgers, Director

As the president of the nation's first black, state-supported, liberal arts college, James E. Shepard was aware of the cultural and humanistic dimension that fine arts could bring to the North Carolina College for Negroes. He envisioned the tangible legacy that a museum could bestow by collecting, preserving, and exhibiting objects of African American cultural importance. However in the 1920s and 30s, priority had to be given to far more pressing matters than building a museum, such as developing strategies to ensure the survival of the school.[1] It was unrealistic, if not unfathomable, to concentrate efforts on the arts although the original charter of the institution supported it.

The creation of a museum for North Carolina Central University had been a goal of several members of the art department faculty since the beginning of the department. When Shepard hired Marion C. Parham in 1942, a step toward the establishment of a museum was taken.[2] Although teaching was her primary responsibility, Parham recognized the importance of a museum and exhibition space. With meager resources, she secured exhibitions from the American Federation of Arts almost from the beginning of her tenure and successfully mounted the first student exhibition in 1954 in room 206 of the Music and Fine Arts Building.

By all accounts, the next department chairman Edward Wilson was an aggressive, determined advocate for a permanent exhibition space. Prior to the fiftieth anniversary celebration of the university in 1960, Wilson was unequivocal in his support of an exhibition space. In his proposal for an art exhibit to be given during the celebration period he stated:

> I must go on record as voicing an objection to attempting a major exhibit on campus, without the proper facilities for showing works of art. As you know, the football team plays on a football field with seats for spectators and with physicians and referees in attendance, the Lyceum programs are presented in an auditorium, the Thespians perform on a lighted stage, the students eat in a dining hall, and even lavatories exist for personal needs, etc. I wish only that we would be granted the opportunity to exhibit art in a gallery.[3]

Wilson would not be successful in garnering support for a museum, but he sounded the clarion call.

Wilson met and was greatly encouraged by William Zorach, a leading American sculptor, who had come to North Carolina Central University in Durham to complete the memorial commission statue of the founder of the university, Dr. James E. Shepard.[4] Today the 7.5 foot statue greets all visitors to the university in its central placement in front of the entrance to the university and the Hoey Administration Building.

By 1958 an exhibition space was set aside in one room of the Fine Arts Building and served as the principal place for showing art work until after Wilson left North Carolina Central University in 1964. Lynn Igoe became the director of the North Carolina Central University Art Museum in 1971, and the first university gallery was formed in a renovated space in the old cafeteria the next year.

Igoe's successor Nancy C. Gillespie continued the advocacy for a permanent exhibition space. Gillespie urged the building of a new Fine Arts Center and outlined detailed plans for space utilization, including a small gallery for the exhibition of permanent acquisitions adjoining a gallery for temporary exhibitions. The forty-seven original works in the collection at the time were the beginning of what would become a premier collection of African American art.[5]

In January of 1976, Norman Pendergraft became director of the North Carolina Central University Art Museum and successfully initiated a comprehensive plan to further advance the museum. Under his watch a strong board of directors was developed and museum acquisitions significantly increased. Pendergraft developed a collecting policy which focused on art by or about African Americans, and he scrupulously acquired works with a discerning eye. By the late

1970s the museum had a solid foundation and existed as an important teaching and stimulating cultural institution within the university. Pendergraft had built a collection that included more than two hundred works of emerging and established African American artists and works by others dealing with the African American experience.

On November 4, 1977, the university broke ground for a new art museum in its current location. In 1986 Irwin Belk made a donation of $59,500 to establish an endowment; the earnings have been used for acquisitions and restorations of works of art. To honor the Belk family, the gallery that houses the museum's permanent collection is named the Carol Grotnes Belk Gallery.

The collection contains works by three major nineteenth-century artists—Robert S. Duncanson, Edward M. Bannister, and Henry O. Tanner. The twentieth century is represented by a generous number of artists active during the Harlem Renaissance of the 1920s and the WPA period of the 1930s, including Richmond Barthé, Romare Bearden, Robert Blackburn, Selma Burke, Elizabeth Catlett, Aaron Douglas, William H. Johnson, Jacob Lawrence, Norman Lewis, Charles White, and Hale Woodruff. Contemporary artists include Sam Gilliam, Barkley Hendricks, and Kerry James Marshall, among others.

William Zorach's sculpture of Dr. James Edward Shepard, founder of North Carolina College for Negroes, now North Carolina Central University.

1. Dr. James E. Shephard founded the National Religious Training School and Chautauqua, now North Carolina Central University, in 1910. Financial support came from student fees and private donations. See the "History and Background of North Carolina Central University" in the 1996–1998 catalogue, North Carolina Central University, pp. 17–18.

2. Thomasina Talley, Diane Dent, and Nannie Dove preceded Parham in providing the nucleus of the formation of an art department. Parham, the first department chairperson, oversaw the transition, from providing support for the liberal arts grounding, to offering a minor, to finally offering a major in art in 1944. In a recent interview, Mrs. Parham said that while there were occasional student shows, ever present financial concerns did not afford the luxury of seriously considering the development of a museum. See Kenneth G. Rodgers, *Re-connecting Roots: The Silver Anniversary Alumni Invitational*, exhibition catalogue (Durham: North Carolina Central University Art Museum, 1997), p. 3.

3. Wilson's proposal for an art exhibit celebrating the fiftieth anniversary of North Carolina College for Negroes at Durham listed many conditions vital to the growth of the art department faculty and students. Edward Wilson to Dr. Helen G. Edmonds, 2 November 1959, North Carolina Central University Archives.

4. In the commission agreement the general terms of the contract were clearly stated. Zorach agreed to produce and deliver a full-size plaster model to afford the James E. Shepard Memorial Foundation the opportunity of seeing how the statue would look in various locations, cast the same in bronze, in addition to furnishing a bronze bust of Dr. Shepard. The contract was signed on April 2, 1956 between William Zorach and the James E. Shepard Memorial Foundation, North Carolina Central University Archives.

5. Nancy C. Gillespie, "North Carolina Central University Museum of Art: A Report to the Board of Directors of Progress Through March, 1973," North Carolina Central University Art Museum Archives. Gillespie's comprehensive report builds a strong case for a campus museum by increasing operating budget, staff (including security), and acquisitions.

# Tuskegee University

Cynthia Beavers Wilson,
Assistant Archivist

Tuskegee University had its beginnings in a bill passed in 1880 by the Alabama State Legislature. This action was generated by two men—Lewis Adams, a former slave, and George W. Campbell, a former slave owner—who saw the need for education among black people in the rural Alabama community. The bill, signed by Governor Rufus Willis Cobb and made law on February 12, 1881, established Tuskegee Normal School for the training of black teachers. Further, a three-man commission, established to serve as the governing board for the school, was authorized to recruit and hire a teacher. After considerable recruiting efforts, the commissioners employed Booker T. Washington, who opened the school on July 4, 1881, thus Tuskegee was born. Thirty men and women from Macon and neighboring counties gathered the first day to attend Alabama's most distinctive normal school for the training of black teachers.

In 1882, Dr. Washington contracted to buy a 100-acre abandoned plantation, which became the nucleus of Tuskegee's present campus. He began a program of self help which permitted students to live on the campus and earn all or part of their expenses by helping to construct the campus.

Dr. Washington soon envisioned the development of a larger institution with a greater diversity of program offerings; however, he realized that such growth and development could not be nurtured by state funding alone, and that financial support from beyond state borders would be essential to fulfilling his dreams. As a result, in 1892 the Alabama Legislature reconstituted and established Tuskegee Normal Institute as a public body and corporation of the State of Alabama with full power of action and authority vested in a board of trustees. Henceforth, Tuskegee could assume the characteristics of a private institution for developmental reasons while continuing partially as a state-supported institution.

During the more than one hundred years since Booker T. Washington opened its doors, Tuskegee University has become a national, independent, coeducational institution of higher learning that has an historically unique relationship with the state of Alabama. Today, while it continues to focus on helping to develop human resources primarily within the African American community, Tuskegee is open to all. Tuskegee's mission has always been service to people—the hand and the heart as well as the mind. Dr. Washington's school was acclaimed—first by Alabama and then by the nation—for the soundness and vigor of its educational programs and principles. This solid strength has continued through the subsequent administrations of the late Dr. Robert Russa Moton (1915–35), the late Frederick D. Patterson (1935–53), and the late Luther H. Foster (1953–81). The university's vitality has been amplified, and new luster added during the current administration of Dr. Benjamin Franklin Payton, who assumed responsibility as fifth president of the university on August 1, 1981. The current administration redefined and upgraded Tuskegee from institute to university status in 1985.

Today, the university has distinctive strengths in the sciences, architecture, business, engineering, health, and other professions, all structured on a solid foundation in the liberal arts. The academic programs are organized into five colleges: The College of Agricultural, Environmental, and Natural Sciences; The College of Business, Organization, and Management; The College of Engineering, Architecture, and Physical Sciences; The College of Liberal Arts and Education; and The College of Veterinary Medicine, Nursing, and Allied Health. The curricula for the five colleges offer fifty-eight degrees including forty-two bachelor's degrees, fifteen master's degrees, the Doctor of Veterinary Medicine, and the Ph.D. in Materials Science and Engineering.

Tuskegee University is rooted in a history of successfully educating black Americans to understand themselves against the background of their total heritage and the promise of their individual and collective future. Over the past century, various social and historical changes have transformed this institution into a comprehensive and diverse place of learning whose fundamental purpose is to develop leadership, knowledge, and service for a global society. In addition, the university's programs focus on nurturing the development of high intellectual and moral qualities among students and stresses the connection between education and the leadership Americans need for highly trained leaders in general, especially for the work force of the twenty-first century and beyond.

View through the Lincoln Gates, Tuskegee University.

Special features in Tuskegee's program include: the George Washington Carver Museum (named for the distinguished scientist who worked at Tuskegee) which preserves the tools and handiwork of Dr. Carver; the Reserve Officers Training Corps Center (Army and Airforce), and the Center for Continuing Education—a nucleus for continuing education.

The educational and cultural environment of the university are enhanced by the Booker T. Washington Monument, *Removing the Veil of Ignorance and Superstition*, by Charles T. Keck, which honors the university's founder; the General Daniel "Chappie" James Center for Aerospace Science and Health Education, honoring America's first black four-star general who was a Tuskegee University graduate; and the Tuskegee Airmen's Plaza, commemorating the historic feats of America's first black pilots who were trained at Tuskegee University; the Kellogg Conference Center, the hub of continuing education at the University and one of only eleven such centers in the United States and England; the Tuskegee University Bioethics Center for Research and Health Care which is preparing to address some of the "critical moral questions that grow out of advancements in science and technology in regard to research on humans and health care;" and the Tuskegee University Library Archives and Washington Collection.

The Archives preserve the history of the university and continue the legacy of nationally acclaimed sociologist Monroe N. Work and the Department of Records and Research by maintaining documents, artifacts, and artistic works pertaining to the lives of African American and black people worldwide. The archives strive to organize and describe the materials so that they are readily available for research. Materials include the papers of Booker T. Washington, Robert Russa Moton, George Washington Carver, and The Lynching Files, composed of sixty-four archival boxes covering lynchings nationwide from 1881–1960.

Romare Bearden
*Early Morning*, c. 1967
Collage, 44 x 56 in.
Collection of Howard University Gallery of Art
© Romare Bearden Foundation/Licensed by
VAGA, New York, NY
checklist 30

# Conserving a Legacy

## Forging a partnership

The history and anatomy of a collaborative conservation, education, exhibition, and publication project

Jock Reynolds

One morning during the spring of 1995, Gary Burger, director of the Williamstown Art Conservation Center (WACC), called a committee of his trustees together for a brainstorming session in Williamstown, Massachusetts. The main agenda for the meeting was to imagine new projects and initiatives WACC might undertake to broaden the center's leadership role in the field of American art conservation. Attending the gathering as the director of the Addison Gallery of American Art and a member trustee of WACC, I was interested in what Burger would propose as new tasks for his volunteer board. For as long as I had known Burger, during trustee service to WACC, he was forever driving himself, his staff, and trustees to strengthen conservation and training programs in every forum that brought together committed arts professionals, educators, and funders. As the sure-handed leader of New England's only regional conservation center, one with a membership of fifty-six collecting institutions, Burger had carefully nurtured the growth of his organization, housed on the grounds of the Sterling and Francine Clark Art Institute. He had steadily increased the center's professional staff, expanded its physical facilities, and most recently led a $1.3 million capital fund drive that successfully endowed post-graduate conservation fellowships, education programs, and technical support services for WACC and its members. Ranging further afield from his work in New England, Burger shared his leadership abilities in chairing the national association of Regional Art Conservation Centers. Throughout 1994 and 1995, he helped the High Museum of Art in Atlanta found the first regional art conservation center in the southeastern states, generously sharing WACC's technical expertise and conservators with Ned Rifkin and Michael E. Shapiro, the High's director and deputy director/chief curator. Somehow Burger also made time in his busy life to advise the Knight Foundation as it explored a concept for creating a national model of inter-museum collection lending. This emerging program, now known as the Museum Loan Network (MLN), directed by Lori Gross from the campus of the Massachusetts Institute of Technology, is now fully operational and funded with substantial multiyear grants by the Knight Foundation and the Pew Charitable Trust. The MLN provides applying museums with grants to support curatorial travel, conservation treatments, and the packing and shipping of artworks identified for long-term exhibition and loan between sister institutions throughout America. The network is encouraging collecting institutions to care for and share their collections in a more generous way—bringing worthy artworks out of storage from lending institutions and placing them on public view at hosting institutions. Everyone benefits in the bargain.

The genesis of the *To Conserve a Legacy* project can be traced to a particular time and a group of people who were actively seeking to broaden communication and collaborative programming efforts between many American cultural and educational institutions. Burger had been a true leader in this regard. It was he who prodded his WACC trustees to imagine more expansive ways the conservation center might engage other institutions in cooperative ventures. Hence, gathering that day to brainstorm in Williamstown was a real pleasure, for the table had already been set.

Our trustee committee discussion began with reminiscences of how difficult it had been to wage WACC's recent capital fund drive. All present noted the severe funding cuts experienced by the National Endowment for the Arts and the National Endowment for the Humanities, whose generous grant programs had been vital to our successful efforts. The Andrew Mellon Foundation, twice a major funder of the WACC campaign, was also cited for its unflagging dedication to conservation and conservation training. Beyond these major funders, however, we acknowledged that contributions to our modest campaign had been hard won. The drive had required a small service organization to spend an inordinate amount of its time on fundraising work it was not really staffed to carry out. As we recalled the efforts that had successfully endowed post-graduate conservation fellowships for WACC, we discussed the importance of alerting students to the field of conservation *earlier* in their undergraduate studies, at a time when a fundamental training in the arts and science might better prepare more young people to pursue rewarding careers in the field of cultural preservation. We noted with concern the lack of racial diversity in the field of American conservation, counting on two hands the number of African American conservators we knew to be professionally active in the field. Burger at this point reminded us that Joyce Stoner, WACC's past board president and the director of the University of Delaware's art conservation program, had actively sought to recruit minority students to her program from the campuses of a number of historically black colleges and universities. Although Stoner's efforts had not yielded the results she sought, she was game for a more concerted effort, one we started to imagine in our discussions. My own thoughts in this regard drifted back to the six years I spent in Washington, D.C. (1983–1989), directing the Washington Project for the Arts, an artists's organization whose mission guided it to support the work of living artists through community-based programs and multicultural exhibitions that most museums were only beginning to imagine at that time.

Wifredo Lam (1902–1982)
*Exodo*, 1948
Oil on burlap, 50½ x 62 in.
Collection of Howard University Gallery
of Art

I will describe for the reader, as I did for my WACC colleagues, one of the first projects I had worked on for the Washington Project for the Arts, an exhibition that artist Keith Morrison, then the Washington Project for the Arts's board chairman and a professor at the University of Maryland, conceived as an important act of cultural memory in the nation's capitol. Morrison's show, entitled *Art in Washington and Its Afro-American Presence: 1940–1970*, set forth the important contributions that African American leaders at Howard University had made to the introduction of modern and contemporary art in Washington during a thirty-year period when few cultural and educational institutions acknowledged and supported such work in public forums (tracing the individual contributions of the Howard University Gallery of Art and Barnett Aden Gallery through individuals such as Alain Locke, James A. Porter, James V. Herring, and many others).

As Morrison wrote in the opening chapter to his exhibition's catalogue:

*It is common belief that art should transcend racial, social, and political problems. In fact, it has not always done so. At different times, people in the arts have had to find innovative ways to thrive in spite of such problems. This exhibition and essay deal with such an era of non-transcendence and with the manner in which artists confronted their environment and survived within it. They were compelled to realize that the idea of the "universal" in art—not black or white—had not yet found community acceptance. They had to await the time when their art was accepted on its own terms regardless of the race of the artist.*[1]

Working on this project had been an illuminating experience which introduced me, a white artist transplanted to the nation's capitol from northern California, to a community whose cultural and racial history I faintly knew and found to be very complex. As the concept for his exhibition and publication solidified, and was generously funded by the Washington Post Company, it was very gratifying to see how eagerly many people and institutions stepped forward to help the Washington Project for the Arts bring Morrison's exhibition to life. The Phillips Collection lent works by artists such as Richmond Barthé, Horace Pippin, Jacob Lawrence, James Lesesne Wells, and Irene Rice Pereira, while the Smithsonian Institution's Anacostia Neighborhood Museum and the Corcoran Gallery of Art also provided significant loans to the show. Individual artists lent generously too, creators such as David C. Driskell, Sam Gilliam, Jacob Kainen, Ed Love, John N. Robinson, and Lou Stovall, as well as private collectors such as Warren Robbins, the director emeritus of the Smithsonian's Museum of African Art, Delilah Pierce, and Ruth Cole Kainen. It was the first instance of extensive cross-racial collaboration by arts organizations, collectors, artists, and scholars I had witnessed.

Anonymous
*Felrath Hines*
Gelatin silver print
Collection of Dorothy C. Fisher

Most illuminating to me was the initial visit I made to the Howard University Gallery of Art, whose collections and history were central to Morrison's project. There I beheld for the first time a collection of artworks assembled by a leading historically black university, one whose holdings included strong representations of African art, broad samplings of nineteenth- and twentieth-century modern and American art, and a small group of early European paintings (works given to the gallery by the Samuel W. Kress Foundation). In searching for particular artworks Morrison wanted to borrow for his exhibition, it was readily apparent that Howard's physical facilities for displaying and caring for its collection were limited and severely overcrowded. This observation could certainly be made of many university and college galleries maintaining collections throughout America, but when I saw major works by Romare Bearden, Wifredo Lam, Edmonia Lewis, William H. Johnson, and others stacked cheek to jowl, it was painfully evident that Howard's cultural treasures deserved better care in climate-controlled galleries and storage rooms to survive in perpetuity.

One of the great works Morrison wanted for his show, Wifredo Lam's *Exodo*, (1948), had suffered a puncture and tear to its canvas and could not be exhibited until it was repaired. At the suggestion of Winston Kennedy, then chairman of Howard's art department, we turned to Felrath Hines, the chief conservator at the Hirshhorn Museum and Sculpture Garden for help. Hines was a multitalented artist who had painted actively in New York and served as Georgia O'Keeffe's personal conservator until Joshua Taylor, director of the National Collection of Fine Arts, beckoned him to work for the Smithsonian in the 1970s. Later still, Abraham Lerner, the first director of the Hirshhorn, enlisted Hines to help care for the avalanche of art that poured into Washington as the result of Joseph Hirshhorn's great cultural gift to the nation. Hines, a well-respected figure in Washington art circles, was a quiet and self-effacing man who worked diligently on his own vein of abstract painting as he conserved some of the greatest art made in the twentieth century. Little did I know that Hines was one of only a handful of African American conservators working in his field, and that he was passionately committed to helping conserve and preserve the art collections of historically black colleges and universities (HBCUs). Our entreaty to Hines for help in repairing Howard University's Wifredo Lam painting was warmly accepted, and he deftly and quickly patched the canvas. An extremely modest invoice accompanied *Exodo* when it was delivered to the Washington Project for the Arts for Morrison's showing, a gesture I now understand as Hines's personal contribution to an exhibition he deemed very important to the art community.

*Art in Washington and Its Afro-American Presence: 1949–1970* was a success in many regards, offering an interested public a fuller view of its community's complicated multiracial and multicultural history, while fostering a forthright forum for interracial cooperation that many individuals and institutions clearly longed to explore in a more substantive fashion. I found it enormously heartening to see museums extending their lending policies to enable the Washington Project for the Arts to borrow important works for Morrison's exhibition, to observe how both black and white scholars generously assisted our volunteer curator in his research and writing, and to watch the Washington Post Company take a leap of faith in providing substantial patronage. The successful endeavor inspired further thought and activity at the Washington Project for the Arts, where we soon began developing other projects we hoped might broaden the cultural and racial equity of the Washington art scene.

My first foray into organizing a retrospective exhibition came about as a direct result of Keith Morrison's project. In his exhibition I had seen for the first time the work of James Lesesne Wells, an accomplished printmaker and painter who had taught at Howard University for almost forty years. Wells had also been a contributor to the Harlem Renaissance as a young man, and a strong producer of graphic art for the WPA/FAP. When I finally met Wells, just after his eighty-fourth birthday, he was still happily producing his art in his Washington home and sitting on a mountain of work that had seldom or never been exhibited. Quite fortuitously, I mentioned the Wells retrospective I was considering to James Fitzpatrick, the Washington Project for the Arts's board president and his wife Sandra, remarking that I would like to locate a young artist/scholar to work with me on the project. "I know just the person for you," replied Sandra Fitzpatrick. "His name is Richard Powell." Powell, a printmaker, turning art historian, was presently ensconced a mere block away from the Washington Project for the Arts at the National Museum of American Art (NMAA) as a Smithsonian Fellow, completing his Ph.D. thesis at Yale University on the life and work of William H. Johnson. Powell was the product of two historically black colleges and universities. He had done his undergraduate work at Morehouse College and earned an M.F.A. in printmaking at Howard University. Powell had also lived with the Wells family for a year during his graduate studies and been well mentored by the venerable artist. I invited the young artist/scholar to lunch, inquired about his research, and learned that Powell was developing a major William H. Johnson retrospective and book for the NMAA, one that would require a significant amount of further study and conservation work on Johnson's estate. Fearing that Powell might be too busy to work with me on the Wells retrospective, I dared to suggest that we co-curate a Wells exhibition. To my delight, Powell said he would love to work on the project, that he deeply admired Wells, and he really wanted to see the elder artist receive broader recognition while he was still alive. With his acceptance a great personal and professional friendship began.

Developing the Wells show took Powell and me into a deeper study of Howard University's history and prompted us to acquire a rudimentary understanding of paper conservation work as we gathered full evidence of Wells's many contributions to American art. Our research also prompted us to share the Wells retrospective with The Studio Museum in Harlem (SMH), in the community where Wells had been an active artist/teacher at the Harlem Art Workshop. Dr. Mary Schmidt Campbell, then director of the SMH and her associate director, Kinshasha Holman Conwill, warmly welcomed the opportunity to host the Wells retrospective during the SMH's twentieth-anniversary year.

The Wells retrospective had a patron saint in the form of the Glen Eagles

Foundation, whose president, Betsy Frampton, heard about the project and offered the Washington Project for the Arts a major grant to support the exhibition and its catalogue. The Glen Eagles grant was thereafter supplemented with funds from the D.C. Commission on the Arts and Humanities and the Washington Post Company, which once again took notice of the Washington Project for the Arts's work in the community and offered financial help which enabled school children and teachers to visit and tour the Wells exhibition. When the show opened in December 1987, it was a day of celebration and aesthetic revelation at the Washington Project for the Arts. The reception for Wells and his work was jammed-packed with people who were amazed by the breadth and quality of the artist's work. At a memorable moment in the reception, Powell and I were approached by a group of teachers who told us, "We love this exhibition, and one of the things we really love about it is that you didn't schedule it in February." The comment brought realization that the Washington Project for the Arts was not perceived as a cultural organization that simply offered up exhibitions of African American artists during Black History Month, but that it was genuinely creating multicultural programs that more and more people in Washington were enjoying.

Jacob Kainen, the former curator of prints for the Smithsonian Institution, printmaker, and painter of national stature, wrote an appreciation for his friend "Lesesne" in the Washington Project for the Arts's Wells catalogue, describing a need so many of us felt— to marshal better support for worthy living artists:

> *Wells has changed his formal approach often since his New York days but through it all he has remained an expressionist, if by that term we mean an artist who goes straight for the jugular in his treatment of a medium. As he has grown older he has become wilder and more visionary. Certainly his late color linoleum prints are among the more memorable ones made recently in this country. It often happens that the most passionate and productive artists are also the most modest, and if their true worth is to be appreciated they must be met more than halfway.*[2]

Kainen and his wife, Ruth, certainly met Wells more than halfway, later backing up their belief in his work by purchasing a number of his late color linocuts and donating them to the National Gallery of Art, the Baltimore Museum of Art, the National Museum of American Art, and the Addison Gallery of American Art.

In the aftermath of the Wells show, I offered Richard Powell the position of director of programs at the Washington Project for the Arts. The dynamic young

James Lesesne Wells
*Negro Worker*, c. 1940
Lithograph on wove paper
14⅝ x 9¹³⁄₁₆ in. (image); 19⅛ x 12⁵⁄₁₆ in. (sheet)
Collection of Howard University Gallery of Art
checklist 252

scholar was soon brewing other major exhibition projects that excited the Washington community and built a large multiracial audience for our artists organization, doing so as the Washington Project for the Arts continued to expand African American representation on its staff and board of directors. Powell's next major curatorial offerings, *From the Potomac to the Anacostia* and *The Blues Aesthetic: Black Culture and Modernism,* further cemented the Washington Project for the Arts's reputation as an institution willing to program boldly and progressively. Philanthropic support for the organization surged ahead too, with the Ford Motor Company providing the corporate sponsorship for an extensive tour of Powell's *The Blues Aesthetic* show. In the midst of all this, two independent offers of employment finally lured me and Powell out of Washington at the end of the 1980s. I was approached by my alma mater, Phillips Academy, to assume the directorship of the Addison Gallery of American Art, while Powell was recruited to join the art faculty of Duke University, where he now chairs the Department of Art and Art History. Neither of us felt we could refuse the wonderful new opportunities afforded us, but neither of us chose to leave the Washington Project for the Arts with anything but great fondness and hope for the organization's continued success.

I have digressed from my account of Gary Burger's WACC trustee committee meeting to tell these stories of another organization and another time, for such stories and many others that might be told—accounts of interconnected institutional histories, important exhibitions, personal friendships, shared collegial interests, and enlightened patronage—importantly shape the values and purposes with which people lead their professional lives. Many of my colleagues who have helped form and direct the *To Conserve a Legacy* project could relay similar narratives were they to present the events and paths that led their lives towards the collaborative work we have been exploring together.

Returning now to the WACC trustee committee meeting that was underway in Williamstown during spring 1995, imagine if you will how the discussion proceeded that day among friends. Mention of Richard Powell, The Studio Museum in Harlem, and Howard University caused all present to realize that if we really were serious about wanting to attract minority students to the field of conservation early in their careers, and if we truly wanted WACC to treat a more diverse range of American art in its conservation laboratories, we needed to work in partnership with strong leaders and institutions active in the field of African American education and culture. It was orally acknowledged that such work would require WACC's board and staff to be proactive in creating new relationships and projects for the conservation center, yet excitement reigned at the prospect and rewards of what might be accomplished.

Having hosted *Homecoming: The Art and Life of William H. Johnson* at the Addison Gallery in 1992, the retrospective exhibition Richard Powell had curated and helped tour for the National Museum of American Art, I remembered a lecture my friend had delivered to Andover students and teachers, one during which he described a long list of HBCU art collections visited while researching the subject of his exhibition. Powell related how his travels had produced surprises at many junctures and awakened him further to rich HBCU holdings of American art. I suggested to my WACC colleagues that we call Powell for a recommendation of potential institutions with which to work, suggesting that Professor Joyce Stoner's idea of recruiting HBCU undergraduate students to the field of art conservation, might begin in some way through a conservation, education, exhibition, and publication project we could co-conceive with a group of HBCUs and WACC. Volunteering the Addison Gallery as an additional organizing partner for such a venture, I suggested that we contact Kinshasha Holman Conwill, now director of The Studio Museum in Harlem, to see if the flagship African American community museum most respected in American cultural circles, might be interested in discussing its potential project participation. We knew that the SMH had worked successfully with many HBCUs in the past, borrowing selected works from their collections for numerous exhibitions that have importantly illuminated African American art and culture for audiences throughout America. The SMH's leadership, it was agreed by all present at our meeting, could be vitally important in helping to form our consortium project.

Assigned to call Richard Powell and Ms. Conwill, I promised Gary Burger and my trustee colleagues that we could get a sense of what might be possible in short order. Such was the case, as Powell and Conwill responded enthusiastically to the gestating concept of organizing an HBCU-based collection care and exhibition project, one that would also involve undergraduate student training. They both sensed that this would be an ambitious and complex undertaking, and that the scale of the project would have to be kept manageable and focused to succeed. They further advised, that out of some twenty HBCUs that possess art collections of some consequence, perhaps only six institutions should be invited to participate in the project. Specific recommendations were made in this regard, since Powell and Conwill were well acquainted with HBCU gallery and museum directors and curators. They stressed the importance of including institutions that had made significant progress in caring for their collections, while including others who had yet to marshal the resources necessary to achieve real progress in such work.

*To Conserve a Legacy* project participants gathered in Andover, Massachusetts, for their first planning meeting, fall 1995.

The pair wisely cautioned that it would be a mistake to arouse public attention to a distorted view of the current state of care of HBCU art collections, and were insistent that the consortium project should accurately represent the accomplishments and challenges that could be cited across the field of HBCU collection care and education. Conwill and Powell also believed the project we were envisioning could arouse a measure of pride and some healthy competition among administrative leaders of HBCUs, as well as their graduates, perhaps stimulating greater resources that could further preserve the cultural legacies of the participating institutions.

Amidst these discussions arose the title for the project: *To Conserve a Legacy: American Art from Historically Black Colleges and Universities.* With it came a recommendation that gallery leaders from Clark Atlanta University (CAU), Fisk University, Hampton University, Howard University, North Carolina Central University (NCCU), and Tuskegee University be invited to Massachusetts to discuss their potential interest in the project.

The Addison Gallery and WACC then set to work organizing an introductory gathering of the potential project participants, one they would host in Andover and Williamstown during October 1995. When the invited leaders from the HBCU galleries came north, the idea was to have them visit the recently renovated Addison for a viewing of the museum's exhibition program, new climate-control systems, and collection study/storage rooms, before moving westward for a tour of WACC's conservation departments and laboratories. The rest of the weekend was to be reserved for meals and discussions of the collaborative work. Subsequently, Tina

Dunkley, director of the Clark Atlanta University Art Galleries, Kevin Grogan, director of the University Galleries, Fisk University, Mary Lou Hultgren, curator of the Hampton University Museum, Dr. Tritobia Hayes Benjamin, director of the Howard University Gallery of Art, Norman Pendergraft, director of the North Carolina Central University Art Museum, and Uthman Abdur-Rahman, professor of fine arts at Tuskegee University agreed to meet in Massachusetts with Dr. Richard Powell, chairman of Duke University's Art and Art History Department and Kinshasha Holman Conwill, director of The Studio Museum in Harlem. Patricia Cruz, the deputy director for programs of the SMH also joined the project's administrative team with SMH Senior Curator Valerie Mercer, as did BJ Larson, the Addison's director of museum resources and public information. WACC trustee Joyce Stoner extended a special invitation to a pair of African American conservators Ted Stanley and Leslie Guy, whom she felt could contribute a great deal of knowledge to our first project meeting. The two professionals readily agreed to join Stoner and the WACC colleagues for the working sessions Gary Burger was scheduling for the Williamstown portion of our impending meeting.

By the time the project participants arrived in Andover for a tour of the Addison Gallery and a dinner on October 28, conversations among the group were already percolating, stimulated by letters and telephone calls that had catalyzed everyone to speculate how a consortium project might be organized. Mary Lou Hultgren, curator of Hampton University's art collections, had earlier in the summer hosted Richard Powell and me for a campus visit with her museum's director, Jeanne Zeidler. The pair gave us a hard hat tour of the Hampton University Museum's major renovation and expansion project.

Arriving in Massachusetts for our group tours and discussions, Hultgren described for her HBCU peers and the other consortium team members Hampton's conservation progress, but allowed that portions of Hampton's collections still required conservation surveys and that the museum's large holdings, like those of almost all museums in America, would greatly benefit from expanded collection care initiatives. Hampton's undergraduate and graduate student programs in museum studies and art, were described for the group—programs from which the Addison Gallery had recruited Andrea Myers, its first education fellow.

Norman Pendergraft offered a snapshot of his much smaller HBCU art collection and museum, one founded in 1972. The NCCU Art Museum had successfully improved its physical plant and collection care practices over the years, doing so through a sustained series of judiciously administered efforts the resourceful director had created with great personal initiative. Pendergraft recalled earlier collection care initiatives that benefited his and other HBCU art collections, citing a project the Ford Foundation funded to help institutions such as NCCU, Fisk University, and Hampton University purchase flat files, object cabinets, and painting screens to improve storage and study conditions for artworks. Professor Uthman Abdur-Rahman of Tuskegee University described a situation of another kind, where within his institution no formal gallery or museum exists to house and exhibit its important paintings, sculpture, drawings, and photographs. He relayed how he and a pair of colleagues, University Archivist Dr. Daniel Williams and Assistant Archivist Cynthia Beavers Wilson, presently oversee the care of Tuskegee's art collections, integrating this important work within many other demands made on their time and material resources.

Tina Dunkley arrived at our first consortium meeting, delighted to relay news of important progress her university was making in advancing the care and display of its outstanding art collection. Dunkley, a dynamo of tenacious energy, had deftly positioned her institution to receive a major grant from the 1996 Atlanta Summer Games Olympic Arts Committee by working with her university's administration to conceptualize a renovation and exhibition project that could be readied for local and international visitors to the Atlanta Games in Clark Atlanta's historic Trevor Arnett Hall. Dunkley's vision foresaw the creation of spacious new galleries for the display of CAU's prized art collection, a project that was commencing its construction phase as she described it to our group. Hope for similar renovations and advances in collection care were conveyed to our consortium participants by Dr. Tritobia Benjamin who brimmed with enthusiasm for the project we were now all imagining with growing interest. Dr. Benjamin spoke candidly and wisely of the important historical role that presidential leadership has played in the life and fortunes of HBCU art collections, adding a brief history of the academic and administrative leadership of Howard University. She professed her strong belief that President H. Patrick Swygert was keenly interested in providing new support for the university's art collections and its longstanding academic programs in the Division of the Arts. Benjamin, Powell, and Conwill also recounted for our group something more of the racial history of education and art in Washington, D.C., discussing how different times and leaders produced eras when Howard University had alternately been more inwardly and then more outwardly directed in its programs and attitudes. Conwill, Hultgren, and Powell outlined the complex racial histories involved in the founding of many HBCUs, noting that the leading institutions had been created by multiracial groups of educators, religious leaders, industrialists, patrons, and politicians devoted to improving educational opportunities for the black population in the aftermath of the American Civil War. They and others added observations that many HBCUs offered early and important educational and spiritual training opportunities to students from American Indian communities and reservations, African countries, the Caribbean, Hawaii, the Philippines, Puerto Rico, etc. Resultantly, as one might reasonably expect, the art collections of many HBCUs had evolved containing a rich diversity of art holdings, each one different and culturally specific to its own institutional history. Our consortium participants agreed that most people still think that HBCU art collections only contain African American art. While discussing this point, our group began to reach its first consensus of opinion, that any project we might undertake together would do well to bring its focus on a full array of American art, work created by American artists in all media represented in the HBCU collections.

To provide the consortium project leaders with a full understanding of the range of conservation and educational services the Williamstown Art Conservation Center could provide the participating HBCUs, Gary Burger had arranged for all of WACC's conservators to give a tour of their laboratories and an overview orientation to their services and programs. The group proceeded to visit the paintings, works on paper, furniture, object, and scientific analysis laboratories, seeing firsthand where and how skilled departments of professionals organized and conducted their work, as well as what range of conservation treatments might be offered to help care for individual artworks owned in HBCU collections. The group also learned from Burger and his WACC colleagues what field and survey services might be offered to HBCU collections and their staffs, as well as what educational programs might be created to interest HBCU students in the field of art conservation.

Joyce Stoner and conservators Ted Stanley and Leslie Guy, described how important it was to get students interested in art conservation as a career while they were still undergraduates. Stanley and Guy spoke compellingly of the value of strong adult role modeling, saying that it would be wise for our project to build in some caring and attentive African American mentors and hosts to help recruited minority students to feel at home in a community that was predominantly white in population. This discussion prompted a broader conversation of what an HBCU intern training program might become within our project. The Studio Museum in Harlem and the Addison Gallery offered the suggestion that they could conceivably augment the student intern project by offering to host HBCU students for working stints supervised by their museum staffs, supplemented with visits to other conservation labs and meetings arranged with other curators, artists, and educators. Another idea that arose from some of the HBCU leaders stemmed from a simple fact of life, that their gallery and museum staffs, already deluged with daily work, were doing all they could simply to maintain the status quo of their collection care and exhibition programs. Could we, these HBCU leaders asked, consider structuring and funding the educational aspect of our project in a way that could pay the student interns during their summer training work and then pay them further to return to their institutions and provide hands-on assistance to their HBCU art collections? Might not such collection care work, rendered upon a return to campus, be seen as a natural culminating experience of internship, one that would have direct practical effect on HBCU collection care efforts? Our group liked this concept and felt internships structured in this manner would also help to spread word of the *To Conserve a Legacy* project throughout university communities. Once again, a group consensus evolved which incorporated these ideas and others into a schematic project design that continued to emerge throughout a weekend of conversations and friendly debates.

*To Conserve a Legacy* participants Kevin Grogan, Mary Lou Hultgren, and Kenneth Rodgers meet at the Howard University Gallery of Art, Washington, D.C., spring 1996.

Many other issues, concerns, and queries arose throughout the discussions—some very practical in nature, others of a more conceptual bent. How would the curatorial process for our project take form? Who could and would attempt to organize an exhibition that would seek to successfully balance issues of aesthetic content and merit with the practical needs of specific artworks that required expert examination and restoration? If the show were not to be curated by committee, which everyone thought was ill-advised, how would the participating gallery and museum directors and curators serve as advisors to a single project curator or a small team of curators? How many venues, others wondered, should the consortium seek for a *To Conserve a Legacy* exhibition? Where in the country should we strive to present the show? How would the number of exhibition venues affect the curatorial selections and the recommendations WACC conservators would make when considering which works could travel safely, and for how long? What challenges would such complexities pose to the project curators? Could they conceptualize and realize a coherent exhibition of American art that would certainly require some flexibility and rotations within its checklist?

Others wondered which cultural institution should premiere the exhibition and perhaps take the leading role in creating the public programs and public relations effort that would introduce the full scope of the *To Conserve a Legacy* project to a national audience. And, of course, another big question arose, one of funding. Where and how would we be able to raise the significant funds needed to tackle a project that was quickly assuming ambitious proportions? How, too, could we administer such a project and keep a consortium of ten institutions readily communicating with one another through what promised to be a four to five-year commitment to work closely together? Where, when, and how often should the consortium leaders continue to meet with one another? Were we all crazy to think that such a project might be undertaken and realized? By the end of the weekend no one thought so, yet there was much more to consider and talk about before such a project might begin in earnest.

As the Williamstown gathering concluded, Dr. Benjamin volunteered to host the next meeting of the project leaders at Howard University. Team members Burger, Powell, Conwill, Cruz, Mercer, Larson, and I agreed to research the conservation, administrative, fundraising, and curatorial logistics the project would require. The HBCU gallery and museum leaders resolved to determine their collection care needs within a conservation and student intern training program that could be discussed in greater detail with the conservators at WACC. The HBCU leaders also wanted to contemplate how they would provide advice and consent to the project's curatorial team, asking that Richard Powell and I jointly undertake this task on the consortium's behalf.

It was concluded that those of us working at the Addison Gallery, SMH, and WACC should work together with Richard Powell to draft a written project proposal, one that would outline what we had all envisioned while meeting with our HBCU colleagues in Andover and Williamstown. The document was then circulated to all project participants for comments and edits. Thereafter, the Addison Gallery began its work as the fiscal agent for the project, developing a budget and grant proposals that could begin to test the worthiness of the project in the non-profit marketplace of philanthropy.

Good fortune in fundraising seemed to attend this project from the onset. A meeting with Ellen Holtzman, the program officer of the Henry Luce

To Conserve a Legacy participants at the Howard University Gallery of Art, Washington, D.C., spring 1996.

Foundation in New York, produced an immediate interest in the project, along with an invitation to submit the first grant application in support of the *To Conserve a Legacy* consortium. Not only did the Luce Foundation's board of directors award the project a generous grant of $150,000 in spring 1996, its imprimatur—as a premiere supporter of many important American art exhibitions and publications—gave our consortium an enormous first boost. BJ Larson, the Addison's able director of museum resources, prepared an application to the National Endowment for the Arts, one that was submitted with real trepidation as the beleaguered federal agency struggled to continue its very existence. It should be said here, that public funding from the NEA, has long been a satisfying indicator of the intellectual and artistic merit of one's creative work. Artistic excellence and good ideas continue to carry real weight in this public funding arena, despite much of what has been written and said in the media and political circles during the last decade. Truth be told, our NEA grant application was submitted on a wing and a prayer.

In advance of the fall 1996 meeting, Dr. Benjamin and Assistant Director Scott Baker, offered me an extended visit to Howard's study/storage rooms and a glimpse of the curatorial pleasures and challenges that lay ahead for me and Richard Powell. We looked into drawers and boxes in the storage rooms, carefully opening them to reveal numerous beautiful and fragile works that clearly would benefit from being conserved, researched, and catalogued within the *To Conserve a Legacy* project. A particularly stirring moment occurred when Scott Baker brought out a cardboard box of papers given to the gallery by Alain Locke, the legendary

Howard professor who promoted African American culture with his teachings and writings. As we unpacked the box together, a folder opened to reveal two stunning ink drawings by Aaron Douglas. Probing deeper into the folder, we found more Douglas drawings, these marked on their borders in pencil marks clearly recognizable as printer's instructions. The images seemed very familiar, and we made a note to see if they had been published in one of Locke's famed volumes. In the same carton we came upon more treasures, gifts from artists to Locke that had been tucked away for years. A stunning Doris Ulmann platinum print emerged, still in its small frame, as did a sheath of prints by James Lesesne Wells, works Richard Powell and I had missed in our preparation of Wells's retrospective a decade earlier. I was already in something of a visual slather when Scott Baker showed me a large group of paintings that he and Dr. Benjamin felt needed attention and conservation. Leafing through these canvases I was astounded to come upon James Weeks's *Jazz Musician*, a remarkable figurative painting. The Howard canvas was from the same series of jazz pictures as the great Weeks painting held in the Bay Area Figurative School collection of the San Francisco Museum of Modern Art (SFMOMA). I had seen SFMOMA's Weeks's canvas often in past years, and knew it to be highly valued among a fine group of other seminal paintings produced by artists such as Richard Diebenkorn, David Park, Elmer Bischoff, and Joan Brown. How did this wonderful work make its way to Washington I wondered, and how might it be conserved to take its rightful place as a true jewel in Howard's collection?

Doris Ulmann
*The Mourner's Bench,* c. 1929–30
Coated platinotype, 8 x 6⅛ in.
Collection of Howard University Gallery of Art
checklist 240

Imagine if you will, a full afternoon of discoveries such as this. Know, too, that the great pleasure of my Howard visit was tinged with the impinging knowledge that Dr. Benjamin and Scott Baker faced considerable challenges in bringing the care of their remarkable collection up to a standard they both strongly desired. The Howard University Gallery of Art was not climate controlled, nor were its crowded storage rooms. Space to prepare exhibitions and to work on the collection was also limited, as were material resources that might provide a sustained conservation program and archival housings for many significant works of art. Our discussion of these issues made it apparent that it would be important to recommend that some of the WACC conservators begin making site visits and conducting collection surveys along with Richard Powell and me as we began our curatorial work. Teamed this way with our HBCU colleagues, WACC's work would proceed within a context of fully integrated conversation, advice, and knowledge. This recommendation was relayed to Gary Burger at WACC as Dr. Benjamin prepared to receive our group. Not surprisingly, Burger had reached a similar conclusion and had already spoken with WACC trustee John Whitney Payson, asking if the Whitney family's Greentree Foundation might be interested in helping support a series of HBCU collection surveys as our consortium project got underway. Payson, a great patron and champion of conservation, readily secured the support required for this work, which gave our project its second significant boost of philanthropy.

By the time our project leaders gathered in Washington during the first week-end of November, Dr. Benjamin had arranged for Howard University President H. Patrick Swygert to greet our group and be briefed on the *To Conserve a Legacy* project. President Swygert's enthusiasm for the project was immediately apparent. During the next year he would make good on his promise to support our work and Howard's gallery by allocating capital funds to climate-control the gallery and its storerooms as the Fine Arts Building underwent renovation.

James Weeks
*Jazz Musician,* 1960
Oil on canvas, 58 x 42 in.
Collection of Howard University Gallery of Art
checklist 249

The Howard meeting allowed our consortium to share the news of our first funding successes and to further define the scope of our future work and how we would divide and imple-ment it among ourselves. The design of the HBCU student intern project was again discussed and the consor-tium agreed to place the intern selec-tion in the hands of the HBCU gallery and museum directors. It was also agreed that the consortium would endeavor to sustain its intern program over two summers and academic years (hosting six students per year—one from each HBCU). The internships would run concurrently with the sum-mer conservation treatments planned for artworks selected from the HBCU collections. The Studio Museum in Harlem and the Addison Gallery con-firmed their willingness to each host three of the HBCU interns for month-long working and study stints at their institu-tions, thus allowing two smaller groups of interns to rotate in and out of WACC's conservation departments. Such an arrangement would help the interns receive closer supervision and personal mentoring attentions. We expected to compensate the students well, and it was concluded that each intern should receive a $5,000 stipend, $1,000 of general expenses, and underwriting for all travel and board associated with the internships. A portion of each intern stipend ($1,500) was to be reserved for HBCU students to earn in service to their home campus collec-tions after receiving their training.

Discussions at the Howard gathering also focused on a consideration of desired venues for the *To Conserve a Legacy* exhibition. It was readily decided that The Studio Museum in Harlem should debut the exhibition in New York, where many HBCU graduates live and major audiences for all manner of art abound. It

Charles White
*Progress of the American Negro*, 1939–40
Oil on canvas, 5 ft. x 12 ft. 11 in.
Collection of Howard University Gallery of Art
checklist 256

was felt that Washington, Atlanta, and Chicago were three major cities that should host the show if possible. Two of these cities were home to participating HBCUs (Howard University and Clark Atlanta University—neither of their galleries would be able to fully accommodate a large-scale exhibition such as the one being planned). The concept of creating partnership venues surfaced, an idea many liked for it suggested a ready mechanism for creating more racially mixed audiences for the show, ones that would hopefully make concerted efforts to visit institutions beyond their normal patterns of attendance. Perhaps, Ms. Dunkley thought, the Clark Atlanta University Art Galleries could share the exhibition with the High Museum in Atlanta and together entice audiences from Tuskegee University to drive up from Alabama to see the show. Similar thoughts visited Dr. Benjamin who revealed that she might wish to have our exhibition presented in its entirety at a major museum in the nation's capitol, while she mounted an additional exhibition of ancillary works from Howard's permanent collection. Kenneth Rogers from North Carolina Central University, who was attending the consortium as the newly named director of NCCU's museum, suggested that NCCU and Duke University collaborate in the project's co-presentation. He and Richard Powell consented to explore this possibility. Everyone present readily agreed that the Art Institute of Chicago, which all noted had been making significant progress in serving its city's large black population more fully, and had long been an academic training ground for many black artists, also ought to be a focus of our attentions. It was observed that Chicago is home to the largest population of HBCU graduates extant in America. Ms. Conwill, Richard Powell, and I were assigned the negotiation of venues and scheduling for the *To Conserve a Legacy* exhibition.

Before leaving the graces of Dr. Benjamin's hospitality at Howard University, our group was treated to a viewing of Charles White's magnificent mural, *Progress of the American Negro*. This work on canvas, which had been stored unstretched and rolled in Howard's storage rooms for more than forty years, was unrolled before our eyes to gasps of appreciation. Not only was the work a clear candidate for conservation, its subject was remarkably entwined with the histories of African American education and some of the particular HBCUs participating in the project. Booker T. Washington and George Washington Carver loomed as giant leaders in White's expansive canvas, along with John Brown, Sojourner Truth, and Marian Anderson, leading a serpentining legion of the people out of a legacy of servitude towards knowledge, modern life, and a fuller participation in American society. Without any hesitation, White's work was immediately placed on the exhibition's checklist and slated for a conservation treatment that would bring it before public audiences once more.

While in Washington that weekend, Ms. Conwill, Ms. Cruz, Ms. Mercer, and I paid a visit to Dorothy Fisher, the recently widowed wife of Felrath Hines, the artist/conservator who had so diligently repaired Howard University's *Exodo* painting by Wifredo Lam for the exhibition Keith Morrison curated for the Washington Project for the Arts. As I watched a beautiful procession of abstract paintings rotate before my eyes in Hines's studio, many of which would hold their own in concert with those produced by artists such as Josef Albers, John McLaughlin, Ad Reinhardt, Ellsworth Kelly, and others, I began to realize more fully how an artist's race could still dictate his or her professional fortunes in America. Hines's widow relayed with quiet resignation how her husband's work had not made it to mainstream galleries and museums supporting abstract and minimalist painting during his lifetime. She recalled, too, how her husband had participated richly in the African American cultural community, but resisted being included in exhibitions that made the subject of his race tantamount to the identity of his art. I thought back again to the first lines of Keith Morrison's catalogue essay:

*It is common belief that art should transcend racial, social, and political problems. At different times, people in the arts have had to find innovative ways to thrive in spite of such problems.[3]*

Indeed, Hines had found a way to thrive in his creative and personal life: to paint as he chose, to conserve artworks he came to know and love in New York and through his work at the Smithsonian, and to serve HBCU collections at Howard, Hampton, and Fisk Universities, where people knew his quiet manner and purposes well.

John Biggers
*Old Man,* 1945
Oil on canvas, 58¼ x 34¼ in.
Collection of Hampton University Museum
checklist 41

I was to see another canvas by Hines when I next traveled to the Hampton University Museum with Richard Powell in December 1996. The painting had been purchased by Jeanne Zeidler and Mary Lou Hultgren for Hampton's collection and spirited the four of us into another discussion of the artist's work as an important creator and conservator. A feeling emerged among us that it might be fitting to dedicate the *To Conserve a Legacy* project to Felrath Hines, an idea which received warm affirmation from our team.

Powell and I had begun scheduling curatorial visits with our HBCU colleagues whenever we could, wanting to view as much material as possible in order to get a feel for which artworks our peers felt needed conservation and which works might suggest an interesting exhibition to our minds and eyes. Powell had visited Hampton many times before, initially while teaching nearby as a young instructor at Norfolk State University, and then later during his doctoral research of William H. Johnson's life and art. From such visits he was well aware of the many gifts the Harmon Foundation had made to Hampton's collection—outstanding works by Johnson and other African American artists. We viewed many of these with Hultgren and Zeidler before delving into other treasures Hampton was hoping to conserve and display. A trio of beautiful early canvases by John Biggers was unrolled before our eyes. *Old Coffee Drinker* and *Old Man* particularly appealed to us. These were works the artist had created at Hampton in 1945 while studying with Viktor Lowenfeld, an Austrian artist and psychologist of Jewish ancestry who had fled Europe and come to teach at Hampton during the World War II era. Lowenfeld had stimulated Biggers and another well-known Hampton graduate Samella Sanders Lewis, to dedicate their lives to art. Biggers recently made a gift of his stunning expressionistic student canvases to his alma mater, not long after completing two very large murals in Hampton University's new Harvey Library. Biggers's beautiful early works cried out to be conserved and restretched after having been stored in the artist's mother's garage for many years. These works were immediately noted as likely candidates for the *To Conserve a Legacy* project, as well as Samella Sanders Lewis's *Waterboy*, another portrait that stood to benefit from a careful cleaning and a new frame. The visit to Hampton also included a stop at the university's Harvey Library, where we viewed a remarkable photographic archive that was soon slated to be rehoused in climate-controlled study/storage rooms in the Hampton University Museum's new building. Mary Lou Hultgren and Hampton's archival assistant, Donzella Maupin, introduced us to a staggering quantity of single images and photographic albums. We soon began paying particular attention to works that documented Hampton's educational programs and community and campus life which included the American Indian programs. As someone who has worked extensively in the field of photography, creating images and curating numerous exhibitions, I was astonished by what I saw at Hampton. There were images of outstanding quality at every turn as Powell and I explored considerable materials that were brought to our study tables. Many of these images record subjects and histories that offer fascinating research opportunities for present and future generations. A rich opportunity awaited our consortium to help Hampton survey its photography holdings and launch a collection care program that might begin to rehouse thousands of fragile cyanotypes, platinum prints, and silver gelatin prints, while conserving particular images and noteworthy albums in the collection for our exhibition.

Powell and I ended our visit with Hultgren and Zeidler, energized by all we had seen and discussed, and then prepared to meet with Kevin Grogan of Fisk University. For me, the trip to Nashville was a first, one I made with Thomas Branchick, WACC's chief painting conservator. We rendezvoused with Grogan and Powell for a viewing of the collections held in Fisk's Van Vechten Collection and Aaron Douglas Galleries, as well as other artworks in Jubilee Hall, the library, and main administration building. Again, visual and historical surprises abounded throughout our visit. Not only had Carl Van Vechten encouraged his friend Georgia O'Keeffe to bestow a major gift of paintings, prints, drawings, photographs, and sculpture from Alfred Stieglitz's estate to Fisk University, a collection which came to be housed in an historic campus building renamed in Van Vechten's honor, the artist had also generously given hundreds of his own photographs to Fisk. Many photographs of cultural luminaries—leading artists, dancers, composers, writers, and musicians—comprised the artist's major gift to Fisk University. I quickly realized that Fisk's Van Vechten Collection richly paralleled the Beinecke Library's broad holdings of the artist's work at Yale University. Once again, the world seemed a very small place.

Grogan gave us a full picture of Fisk's collection care needs in short order. A tour of Jublilee Hall revealed the heartening results of a major conservation project, one that had recently been undertaken on a huge nineteenth-century oil painting sited in the campus's most historic building. The restored painting of the famed Jubilee Singers was a result of their London performance which so moved Queen Victoria that she ordered their portrait painted in 1873 by Edmund Havel. Revenues from previous United States tours of the Jubilee Singers purchased the land that Fisk currently occupies.

A daunting conservation challenge for Fisk University existed elsewhere within its own administration quarters, where an extensive mural project Aaron Douglas had executed on canvas was applied on walls of the second floor of another historic building. The mural had been stabilized but the building was in a state of alarming deterioration, awaiting restoration scheduled for 1999–2000. Other easel paintings executed by the artist, classic works in the gallery's collection such as *Building More Stately Mansions* and *Noah's Ark*, had been carefully conserved by Felrath Hines, who had earlier tended Fisk's Alfred Stieglitz Collection as a consulting conservator. Grogan showed us where other conservation challenges

Carl Van Vechten
*Horace Pippin*, 1940
Gelatin silver print, 10 x 8 in.
Fisk University
checklist 244

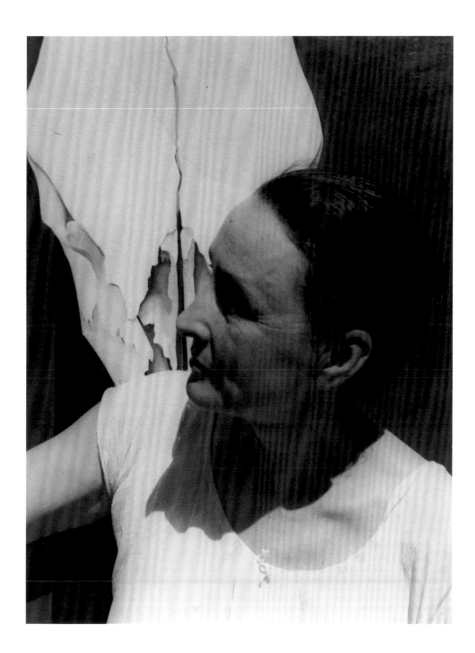

Carl Van Vechten
*Georgia O'Keeffe*, 1935
Gelatin silver print, 10 x 8 in.
Fisk University
checklist 243

water and selected quotations that commemorate the potent ideas and forces that guided the great man's life and swept him deeply into the American consciousness. The next morning we began our work by searching out two sculptures created by Edmonia Lewis, an artist who trained and worked in Europe and America during the nineteenth century. Lewis's *Awake* and *The Old Arrow Maker and His Daughter*, two beautiful marble carvings, were uncrated for our examination. Immediately they revealed themselves as candidates for our conservation project, needing cleaning and minor repairs. Another storage room contained a marvelous cache of important paintings and works on paper that Richard Powell had seen on his first research visit to Tuskegee. These works called out to be conserved and seen in public once again—notable examples of art by William H. Johnson, William Harper, and William E. Scott.

Cynthia Beavers Wilson, assistant archivist, in the files of Tuskegee University.

It was our visit with Dr. Daniel Williams and Cynthia Beavers Wilson, Tuskegee's archivist and assistant archivist, however, that opened a floodgate of important visual imagery and historical material before our eyes. The archive's photographic collections were simply remarkable. Beautiful images recorded by Arthur P. Bedou, Cornelius M. Battey, Leonard Hyman, P.H. Polk, and many others who had chronicled the life and leaders of Tuskegee's early years, were spread before us as we made queries and requests of our hosts. It was readily apparent that a conservation study and survey of Tuskegee's photography collections should be undertaken within the scope of our project.

Having worked on exhibition and artist projects within the collections of various California libraries and archives when living in San Francisco, I was accustomed to researching and locating artistically important photographs within large caches of photographs catalogued merely by title and/or subject. Richard Powell brought a deep knowledge of HBCU history and African American history to help aid our selective viewing, and Thomas Branchick noted the conservation and collection care issues facing our Tuskegee colleagues. In our discussions it was agreed that WACC should send Lyzanne Gann, its photograph conservator, to Alabama to conduct the study of the photographic materials collection held in the Tuskegee University archives. In this way the *To Conserve a Legacy* project could produce some immediate recommendations for the collection's future care. Consensus among us held that WACC should receive the cache of paintings, sculptures, and works on paper that Powell, Branchick, and I selected. We deemed these works as likely candidates to be placed on the *To Conserve a Legacy* exhibition's checklist, and it was agreed that treatment proposals for these works could be prepared right away, as Tuskegee had no gallery in which to exhibit these artworks, nor a proper climate-controlled space in which to store them. Dr. Williams and Ms. Wilson welcomed us to begin active curatorial research within their photography collection, something Powell and I planned to do through future visits. A mere glimpse of what was contained in these holdings had quickly convinced Branchick, Dunkley, Powell, and me that HBCU archives likely contained many unknown and little-known photographs of great importance.

Returning north through Atlanta, Branchick, Dunkley, Powell, and I discussed the new conservation lab that WACC was helping the High Museum of Art to

Cornelius Marion Battey
*Carpentry Division*, c. 1920
Gelatin silver print, 7⁵⁄₁₆ x 9³⁄₁₆ in.
Collection of Tuskegee University
checklist 26

Cornelius Marion Battey
*Class in Tailoring, Tuskegee Institute, Mr. E. Carter
Instructor*, c. 1920
Gelatin silver print, 7 x 9 in.
Collection of Tuskegee University
checklist 27

open, and agreed that Ned Rifkin, the High Museum of Art's energetic director, might be a perfect partner with Tina Dunkley and CAU for the public display of the *To Conserve a Legacy* exhibition. Rifkin's interest was soon aroused and the High later committed to co-host the show in Atlanta.

The next research trips took me to Howard University again and then to Durham, North Carolina, where meetings with Kenneth Rogers of NCCU, Richard Powell, Michael Mezzatesta, director of the Duke University Art Museum, and Iris Tillman Hill, director of Duke's Center for Documentary Studies, produced another group of colleagues interested in sharing a venue for the *To Conserve a Legacy* project. The visit to Durham was an opportunity to view and visually memorize much of the NCCU collection. There we began a tentative checklist of works we might wish to borrow from the NCCU collection.

*To Conserve a Legacy* participants at the new Hampton University Museum, Hampton, Virginia, hosted by Jeanne Zeidler, director.

By the time all the *To Conserve a Legacy* project leaders met again in the new home of the Hampton University Museum, May 1997, a tentative, preliminary exhibition checklist for the project was evolving and three shipments of artwork had been sent to WACC for examination. Treatment proposals for artworks received from Tuskegee, Howard, and Hampton Universities were well underway in Williamstown as WACC, the Addison Gallery, and The Studio Museum in Harlem readied their staffs, guest speakers, and mentors to receive the first six HBCU student interns. Each HBCU leader attending the Hampton gathering presented a brief profile of the student selected to represent their university, and the consortium members shared news that was developing on a number of fronts. The funding of the consortium project had increased in healthy fashion with the receipt of a $125,000 grant from the National Endowment for the Arts, an award of public support that sent our spirits soaring. Other important funds were awarded the consortium from the LEF Foundation and the Joseph Harrison Jackson Foundation—the latter grants being earmarked to support the *To Conserve a Legacy* student intern program. Funding proposals being prepared for the AT&T Foundation and Ford Motor Company were discussed by the consortium leaders developing the project's fiscal resources, as was the important news that Gary Burger was leaving his post at WACC to become the new director of cultural programs for the John S. and James L. Knight Foundation in Miami, Florida. It was also announced that Thomas Branchick, who had conducted much of the center's fieldwork in helping to organize the *To Conserve a Legacy* project, would shortly become WACC's interim director, a position he would hold while a search for Burger's replacement proceeded. He, too, joined the project meeting in Hampton, Virginia.

Those of us already inspired by the recent progress Clark Atlanta University and Howard University were making in renovating their galleries and collection care facilities, were in for another treat when touring the new Hampton University Museum with Director Jeanne Zeidler and Curator Mary Lou Hultgren. Not only had the museum staff's and President William Harvey's capital fundraising efforts been very successful, the resultant remodeling of historic Huntington Library yielded elegant, spacious, and efficiently organized permanent collection and temporary exhibition galleries, education facilities, well-equipped offices, and a new museum shop. The museum complex also included a newly expanded collection storage and office annex, one easily accessed from an ample loading dock that was adjacent to a large freight elevator and other "back of house" amenities supported with new climate-control systems.

The careful planning efforts pursued by Zeidler, Hultgren, and others had clearly helped create a first-rate museum facility that would enable Hampton University to conserve its growing cultural legacy for future generations. Efforts were already underway to install the remainder of their new and expanded permanent collection galleries. A series of temporary exhibitions was taking shape, and expanded educational and collection care programs were being developed.

Back in Williamstown, Andover, and New York, the staffs of WACC, the Addison, and SMH were preparing to receive the first six HBCU student interns in two groups. They arrived the third week in June; Carol Cooper, Howard University; Jonique Gilliam, Clark Atlanta University; and Julian Weaver, North Carolina Central University, accepted the first tour of conservation training at WACC. Traveling to Andover for a program of museum collection care, community-based field trips, and mentoring were Kelli Hall, Fisk University; Tamara Holmes, Hampton University; and Pierre Blackman, Tuskegee University.

The six interns had been split into groups of three for practical and conceptual reasons. WACC's conservators felt that they could provide the very best educational experience to the interns through hands-on learning pro-

Jock Reynolds (left) discusses project works with student interns, project participants, and staff conservators at the Williamstown Art Conservation Center, summer 1997.

jects executed directly on the works arriving from the HBCU collections, rotating these projects within all departments of the conservation center. Reasonable limits of work space and equipment dictated that the intern groups be kept as small as possible, yet also cohere as intimate peer-learning seminars. Knowing from our initial curatorial research that Fisk, Hampton, and Tuskegee Universities possessed extensive photographic holdings, it was suggested that the Addison Gallery, which possesses a particularly rich collection of American photographs, host a trio of students from HBCUs with complementing collection strengths during the two-year training program that lay ahead. This logic was accepted and it was further agreed that The Studio Museum in Harlem would host a trio of students from Clark Atlanta, Howard, and North Carolina Central Universities each summer, providing them with a month-long program of museum studies, community-based field trips, and mentoring after they had acquired their initial conservation training at WACC. We decided to bring all six interns together with the consortium project leaders each summer in Williamstown, close to the time when the trios would be rotating to their next institutional hosts. This would enable the group as a whole to meet and talk about the *To Conserve a Legacy* project, examining and encouraging the work the HBCU student interns and WACC conservators were conducting and discussing the curatorial premises that would be evolving for the project's exhibition and publication.

Insight into the learning and conserving that commenced in the summer of 1997 can be readily gleaned from the journal kept by Carol Cooper, Howard

University's first student intern. Remarking on the first day spent at WACC, she wrote of being "surrounded by people who truly love what they do and work collectively well too. . . . I've learned about basic elements and their importance—glue and people." On their first day of work, Carol Cooper, Jonique Gilliam, and Julian Weaver were taught how to clean paper by Leslie Paisley and Rebecca Johnson, WACC's paper conservators. They learned how to make paste for hinging and securing paper art to mattes, and brushed up math skills to calculate precise methods for cutting and fabricating mattes. By the second day of her internship, Ms. Cooper was carefully helping unpack:

*lots of paper pieces from Howard—lots of William H. Johnsons, early James Wells, and a couple of Tanners and lots of Dox Thrash. . . . It was like my birthday or Christmas—unwrapping the treasures. Unwrapping the pieces gave me such a connection with the artist. I felt honored to handle their works. I began working in paper conservation on two Aaron Douglas pieces. Years ago I began a special kinship with him because we are from the same part of the country, the Midwest (he from Kansas—me from Missouri—he even taught at Lincoln High School in Kansas City, MO). I loved cleaning and hinging the works. And yes, I prayed to the Matte God first so I wouldn't make big mistakes.*[4]

Howard University intern Carol Cooper (right) discusses her conservation work with *To Conserve a Legacy* curators, project participants, and student interns in Williamstown Art Conservation Center's paper laboratory, summer 1997.

As conservation projects for the HBCU student interns working in Williamstown burgeoned, other learning experiences were afoot in Andover. There, the trio of HBCU student interns was helping the Addison's staff survey, clean, mount, and catalogue a large trove of Philippe Halsman photographs in the gallery's collection. They also toured other museums and conservation laboratories, and were warmly received by Edmund Barry Gaither, the founding director of the Museum of The National Center of Afro-American Artists and the conservation staff of the Isabella Stewart Gardner Museum. African American mentors such as Gaither, and venerable Boston artist, Allan Rohan Crite, were especially interesting to the HBCU student interns. Gaither spoke eloquently of the programs his institution had produced and the continuing economic and racial issues that presented special challenges to his community-based museum. Crite concurred, but added a working artist's perspective to the picture from his almost ninety years of living, doing so in the welcoming company of his wife Jackie Cox-Crite, director of the Allan Rohan Crite Research Institute, who had graciously agreed to host HBCU student interns visits. As they surveyed Crite's paintings, prints, and books of drawings, I alerted the student interns that they would be encountering an early painting of Mr. Crite's at WACC during their next stint of summer training. We had already selected Crite's *Beneath the Cross of St. Augustine* (1936) as a canvas that should be conserved and exhibited within the *To Conserve a Legacy* project. I was pleased to realize that once again we had the ability to create what Carol Cooper had described in her journal as "a direct connection to the artist."

Aaron Douglas
*Rebirth,* c. 1925
Ink and graphite on wove paper, 12¹⁄₁₆ x 9 in.,
Collection of Howard University Gallery of Art
checklist 78

Aaron Douglas
*Sahdji,* c. 1925
Ink and graphite on wove paper, 12¹⁄₁₆ x 9 in.,
Collection of Howard University Gallery of Art
checklist 80

The planned summer meeting of all the HBCU project participants took place in Williamstown during the last weekend in June, a time during which the first trio of HBCU student interns proudly displayed the work they had accomplished with the WACC conservators. Richard Powell and Valerie Mercer, offered the entire intern cadre an informative slide lecture and led a discussion of African American art, placing its traditions of visual expression within the broader context of American art.

Powell and I examined all of the artworks that had to date been sent north for the WACC conservators to examine. Specific treatments were discussed and recommended by the conservators as they spoke before the exhibition co-curators and the HBCU student interns and leaders. These discussions made clear how complex our choices might become in the future, and helped suggest the manner through which works should be prioritized for conservation on the basis of aesthetic merit, need for treatment, cost of treatment, and availability to the *To Conserve a Legacy* exhibition. Many ideas governing our basic working process had to be ironed out, with ground rules established as to how our work would proceed. As co-curators, Powell and I were recognizing that this was going to be a challenging exhibition to organize—one that would attempt to synthesize some important historical and artistic ideas through a large group of artworks produced in multiple media, a good number of which would be rotated in and out of the exhibition as stipulated by the recommendations of conservators and the needs of the HBCU museum and gallery directors. All present agreed that this mammoth effort would require clear communication and unwavering good will. Kinshasha Conwill offered a basic premise to guide our work—that the artistic excellence of our project should be the very best it could be, in both form and content, when we presented it to general audiences in the public forums that will receive our traveling exhibition.

Allan Rohan Crite with *To Conserve a Legacy* student interns Tamara Holmes, Kelli Hall, Jackie Cox-Crite, and Pierre Blackman, in his Boston studio, summer 1997.

The basic goodwill and generosity fueling our collective work was reinforced at a dinner for the participants hosted by Donald Friary, chairman of WACC board of trustees, and Michael Conforti, WACC trustee and director of the Sterling and Francine Clark Art Institute. Friary, also director of Historic Deerfield, warmly welcomed the project participants, as did Conforti. Linda Shearer, a former WACC trustee and director of the Williams College Art Museum, added her greetings to the project participants and later provided a tour of her teaching museum.

As the Williamstown summer meeting ended, farewell toasts were offered at a dinner celebrating Gary Burger, who was heartily thanked for his longtime leadership of WACC and for helping to launch the *To Conserve a Legacy* project.

The HBCU leaders departed; a new spate of work began for the two trios of HBCU student interns. Those hailing from Clark Atlanta, Howard, and North Carolina Central universities were immersed in numerous learning experiences at The Studio Museum in Harlem and exposed to some of the vast cultural resources of New York City. Forays to nearby conservation programs were also arranged for the student interns. WACC trustee Margaret H. Ellis, chairman of

Allan Rohan Crite
*Beneath the Cross of St. Augustine,* 1936
Oil on canvas, 20 1/8 x 36 in.
Collection of Howard University Gallery of Art
checklist 63

the conservation center at the Institute of Fine Arts at New York University (NYU), arranged a tour of her center, guided by Shelley Fass. A visit was set up at the conservation laboratory of Rustin Levenson, where the HBCU student interns spoke with Harriet Irgang, who had worked on the restoration of the Charles Alston murals at Harlem Hospital. Later in July, the student interns met with Cheryl LaRouche, an architectural conservator working to care for the historic black burial grounds extant on Manhattan Island. From LaRouche and Camille Billops of the Hatch-Billops Collection, the interns felt they ended their SMH residency with many new insights into the complicated racial, political, economic, and cultural issues that confront African American artists, scholars, curators, conservators, and collectors.

Back in Williamstown, the other trio of HBCU student interns worked diligently to carefully organize and archivally sleeve the thousands of photographs that comprised Hampton University's historic Camera Club collections. They also assisted WACC's Lyzanne Gann, Leslie Paisley, and MK Lalor in conducting surveys and treatment on the Hampton and Dakota albums, while also studying many other photographs. The HBCU student interns were trained to begin the cleaning of Tuskegee's two Edmonia Lewis sculptures, which underwent their initial treatment as the first summer of HBCU student intern work came to an end.

Exciting discoveries of many sorts were made that summer, illuminations that delighted all of us working on the project. One worth mentioning involved the combined efforts of WACC's object and paper lab conservators, who were intent on learning something more about William Artis's terra-cotta *Bust of Miss Coleman* as they prepared to treat the sculpture. The work from Howard University's collection had broken in two pieces and arrived at WACC accompanied with two photographs I had found in the Howard University Gallery of Art's storage room. The photographs recorded Artis himself sculpting Miss Coleman's portrait before a class of Howard University art students. Miss Coleman was posing "live" for the artist as he worked. The images were immediately

left: *To Conserve a Legacy* project participants, student interns, curators, and conservators at the Williamstown Art Conservation Center, summer 1997.

above: Conservator Lyzanne Gann (center) and interns Carol Cooper, Kelli Hall, Jonique Gilliam, Julian Weaver, Tamara Holmes, and Pierre Blackman viewing artworks at the Williamstown Art Conservation Center, summer 1997.

helpful to the object conservators who were studying the manner in which Artis's piece had been fabricated, then mysteriously fractured, and might now be repaired. Leslie Paisley recommended that she carefully separate the images from their thick acidic mounts. Upon receiving Dr. Benjamin's permission to proceed with the proposed treatment, Paisley soon discovered that the photographs had been taken by the Scurlock Studio of Washington, D.C., that had chronicled Howard University's history and community life in the nation's capitol for many years. The Scurlock Studio stamp was clearly evident on the back of each image once WACC's conservator had cleaved the photographs from their nonarchival mounts.

At the end of summer 1997, the HBCU interns returned to their respective campuses to resume their academic studies and to serve their galleries and museums in earning the final portion of their project stipends. BJ Larson and I accelerated our fundraising efforts at the Addison Gallery, fortified with discussions and foundation meetings that Kinshasha Conwill and Patricia Cruz helped us orchestrate from their offices at the SMH. The Addison and SMH leaders worked closely

Addison Scurlock
*William Artis, Giving a Demonstration,* (Portrait
Sculpture Class: "Bust of Miss Coleman"), 1946
Gelatin silver prints
Each 8⅛ x 10 in. (image); 9¼ x 11¼ in. (sheet)
Collection of Howard University Gallery of Art
checklist 214, 213

William Artis
*Bust of Miss Coleman*, 1946
Terra-cotta with wood base, 14 x 8 x 9 in.
Collection of Howard University Gallery of Art
checklist 21

together with Richard Powell to begin shoring up institutional hosts and co-hosts for the *To Conserve a Legacy* exhibition. Fruitful discussions with the Corcoran Gallery of Art's director, Jack Cowart, and curator of photography and media, Philip Brookman, produced an important venue for the show in the nation's capital, while similar talks and correspondence with the Art Institute of Chicago's director, James Wood, and curator of twentieth-century art, Jeremy Strick, led another great American museum to add the project to its future exhibition schedule. Paired presentations for the exhibition also firmed up between the CAU Art Galleries and the High Museum, with Tina Dunkley and Ned Rifkin securing their working agreement. Another partnership formed between Jeanne Zeidler of the Hampton University Museum and William Hennessey, the newly named director of the Chrysler Museum of Art. Fisk University's Kevin Grogan worked diligently in his community to finalize a pairing of his Nashville institution with the Tennessee State Museum, directed by Lois Riggins Ezell. The three-way partnership of North Carolina Central University's Art Museum, Duke University's Art Museum, and the Center for Documentary Studies also jelled.

Amidst all of this busy work, very heartening news arrived from the AT&T Foundation, whose cultural programs director, Suzanne Sato, had invited the *To Conserve a Legacy* consortium to submit a funding application earlier in the year. AT&T's board of directors, long committed to supporting important museum exhibitions throughout America, as well as educational initiatives aimed to strengthen HBCU education, granted our project a $250,000 award. Mabel Cabot, director of the Ford Motor Company's cultural programs, called with more welcome news, relaying that her directors were processing our request for a grant of $250,000, support which would provide a powerful partnership of national corporate funding for the *To Conserve a Legacy* project. Ms. Cabot and the Ford Motor Company have a strong history of seeking out and supporting exhibition and education programs developed by some of our consortium project leaders, notably Richard Powell's *The Blues Aesthetic: Black Culture and Modernism* show.

It should be said now, and remembered at every turn, that had a successive number of enlightened funders not continued to step forward to support the *To Conserve a Legacy* project, our collective efforts to research, conserve, exhibit, and document important American artworks held in HBCU art collections, would have stalled and floundered. A sustained force of committed philanthropy has shadowed every advance that was made in the work that has transpired within this consortium project. The faith and ideals that helped fuel such patronage was abundantly genuine, leading our project leaders to hope that other funders will be inspired to share more actively in the risks and rewards that attend daring cultural work.

Feeling confident that sufficient project funding was in place to fully support the curatorial premises that Richard Powell and I were evolving through repeated

Josef Albers
Study for *Homage to the Square,* 1957
Oil on board, 20 x 20 in.
Collection of Hampton University Museum
checklist 3

Alma Woodsey Thomas
*Orange Glow*, 1968
Acrylic on canvas, 50 x 60 in.
Fisk University, Nashville, Tennessee
checklist 231

institutions and collections, and to participate as scholars in researching and authoring selected entry essays for the publication. Since conservation was the central premise guiding the *To Conserve a Legacy* project, it was anticipated that WACC's conservators would write of their service to the HBCU collections, bringing broader attention to the science and art that guides their important professional work. Thomas Branchick, who has now become the new director of WACC, agreed to organize each of the center's departments to write an essay detailing a particularly interesting conservation issue and/or treatment project that arose from the study of artworks sent to Williamstown. Richard Powell and I also suggested that we consider offering a wider group of young scholars the opportunity to write some of the individual entry essays we sought for the catalogue, providing

left: *To Conserve a Legacy* student interns Amhad Ward, Rayna Gardner, Rodney Bennett, and Hollie Hallowell, summer 1998.

center: Intern Elee Elijah Stewart and Rebecca Johnston, conservator, summer 1998.

right: James Herring, student intern, and Leslie Paisley, conservator, summer 1998.

yet another forum for encouraging a new generation of thinkers and doers to enter the field of American art and learn more of the rich HBCU holdings. Powell also volunteered that he had a seasoned publication editor in mind, Louise Stone, who was later retained to oversee yet another very complex series of tasks and working deadlines for our consortium.

Discussion of the project catalogue also included a stated interest by Roger Conover, director of MIT Press, that his educational institution wanted to serve as the partnering publisher for our project. Conover and MIT Press had just finished working closely with the Addison Gallery and The Phillips Collection (Washington, D.C.) to produce a beautiful catalogue documenting *Arthur Dove: A Retrospective*, so all agreed the Addison should solidify another working agreement with Conover, whose publications are well chosen and broadly marketed to national and international audiences.

Another meeting of the consortium was held at Howard University, where Dr. Tritobia Benjamin showed us the reinstallation of the university's African collection and described the progress that had been made in adding new mechanical and climate-control systems to Howard's main galleries and storage rooms. Our agenda included time for our HBCU leaders to describe the second group of students they had selected to participate in the coming summer's intern program as well as hours to review the exhibition checklist, discussing item by item the availability of works Powell and I were proposing for public viewing. Thomas Branchick discussed the further review of the artwork his WACC conservators would make in the months ahead, cautioning that discoveries made during laboratory examinations and treatments would likely lead to some recommendations that would limit the number of venues and the light levels some of the checklist's artworks could healthily endure.

Branchick also readied the consortium leaders for the third 1998 meeting in Williamstown and reported that many visitors to WACC's laboratories were taking an active interest in our project. He relayed how writer Pete Filkins had arrived one day to observe the treatments underway on various HBCU artworks, including two of Tuskegee's William H. Johnson paintings Branchick was treating. Impressed by what he saw going on in the lab, Filkins was inspired to begin writing a major article on the *To Conserve a Legacy* project for *Conservation Magazine*. Branchick also described how Michael Conforti, of the Sterling and Francine Clark Art Institute, intrigued by all that was happening in the conservation center, had generously provided funds from the Clark's budget to pay for the conservation of Howard University's large Charles White mural *Progress of the American Negro*. Subsequent research by Scott Allan would provide a catalogue entry essay on White's painting and lead to a public symposium the Clark would offer on the artist's work and HBCU collections.

Valerie J. Mercer, Tina Dunkley, Uthman Abdur Rathman, Tritobia Hayes Benjamin, Thomas Branchick, and Kenneth Rodgers view works on paper at the Williamstown Art Conservation Center, summer 1998

Dr. Benjamin and Thomas Branchick also shared news of another welcome development, one arising directly from the professional membership of the American Institute of Conservators (AIC). The AIC, which in recent years had taken a proactive role in recruiting minority students into the field of conservation and was well known to Hampton University Museum's staff through a volunteer project the AIC had conducted for them in 1996, was now offering its member services to assist the Howard University Gallery of Art. Through a collection care project being organized by the AIC's Michele Pagan, its members were preparing to help Dr. Benjamin and her staff rehouse Howard's sculpture and ceramic collection in protective foam nesting units, to archivally store numerous works on paper, and to provide numerous paintings in the gallery's collection with new protective backings and hanging hardware. All this work was accomplished during an intensive two-day workshop of AIC's membership on May 30 and 31; one that ended with a festive "thank you" reception hosted by Dr. Benjamin. Heading off to coordinate the second stage of the student intern program, our consortium members coordinated calendars once more and agreed to meet again in Williamstown at summer's end.

Returning to Andover, I found the Addison's staff eager to receive our three new interns. Rayna Gardner from Tuskegee University, Hollie Hollowell from Fisk University, and Ahmad Ward from Hampton University soon arrived in our midst and immediately began working with our curators, registrar, and preparators, learning how exhibitions are organized. During the intern's first week in residency, extra work stations were installed in the Addison's preparations department so the students could assist in matting and framing a group of Hans Hofmann drawings and watercolors and all of Robert Frank's photographs from *The Americans,* bodies of work that were being readied for display from the museum's permanent collection.

That same week I attended WACC's annual summer trustee meeting in Williamstown and there met the second trio of HBCU interns; Rodney Bennett, NCCU, James Herring, Howard University, and Elee Elijah Stewart, Clark Atlanta University. Walking into WACC early on a Friday morning, I found Bennett and Stewart working diligently with the conservators in the paper laboratory, carefully surface cleaning photographs and photographic albums from Hampton's and

William Edouard Scott
*Woman at Rest by Candlelight*, c. 1912
Oil on canvas, 18 x 22 in.
Collection of Clark Atlanta University Art Galleries
checklist 211

Leigh Richmond Miner
*Candle Lightin' Time*, 1901
Digital reproduction from original cyanotype
7½ x 4½ in.
Collection of Hampton University Archives
checklist 174

Leigh Richmond Miner
*Candle Lightin' Time*, 1901
Digital reproduction from original cyanotype
7⁵⁄₁₆ x 4⁷⁄₁₆ in.
Collection of Hampton University Archives
checklist 175

Memorable moments proliferated during the Williamstown meeting, but some stand out in my mind. Elee Elijah Stewart, the student from Clark Atlanta University, spoke eloquently before our assembled group while displaying John Wilson's *Negro Woman*, describing the careful cleaning process that had restored this beautiful painting. The young man treated all of us to a brief and fascinating lecture on chemistry, relaying what he had learned about human saliva—its powerful and gentle cleansing powers—and why it is still used today in conservation labs along with other mild synthetic chemical cleaning solutions. The pride Stewart took in his learning and work was abundantly evident in his talk.

Another treat that day was offered at the invitation of painter conservators Tom Branchick and Sandra Webber, who rotated our numbers through a room that could be darkened to view the John Biggers's *Old Coffee Drinker* and *Old Man* under ultraviolet lighting. The two canvases had been fastidiously restored by Kirsten Younger, an advanced WACC postgraduate intern from NYU's Institute of Fine Arts. Her delicate inpainting of Biggers's works was now only visible to the human eye under ultra-violet examination lamps. There in the darkness, one could see how the two canvases, long rolled and cracked in storage, had been beautifully repaired and readied for exhibition.

Other treatments that painting conservators Michael Heslip and Montserrat LeMense were undertaking

Williamstown Art Conservation Center's staff conservators Sandra Webber and Michael Heslip, and *To Conserve a Legacy* curator, Richard Powell discuss Howard University's *Charles Wilson Fleetwood Jr.*, 1858 by Thomas Waterman Wood, an unattributed work prior to conservation for the project.

rested on easels in another portion of WACC's painting laboratory. There Thomas Waterman Wood's portrait of *Charles Wilson Fleetwood Jr.* (1858) was being visually transformed by the skilled Heslip, who had discovered the signature of the artist while cleaning the base of an architectural column framing the painting's subject within its composition. This aesthetically and historically important work from the antebellum period was recorded and known to expert scholars of American art, but the painting's whereabouts had been a mystery for many years. It happened that the canvas was donated to Howard University's art collection in 1954 by Dr. Annette Hawkins Eaton where it remained accessioned as an unattributed work until Wood's signature became visible during Heslip's treatment.

Another modern painting of great beauty, *Full Blown Magnolia*, was also being restored by Heslip. This stunning canvas by Suzanna Ogunjami, an African painter who had settled for some time in America and returned to live in Africa, had been given to the Hampton University Museum by the Harmon Foundation, but it had not been displayed for many years because it needed significant restoration. Receiving the care it richly deserved at WACC, the painting now appeared as a remarkable work, an image executed with the same charged passion and formal strengths one sees in similar canvases painted by Martin Johnson Heade and Georgia O'Keeffe. Viewing the painting as Heslip spoke about his treatment was Andrea Barnwell, a doctoral candidate in the Department of Art and Art History at Duke University, who now works for the Art Institute of Chicago. MacArthur Fellow Barnwell had been commissioned to write the *To Conserve a Legacy* catalogue entry essay for Ogunjami's virtually unknown painting and had traveled with her colleague Daniel Schulman, associate curator in the Department of Twentieth-Century Paintings and Sculpture, Art Institute of Chicago, to be present at the Williamstown consortium meeting. She stood transfixed before Heslip's easel as he described the decisions he was making in conserving the painting. Seeing the vivid original colors of Ogunjami's painting emerging before Barnwell's eyes, one could sense another magical moment of learning and inspiration taking place.

Side by side with Heslip, conservator Montserrat LeMense had on her easel an unattributed nineteenth-century genre painting from Howard University's collection. This work had caught my eye at Howard University during my first visit to its gallery's storage rooms. There the canvas darkened by age, dirt, and discolored varnish, had suffered a bit of water damage and appeared to be unsigned. Yet, on its stretcher bar there was a small label questioning the canvas as a possible work by Eastman Johnson. Sent to Williamstown for an examination by Heslip and LeMense, the anonymous canvas seemed more likely to be of the hand of Harry

*To Conserve a Legacy* curator, Richard Powell in the painting laboratory at the Williamstown Art Conservation Center, summer 1998.

Roseland, another nineteenth-century American painter. Its composition presented a moving scene of human sharing, one portraying a black family hosting a passing stranger at its dinner table within a humble cabin home. When first viewed in its pretreated state, the painting was very clouded and murky. Many of the details in the composition could simply not be seen. Now, a year later, cleaned and carefully restored by LeMense's hand, the painting had come fully to life once more. The simple meal being offered the stranger by the daughter of the family steamed with immediacy, color, and flavor. Behind the family, on the cabin walls, one could now see objects that were in use in daily life—books, pictures, a banjo, tools, and the like. Richard Powell and I were astounded by how closely the painting's composition and imagery paralleled photographic images we had gleaned for conservation from Hampton University's photographic archives. Discoveries such as these cropped up continually throughout the development of the *To Conserve a Legacy* project, creating many moments when students, faculty members, conservators, and museum professionals became exhilarated by what they were seeing and learning while working together to restore and study a small portion of America's cultural riches.

Concluding this essay at summer's end, a major transition in my personal life is underway. I am leaving the directorship of the Addison Gallery of American Art and my alma mater, Phillips Academy, to become the director of the Yale University Art Gallery. As I take leave of Andover, a small show of Hans Hofmann's work—celebrating the fiftieth anniversary of the artist's 1948 Addison retrospective—is being installed in the gallery next to an exhibition of Frank Stella's current work. The two shows link creators of different generations and visually demonstrate the influence Hofmann exerted on a fellow artist who first saw his landmark abstract expressionist works in Andover's teaching museum as a teenage student. The Addison's ever insightful education coordinator, Julie Bernson, called attention to a quote Hofmann offered to my former teacher, Bartlett Hayes, in his book *Search for the Real* (1948). I think it is worth sharing as one considers what still remains to be done to strengthen the many worthy teaching collections, schools, and universities that exist throughout this land. In Hofmann's words:

> When America adds a developed culture to its economic richness it will be one of the happiest countries in the world. Providing leadership by teachers and support of developing artists is a national duty, an insurance of spiritual solidarity. What we do for art, we do for ourselves and for our children and for the future.[5]

Anonymous Camera Club photographer
*The Old Folks at Home, (Cabin Interior–Sheppards at dinner)*, 1900
Digital reproduction from original cyanotype
7³⁄₈ x 9⁵⁄₁₆ in.
Collection of Hampton University Archives
checklist 13

The last sentence of Hofmann's pithy statement reminds me of another phrase I heard uttered on more than one occasion by my African American colleagues during our work together on the *To Conserve a Legacy* project. "We stand today on the shoulders of those who came before us" is a phrase that also powerfully expresses the enduring connections that exist between generations and bind us all to cultural legacies that deserve and need to be conserved to tell a larger story of American art more fully.

It is certainly the hope of all the active participants in this consortium project that others will continue to expand the work our collective project has begun, which, of course, is only a modest continuance of work many others have been pursuing for years and for lifetimes before us. For young artists, teachers, scholars, alumni/ae, and philanthropists considering the opportunities that await you within historically black colleges and universities, we hope this project proves to be something of an inspiration and an invitation.

1. Keith Morrison, *Art in Washington and Its Afro-American Presence: 1940–1970*, (Washington, D.C.: Washington Project for the Arts), p. 11.

2. Richard Powell and Jock Reynolds, *James Lesesne Wells: Sixty Years in Art*, (Washington, D.C.: Washington Project for the Arts, 1986–1987), p. 3.

3. Keith Morrison, *Art in Washington and Its Afro-American Presence: 1940–1970*, (Washington, D.C.: Washington Project for the Arts), p. 11.

4. Carol R. Cooper, *To Conserve a Legacy*, journal entries with slides and photographs, December 1997, pp. 1–2.

5. Hans Hofmann, *Search for the Real and Other Essays* (Andover: Addison Gallery of American Art, 1948), p. 58.

Anonymous (possibly Harry Roseland)
*Guest at Dinner*, c. 1869
Oil on canvas, 33½ x 43½ in.
Collection of Howard University Gallery of Art
checklist 19

Alfred Stieglitz
*North from an American Place*, c. 1931
Gelatin silver print, 10 x 8 in.
Fisk University
checklist 222

Alfred Stieglitz
*Radio City from Shelton Hotel*, 1930
Gelatin silver print, 8 x 10 in.
Fisk University
checklist 225

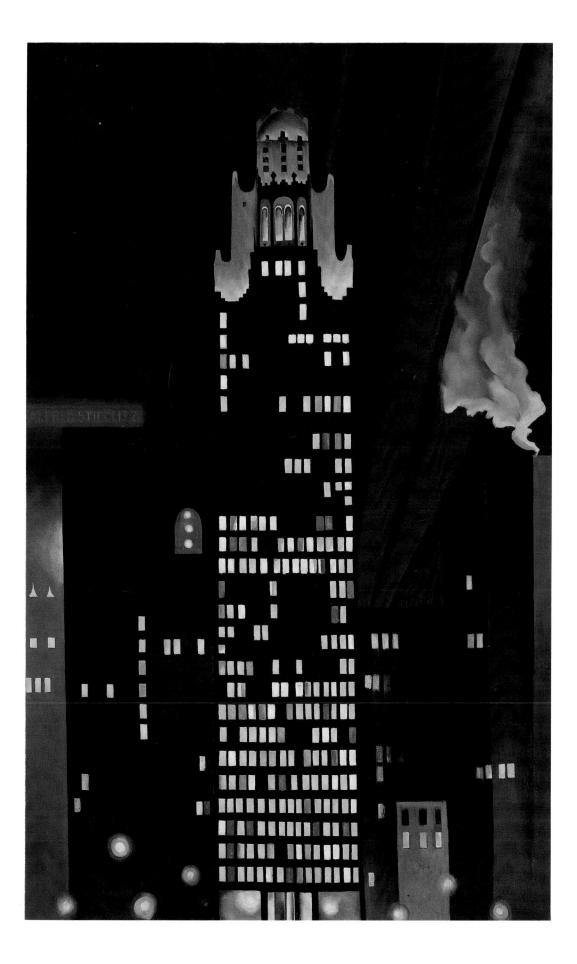

Georgia O'Keeffe
*Radiator Building—Night, New York*, 1927
Oil on canvas, 48 x 30 in.
Fisk University
checklist 191

Archibald J. Motley, Jr.
*Black Belt*, 1934
Oil on canvas, 31⅞ x 39½ in.
Collection of Hampton University Museum
checklist 186

Archibald J. Motley, Jr.
*The Liar*, 1936
Oil on canvas, 32 x 36 in.
Collection of Howard University Gallery of Art
checklist 188

Romare Bearden
*Jazz: (Chicago) Grand Terrace Ballroom—1930s*, 1964
Photomontage, 49¾ x 68¼ in.
Collection of Howard University Gallery of Art
© Romare Bearden Foundation/Licensed by VAGA,
New York, NY
checklist 31

Jacob Lawrence
*Strike*, 1949
Opaque watercolor on board, 19¹⁵⁄₁₆ x 23⁷⁄₈ in.
Collection of Howard University Gallery of Art
checklist 157

Mr. and Mrs. C.B. Miller
*Miller Album: Yazoo City Public School*, c. 1908
Gelatin silver print in bound volume
4⁷⁄₈ x 6¹³⁄₁₆ in.
Collection of Tuskegee University
checklist 172

C.D. Robinson
*State Road Public School—Perry Co., Ala Old*
*Building,* c. 1915
Gelatin silver print, 10 x 8 in.
Collection of Tuskegee University
checklist 204

C.D. Robinson
*Trustee Board*, c. 1915
Gelatin silver print, 10 x 8 in.
Collection of Tuskegee University
checklist 205

C.D. Robinson
*Greensboro Public School, Hale County, AL Old Building*, c. 1915
Gelatin silver print, 7¹¹⁄₁₆ x 9¹¹⁄₁₆ in. (image); 8 x 9¹⁵⁄₁₆ in. (sheet)
Collection of Tuskegee University
checklist 203

Jane Eliza Davis
*Untitled, Family along fence*, c. 1900
Digital reproduction from original cyanotype, 3¾ x 6¹⁄₁₆ in.
Collection of Hampton University Archives
checklist 66

William Christenberry
*Tingle House, Near Akron, AL*, 1962
Gelatin silver print, 3³⁄₈ x 5¹⁄₁₆ in. (image); 8 x 10 in. (sheet)
Collection of Hampton University Museum
checklist 60

Hale Aspacio Woodruff
*Erosion in Mississippi*, n.d.
Pastel on wove paper, 17¾ x 22¼ in.
Collection of North Carolina Central University Art Museum
checklist 261

John N. Robinson
*Anacostia Hills*, 1944
Oil on canvas, 23¾ x 29⅞ in.
Collection of Howard University Gallery of Art
checklist 206

Claude Clark, Sr.
*Jumpin' Jive*, c. 1940
Color etching on heavy-weight wove paper
7½ x 9 in. (image); 9¾ x 11¹³⁄₁₆ in. (sheet)
Collection of Howard University Gallery of Art
checklist 61

William M. Hayden
*Saturday Night Function*, c. 1950
Oil on canvas, 36 x 48 in.
Collection of Clark Atlanta University Art Galleries
checklist 105

William Henry Johnson
*Woman in Blue/Ida*, c. 1939
Oil on burlap, 32 x 24¼ in.
Collection of Clark Atlanta University Art Galleries
checklist 134

William Henry Johnson
*Mom Alice*, c. 1944
Oil on cardboard, 31 x 25 in.
Collection of Howard University Gallery of Art
checklist 126

Humbert Howard
*Portrait of My Wife*, 1950
Oil on canvas, 32 x 24¼ in.
Collection of Howard University Gallery of Art
checklist 111

William Henry Johnson
*Doug*, 1930
Oil on canvas, 28 x 20 in.
Collection of Howard University Gallery of Art
checklist 121

Aaron Douglas
*Still Life*, n.d.
Watercolor and graphite on laid paper, 18⅝ x 20⅝ in.
Fisk University
checklist 81

Charles Demuth
*Oranges and Artichokes*, 1926
Watercolor on paper, 13¾ x 19⅝ in.
Fisk University
checklist 72

Suzanna Ogunjami
*Full Blown Magnolia*, c. 1935
Oil on burlap, 20 x 24 in.
Collection of Hampton University Museum
checklist 192

Charles Demuth
*Calla Lilies,* 1927
Oil on composition board, 42¹/₈ x 48 in.
Fisk University
checklist 69

William Harper
*Landscape*, c. 1906
Oil on canvas, 36⅛ x 36⅛ in.
Collection of Tuskegee University
checklist 97

Henry O. Tanner
*Disciples Healing the Sick*, c. 1930
Oil on board, 40 x 52 in.
Collection of Clark Atlanta University Art Galleries
checklist 226

Herbert Pinney Tresslar
*William J. Edwards and the teachers at Snow Hill Institute*, n.d.
Gelatin silver print
6⁵/₁₆ x 8¹/₄ in. (image); 8⁵/₈ x 11¹/₂ in. (sheet)
Collection of Tuskegee University
checklist 239

# To Conserve a Legacy

## American Art from Historically Black Colleges and Universities

Richard J. Powell

Dedicated to Richard A. Long

*In his typically understated, yet profound way of speaking, Richard A. Long, Atticus Haygood Professor of Interdisciplinary Studies at Emory University, said (of the future of the visual arts at historically black colleges and universities) that "people create their own future to a certain extent." This quiet call to individual and institutional self-agency also defines the cultural advocacy and staunch pragmatism that Professor Long has professed and practiced his entire career. As a former professor at four black institutions of higher education—West Virginia State College, Morgan State College, Hampton Institute, and Atlanta University—Professor Long knows all too well of the many challenges and occasional triumphs in maintaining a visual arts program at these and other black institutions. A graduate myself of Morehouse College and Howard University, I could not have conceived of, initially, being a visual artist and, now, being a professor of art history, without first having been painstakingly taught and artistically inspired by Professor Long. I am deeply indebted, like countless other scholars of African American art and culture, to Professor Richard A. Long for his commitment to higher education, regard for the arts in all of their manifestations, and dedication to the people and programs at historically black cultural institutions.*

### Introduction: Through an African American Lens

In Joshua C. Taylor's preface to the catalogue that accompanied the important bicentennial exhibition *America as Art*, he queried himself about the wisdom in organizing a major exhibition of American art that "includes no works by Copley, Homer, Eakins, or Sargent." What Taylor and his exhibition coordinator Richard Murray had assembled (minus major works by Copley and the others) was a visual/cultural excursion through American symbols, ethnic and class-based identities, and other assorted ideas and themes, realized largely through popular art forms (like printmaking and the applied arts), as well as paintings and sculptures by what most scholars would consider "minor artists." Taylor answered his own, initial question with the admission that, along with concentrating on works and aspects of art in America that are "less well known," the intention of *America as Art* was to think about "the identity of art with our cultural past": an endeavor that, in his estimation, can provide "unexpected pleasures" and "joy to the eye."[1]

I thought about Taylor and Murray's ground-breaking exhibition and inquiry into the visual imagination of America as I pondered with co-curator Jock Reynolds our selections for the exhibition *To Conserve a Legacy: American Art from Historically Black Colleges and Universities*. Admittedly, Mr. Reynolds and I were less likely to point out or bemoan the absence of works by Copley, Homer, Eakins, or Sargent in this exhibition, preferring instead to encourage audiences to take "pleasure" in seeing and thinking about the unexpected in American art, and in what these institutions would call the "culturally definitive" nature of their holdings. Although questions of what constitutes an "American art canon" and the "culturally definitive" emerged, our intention in *To Conserve a Legacy* is to answer these questions by way of surveying the art collections of six of these institutions—Clark Atlanta University, Fisk University, Hampton University, Howard University, North Carolina Central University, and Tuskegee University—and, based on these surveys, exhibiting the most culturally representative works.[2]

Returning to Taylor's provocative notion of *"America-as-Art-without-four-great-American-painters,"* another series of questions emerges: Is it possible to think about American art from a variety of cultural and/or curatorial perspectives? Is there the chance that portraits, history paintings, genre scenes, landscapes, and studies by Copley, Homer, Eakins, and Sargent are not so much *definitive* of the American character but, rather, *exemplary of one particular collection of many American characters and qualities:* cultural representations which multiply and diversify as we open our eyes, broaden our vistas, and embrace the entirety of American history? Can one, in lieu of the above "big four," successfully examine American art using, for example, works by George Catlin, Paul Cadmus, Georgia O'Keeffe, and Andy Warhol (as Taylor did in *America as Art)* or Henry Ossawa Tanner, Archibald J. Motley, Jr., Elizabeth Catlett, and Sam Gilliam (as we do in *To Conserve a Legacy)*?[3]

*To Conserve a Legacy: American Art from Historically Black Colleges and Universities* responds to these questions through artists and art works not customarily considered visual conduits of an American character and identity. As one might expect, the most frequent subject of the art works in these collections is black America *itself:* its heroes, communities, pastimes, problems, and dreams, all given concrete, palpable forms, and fashioned with equal doses of fantasy, reality, and abstraction. In an ideal world, one need not argue that an artistic perspective or worldview informed by African Americans is no less universal (or biased) than one shaped by European Americans, but since this world is *not* ideal, let the claim for relativity go on record. What is of particular importance to the conceptual framework behind *To Conserve a Legacy* is that the cultural criteria for this exhibition—each art work's intrinsic place within a set of American themes and/or viewpoints—is commensurate with other art historical examinations of American culture. The *difference* is that these American themes and viewpoints—i.e., freedom, the sublime, arcadia, everyday life, modernism, political activism, etc.—come into being and take shape through artists for whom the

Anonymous
*Untitled (Woman at a gate holding a cat),*
c. 1890s
Gelatin silver print, 8⅞ x 7¼ in.
Collection of Tuskegee University
checklist 11

black experience is the key, cultural paradigm. These artists and art works provide an experiential thermometer for gauging this nation's social, psychological, and political temperature.[4]

An anonymous photographer, working in the rural South during the first few years of the twentieth century, intuitively understood this notion of an African American-centered universe and, by association, a normative view of black life. The focal point of this photographer's African American worldview—a plump and attractive black woman, standing at the gated entrance to a yard and house, and affectionately holding a calico cat in her arms—moves between the aforementioned subject *proper* and a subliminal message about order, position, and boundaries. This image of black domesticity—on the one hand, utterly commonplace yet, on the other, idyllic and quite lovely—recalls W.E.B. DuBois's remarks in *The Souls of Black Folk* (1903) about "the place of the Fence in civilization." Describing rural communities and landscapes in the South's "Black Belt," DuBois observed that " . . . now and then, the criss-cross rails or straight palings break into view, and then we know a touch of culture is near." DuBois's statement—a fitting caption for this photograph from the rural South—links African American enterprise and a planned environment with progress, social refinement, and an enlightened picture of the industrial South.[5]

That "civilization" and "culture" could, in fact, be found among the black masses in the turn-of-the-century southern United States was actually an idea that many social reformers and progressives espoused at that time. For example, at Tuskegee Normal and Industrial Institute (where the above mentioned photograph was originally commissioned and, as Tuskegee University, is now housed), its founder and spiritual leader Booker T. Washington exhorted his students to "cast down [their] buckets where [they were]," and to take their lessons of productivity, perseverance, and thrift to the black poor and illiterate. In the mind of Washington, this errand into a post-Reconstruction era, economically driven, southern wilderness, would help bring Negroes out of psychological slavery and agrarian peonage and, instead, into "a new heaven and a new earth."[6]

Washington's utopian vision for blacks in the South—seemingly light years removed from comparable, white evangelical and elitist visions of America—reveals how the leadership (and, by extension, the cultural advocates) of selected black institutions of higher learning participated in the greater nineteenth-century obsession with symbolic readings of nationhood and citizenship. The founder of Tuskegee Institute (along with his counterparts at other historically black colleges and universities created in the aftermath of the Civil War) envisioned an America where former slaves and other free men and women of color had a place at America's proverbial banquet table, partaking of such provisions as the vote, civil rights, land-and-property-ownership, the use of public accommodations, and access to public education, to name just a few. In the South, wrote DuBois:

> amid a wide desert of caste and proscription, amid the heart-hurting slights and jars and vagaries of a deep race-dislike, lies this green oasis, where hot anger cools, and bitterness of disappointment is sweetened by the springs and breezes of Parnassus; and here men may lie and listen, and learn of a future fuller than the past, and hear the voice of Time: "Entbehren sollst du, sollst entbehren."

The moral oasis and Parnassus-like setting that the historically black colleges and universities became (despite being surrounded on all sides by prejudice, discrimination, and often racial violence) triggered in its students, teachers, and patrons not only the ability to "learn of a future" and to "hear the voice of Time" (as DuBois noted) but to *picture* a world where African Americans embodied culture and civilization (as seen in the Tuskegee Institute photograph of the lady standing before an open gate).[7]

### Forever Free: Emancipation Visualized

A core group of these historically black colleges and universities—Atlanta University, Fisk University, Hampton Institute, and Howard University—were founded as a result of President Abraham Lincoln's 1863 Emancipation Proclamation and efforts by the Freedmen's Bureau, the American Missionary Association, and other religious organizations to assist and educate former slaves. It is not surprising, therefore, that part of the self-defining process for these institutions (upon their creation and long afterwards) entailed the gathering of published documents, memorabilia, and works of art that depicted and/or visualized emancipation. While the general theme of freedom—both literal and figurative—is in evidence at various moments in American art history (e.g., during the federalist period in paintings about the American Revolution, and in mid-to-late nineteenth-century paintings and sculptures exploring Western themes), the specific theme of the emancipation of enslaved black men and women began to appear in American art in the years immediately following the 1863 presidential edict.[8]

The canonical work on the theme of emancipation—Edmonia Lewis's marble sculpture *Forever Free* (1867)—satisfied most of the artistic expectations that audiences would have had for a work on this topic: e.g., the reverential, upward gazes; the gestures of gratitude and victory; and the former slaves's humble attire. Yet, Lewis seems to have problematized the subject, as seen in the sculpture's distinctly gendered responses to emancipation, the racial ambiguity of her subjects, and the proportion and scale disparities between the two figures. While some might attribute these problems in form and interpretation to an overt display of nineteenth-century sexual and racial mores, as well as to Lewis's inexperience at this stage in her development as a sculptor, one could also argue that throughout her career (and in her public persona) Lewis often defied the representational conventions of her day. In the case of *Forever Free,* the political and psychological phenomenon of emancipation was an appropriate vehicle upon which she could impose issues of racial difference, contradictory reactions based on gender, and even questions of decorum and competency. Despite the cool white marble and superficial overtures to other contemporary sculptors (like Harriet Hosmer and Hiram Powers), Lewis's impassioned, decidedly anti-neoclassical *Forever Free* was perhaps matched in psychological complexity and artistic tenor by the emotionally wrenching slave narratives/emancipation sagas of her literary counterparts, such as Harriet Jacobs and Sojourner Truth.[9]

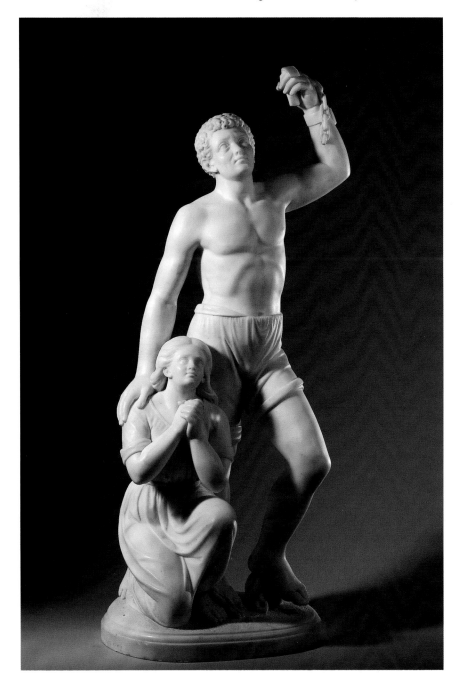

Edmonia Lewis
*Forever Free,* 1867
Marble, 41¼ x 22 x 17 in.
Collection of Howard University Gallery of Art
checklist 158

But representations of emancipation and freedom were capable of being more than just images of broken shackles or genuflecting slaves. For some, the very idea of an African American operating outside of the sphere of slavery was enough to signify bodily freedom. Similarly, for many painters and sculptors of color the avoidance of the black subject altogether and the conscious demonstration of artistic skills and a command of the academic ideals of art denoted another kind of emancipation: freedom from the vexing, worrisome subject of a democracy gone awry; sovereignty from a *de facto* American caste system; and independence from assumptions of black inferiority. When in 1903 DuBois wrote "I sit with Shakespeare and he winces not. Across the color line I move arm in arm with Balzac and Dumas . . . ," he was, in effect, temporarily identifying with this latter category of interpreters of emancipation: advocates of a liberating, European-centered notion of "the universal" that manifested itself in a non-confrontational, sublime, and often escapist art.[10]

So almost simultaneous with Edmonia Lewis's socially engaged *Forever Free* was Robert S. Duncanson's *Cottage at Pass Opposite Ben Lomond* (1866): a homage to Celtic romanticism begun during the artist's 1865 tour of the Scottish

Robert S. Duncanson
*Cottage at Pass Opposite Ben Lomond,* 1866
Oil on canvas, 12³/₈ x 20³/₈ in.
Collection of North Carolina Central
University Art Museum
checklist 89

Highlands. Duncanson's audiences would have been hard-pressed to thematically link this painting to a still-cleaved, post-Civil War America, or to a politically astute black artist. More likely the art viewing public would have immediately associated this painting with one of several schools of American landscape painting, whose images of the wilderness, westward expanding civilization, and imaginary, idealized vistas were coveted by the country's leading art collectors. For Duncanson, his success with this part-observable, part-literary, and part-invented genre was a clear indication of his own emancipation and artistic independence: a victory over society's presumptions of what an artist of color should create. "Mark what I say here in black and white," Duncanson wrote to his son (who wanted him, in words and deeds, to be more proactively black American), "I have no color on the brain; all I have on the brain is paint." Such a pronouncement sheds a different, interpretive light on *Cottage at Pass Opposite Ben Lomond,* one that highlights this painting's social core and liberating effects, despite its surface serenity and assumed distance from the topical and ideological.[11]

Because of the efforts of historians and artist/teachers at many historically black colleges and universities, *Forever Free* and *Cottage at Pass Opposite Ben Lomond* have become important visual tools for teaching students about concepts of freedom, art, and culture in nineteenth-century America, and the African American experience *sui generis.* By the time these two works of art entered into the permanent collections at Howard University *(Forever Free,* during the late 1960s) and North Carolina Central University *(Cottage at Pass Opposite Ben Lomond,* during the mid-1980s), histories of African American art and artists were being rewritten to acknowledge the range and scope of subject matter, aesthetic sensibilities, and artistic intentions among this group of cultural arbiters; however, exploring the educational uses and potential of visual art at historically black colleges and universities began neither in the twentieth century, nor with works solely by African American artists.

**The First Americans**

Almost from its inception, Hampton Institute's faculty, staff, and students viewed the collecting of art, artifacts, and folklore as a major component of their mission. Beyond the Institute's historic emphases on manual training and a broad, liberal arts education, the material and oral traditions of peoples of color have played a key role in Hampton's curricular and extracurricular undertakings. General Samuel Chapman Armstrong, Hampton Institute's founder and first principal, proclaimed the centrality and importance of Negro and American Indian art forms to the greater cultural enterprise when he asserted that "The Negro has the only American music; the Indian has the only American art." Alluding here not only to American cultural production, but to Hampton Institute's specific calling to educate the sons and daughters of former slaves, other free men and women of color, and displaced American Indians, Armstrong saw the intrinsic value of providing Hampton students with a truly diverse, learning environment. "The mingling of the students there is good for both," wrote Armstrong some years later, "pushing the Indians by the force of surrounding influences quickly and naturally along, and reacting finely upon the Negro by the appeal to his sympathies and better nature. The work for another race broadens and strengthens our movement and adds, if possible, to its inspiration." As racially paternalistic as these pronouncements may sound today, Armstrong's views on a coeducational system—for blacks and Indians, as well as for women and men—were considered extremely radical in his day, and clearly in opposition to the American majority who would have preferred to ignore the plight of thousands of recently emancipated slaves and disentitled Indians.[12]

Of course, Hampton Institute's teachers—white, Protestant, and many from prominent New England families—also benefited from the intermingling and exchange of ideas between Hampton's various cultural groups. As seen in a well-known, turn-of-the-century photograph from Hampton (Class in American History), everyone at the school was potentially a student, especially in regard to studying the history, material culture, and folkways of American Indians. The teacher in Class in American History is an observer like the rest of the class, and just as much of a spectacle and curiosity (for photographer Frances Benjamin Johnston and viewers) as are the uniformed students and the young American Indian student-turn-model, bewigged and dressed in buckskin. Like the stuffed bald eagle to his right, this flesh-and-blood Indian provided this history class with a visceral example of Americana: specimens plucked from the American field, and images of those "first Americans" who, in this age of industrialism and territorial expansionism, were the most susceptible to extermination or extinction. Caught between being the ethnographic observer and the focal point of America's often prejudicial gaze, the proponents of Hampton Institute's multicultural experiment insisted upon placing their American Indian students in close proximity to their Negro students for sociological, educational, as well as politically strategic reasons.[13]

But as evidenced in Class in American History, Hampton Institute's intellectual fascination with Native American culture, coupled with the expectation that students should fully assimilate into a white, Anglo-Saxon, Protestant work ethic, created a psychological split among the school's American Indians. Again, the simultaneous "observer/subject" position that this American History class imposed on its Indian students—a paradoxical situation of which Johnston was certainly aware—underscores one of the true ironies of the Hampton experiment. A nostalgia for the Native American past that was capable of being paired with and, at times, co-opted by the apparent social and material advantages of Western civilization was an idea that had Native American sources as well, as seen in a letter from a reservation-bound father to Hampton's administrators, telling them that "I see [my son's] picture when he has on white man's clothes which contain

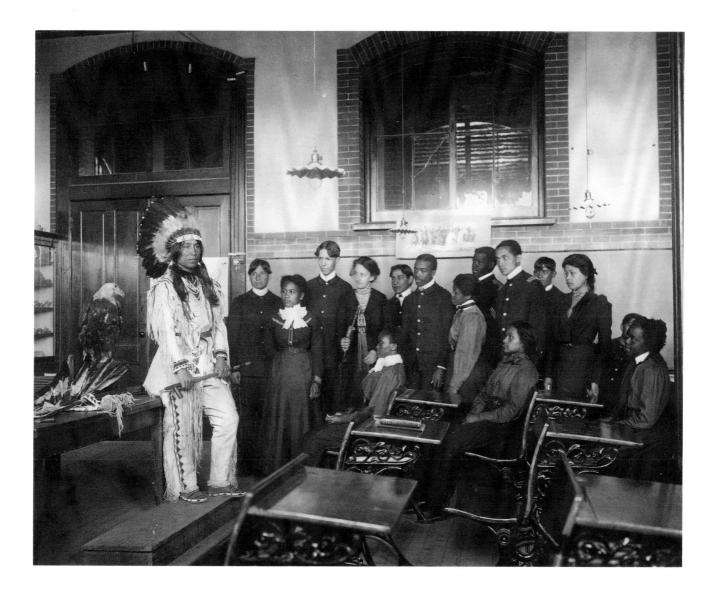

Frances Benjamin Johnston
*The Hampton Albums: Class in American
History*, 1899–1900
Platinum print, 7½ x 9⅜ in. (image);
9½ x 11½ in. (sheet)
Collection of Hampton University Archives
checklist 137

Clara Darden
*Covered baskets*, c. 1904
River cane, pigment
Sizes vary from 2⅞ to 6 inches in height,
width, and depth
Collection of Hampton University Museum
checklist 64

many places to put money in pockets, and I know you hold my son well for me."[14]

This comingling of pride, gratitude, and unmasked capitalism suggests that Hampton Institute's call for assimilation had implications far beyond questions of cultural suppression or expressivity. When, in 1905, Hampton acquired a collection of seventy-two baskets from the Chitimacha peoples of the Lower Mississippi Valley, the reasons for accepting these baskets were three-fold: ethnological (their stylistic links to baskets made by the ancient Aztecs); revivalist (in hopes that Native American students would study these baskets and resuscitate their archaic designs and forms); and commercial (in anticipation of them providing students with models upon which to manufacture similar ones for sale). These same impulses (with varying degrees of emphasis) also resided within Hampton's African American student population, motivating them to embrace the school's mantra of "education of the hand, education of the mind, and education of the character." Realizing the almost insurmountable obstacles that their students faced as they graduated and entered the bigger world of racial prejudice and economic hardships, Hampton's teachers pressed into their African American and Native American students not only the necessary educational background and specializations in trades, but the required social skills, time management acumen, and coping mechanisms that would enable them to meet the challenges of an increasingly industrialized America.[15]

### Training the Head, the Hand, and the Heart

Hampton Institute's message—a mixture of liberal Protestantism, manual training theory, and missionary zeal—formed the pedagogical bedrock for the mission statements and philosophies of several historically black colleges and universities during the period between the end of the Civil War and the beginning of the twentieth century. The strict, authoritarian tenor of student life at these schools, and the highly structured mixture of liberal arts and trade-school education that they advocated were viewed as the requisite cures for decades of poverty, ignorance, and moral dissolution in black communities. In order to turn the tides of social, psychological, and material bankruptcy that centuries of slavery had imposed on black Americans, a select group of white educators (most from the northeastern sector of the United States, and many with religious and/or military backgrounds) moved to the South and started these schools for the freedmen and their children.[16]

The students's curriculum was a curious combination of a classical and practical education—e.g., Latin, Greek, natural philosophy, geometry, and industrial training. The schools that these educators built (usually with local, black labor) were frequently situated amidst acres of farmland, dotted with vegetable gardens and greenhouses, and consisted of vernacular classroom buildings, spare but spotless dormitories, and (for the most affluent in the group) majestic Romanesque chapels, and grand, two-storied, shingled houses for the president, his family, and the faculty. These were palatial settings compared to the crowded, often depressing environments that the students had left behind. Rather than seeing the mandatory daily chapel attendance, the high-collared and long-sleeved uniforms, the unrelenting study and work schedules, and the puritanical rules regarding male-female fraternization as a burden, students accepted this cloistered and

regimented lifestyle if it meant being allowed to attend school, improve one's condition, and to take that knowledge and ability back to his or her community. "I was
dazed at the splendor of Tuskegee," recalled William H. Holtzclaw, a Mississippi
school principal, about his first days on the campus. He continued his reminis-
cence with other memories:

> I saw more activity among Negroes than I had ever seen before in my life. Not only
> was everybody at work, but every soul seemed to be in earnest. I heard the ringing
> of the anvil, the click of machinery, the
> music of the carpenters' hammers.
> Before my eyes was a pair of big fat
> mules drawing a piece of new and im-
> proved farm machinery, which literally
> gutted the earth as the mules moved. . . .
> Then there were the class-rooms, with
> their dignified teachers and worthy-look-
> ing young men and women. Amid it all
> moved that wonderful figure, Booker T.
> Washington. I began at once a new
> existence. I made a vow that I would
> be educated there, or I would die and
> be buried in the school cemetery . . .

Leigh Richmond Miner
*Portia ironing*, 1907
Digital reproduction from original cyanotype
6⁹⁄₁₆ x 4⁹⁄₁₆ in.
Collection of Hampton University Archives
checklist 177

Holtzclaw's animated description
of Tuskegee Institute and his fervent
desire to be a part of its "great work"
have reverberations during this period
in the writings of countless other
alumni from historically black colleges
and universities. Impassioned reflections such as this one functioned both
as personal testimonies of individual
achievement, as well as the best kind
of publicity, promotional material, and
fundraising tools for the school.[17]

Often working in tandem with
narratives like William H. Holtzclaw's
were photographs of historically
black colleges and universities. These
pictures documented the physical
layout of the campuses, the scale
and architectural details of assorted
buildings, classroom and laboratory
activities, teachers and students hard
at work, and, without exception, the
often imposing and impressive figures of the college and/or university presidents.
If the published accounts of the school's activities were not entirely capable of
transmitting information about the operations and agendas of these institutions
to the wider public, then the photographs of these activities and of the people
engaged in them made the stories and institutional objectives apparent for one
and all to see. Frances Benjamin Johnston's famous photographic portfolio of
Hampton Institute (which includes her photograph *Class in American History*)
certainly functioned as a visual supplement to that institution's printed facts and
figures. Similarly, a 1907 series of photographs (taken by Hampton's Director of
Applied Arts Leigh Richmond Miner for the school's display at the Jamestown
Tercentennial Exposition) also served public relations needs. These photographs—

documenting the work and leisure activities of two "typical" Hampton students, Portia Peyton and Almancy Lee Evans—were the irrefutable "evidence" for the cynical and the curious that Hampton Institute's unique educational system was successful in improving the lives of its students. Staged, designed, and lit by Miner, photographs like *Portia ironing* turned the real-life drudgery of manual labor into something morally uplifting and visibly lovely, resonating with the works of other pictorialist photographers of that same period (e.g., Edward J. Steichen, Clarence H. White, and Gertrude Käsebier).[18]

Charles. T. Keck
*Booker T. Washington Removing the Veil of Ignorance and Superstition*, 1922
Bronze
Collection of Tuskegee University

Students like Portia Peyton knew how alluring, communicative, and self-empowering these photographs could be, which is apparent in the scores of other photographic portraits and documentary images taken of students from historically black colleges and universities c. 1900. School administrators like Hampton Institute's Hollis B. Frissell and Tuskegee Institute's Booker T. Washington knew how effective documentary photography was in elevating the public profiles of their respective schools, as well as for capital campaigning and fundraising. For many of these students, teachers, and alumni, to have one's institution, community, and activities photographed for promotional purposes and for posterity was, in effect, to have one's existence and purpose in life validated. The photograph of Tuskegee alumnus William J. Edwards and his teaching staff on the front porch of the Snow Hill Normal and Industrial Institute (in Wilcox County, Alabama) certainly conveyed his personal sense of pride in the creation of this rural academy, and the entire staff's sense of dedication to the formidable task of "uplifting the submerged." Edwards's visions for a school (designed on the Tuskegee model) that "would train men and women to be good workers, good leaders, good husbands, good wives," and to be "fit citizens of the State, and proper subjects for the kingdom of God" are clearly revealed here. Pictures like this one—depicting young, attractive, and well-dressed African American men and women, who radiated a serious, scholarly aura, and are clearly unified in their duty to God and community—were understood by one and all to be ammunition against those in society who would deny African Americans their rights and privileges as full citizens, not to mention a visual contestation against the legion of racist images that proliferated throughout America during this same time period.[19]

Tuskegee Institute was the source for another important didactic image when, in 1922, sculptor Charles T. Keck presented his bronze statue *Booker T. Washington*

*Removing the Veil of Ignorance and Superstition* before a widely attended Founder's Day audience. Keck's earlier apprenticeship with the acclaimed sculptor Augustus Saint-Gaudens was in full evidence in this piece, as seen in his allegorical depiction of Washington literally (and figuratively) uncovering a heavily cloaked, crouching black man. By depicting Washington in the stance of an ancient hero and in the act of pulling away "the pall of ignorance and superstition" from this personification of a backward, illiterate people, Keck was able to turn what otherwise might have been a fairly routine sculptural portrait into a *tableau vivant:* a public morality play about racial uplift, Social Darwinism, and the cults of personality and leadership.[20]

Several years later, the Harlem Renaissance painter, muralist, and book illustrator Aaron Douglas would embrace a similar didacticism in his gouache drawing *Rise Shine for Thy Light has Come* (c. 1927). By incorporating the first line and musical bar of a traditional Negro spiritual into a geometric, stylized, and chromatically graduated image of an upward gazing woman, Douglas inadvertently continues the black institutional stratagem of constructing visual narratives and pictorial signs that proclaim African American sovereignty, ingenuity, and promise. Douglas's drawing—with its understated patterning and rhythmic interplay of chevrons, waves, and bands—reveals its indebtedness to his teacher, the German artist and designer Winold Reiss. Several years prior to the creation of *Rise Shine for Thy Light has Come,* Douglas had been Reiss's student and was encouraged by Reiss to adopt a more African art-centered sensibility. Fusing these "Afro-Deco" design tenets with the philosopher Alain Locke's theory of a culturally reawakened and cognizant "New Negro," Douglas placed his visual modernism in service to an emerging black intelligentsia, as well as to the unlettered, but politically nascent, urban black masses. Apparently Alain Locke (who would eventually acquire *Rise Shine for Thy Light has Come* and bequeath it to Howard University) already had a similar notion about the modern uses of the Negro spiritual, since the same line and musical bar in Douglas's drawing appeared on the dedication page of Locke's important collection of African American essays, fiction, poetry, and visual art, *The New Negro* (1925).[21]

Although Douglas was not affiliated with a historically black college or university when *Rise Shine for Thy Light has Come* was created, he was already familiar with this musical line from Locke's book and knew that this spiritual had originally been transcribed and published by John Wesley Work (1873–1925), a Fisk University composer, a former conductor of that school's legendary Jubilee Singers, and the author of *Folk Song of the American Negro* (1915). After a series of visits to Fisk University (during which he painted a multipaneled mural cycle in the University Library), Douglas accepted a teaching position there in 1937, which could be interpreted as taking his career-long interest in a morally instructive art to the next, logical step—becoming a full-time university professor of art.[22]

The curricular objectives and teaching strategies that Douglas helped implement at Fisk University in the late 1930s were light years apart from Hampton and Tuskegee's pioneering experiments in manual training and moral instruction in the late nineteenth and early twentieth centuries. While the two educational systems sprang from the same "training for life" philosophy that most historically black colleges and universities were founded under, the rapidly changing status of African Americans in the post-World War I years caused many educational institutions to modify their departmental structures and instructional approaches. These new economic realities, coupled with an increased interest in alternative fields of study and social questions pertaining to African Americans (e.g., demographics, labor, health, acculturation versus segregation, etc.) shifted the pedagogical focus (especially at schools like Fisk and Howard) away from vocational training and an emphasis on a classical education towards a more theoretical, society-centered,

Aaron Douglas
*Rise Shine for Thy Light has Come,* 1924
Opaque watercolor and black ink on paper board, 11¾ x 8¼ in.
Collection of Howard University Gallery of Art
checklist 79

and problem-solving curriculum. Framed by a heightened race consciousness, sense of community obligation and social optimism, Douglas's *Rise Shine for Thy Light has Come* represented not only black visual modernism, but a new intellectual model and missive for African Americans that promoted cultural and social engagement.

Ironically, anchoring such a progressive statement in art was the grassroot wisdom and moral compass of the Negro spirituals and, by association, traditional African American religion. In contrast to the largely secular and sometimes agnostic milieu of many predominately white American institutions of higher education, historically black colleges and universities have always had a prominent place for religious studies in their curriculum, and an essential role for the major African American religious denominations in their organizational structures. Indeed, the theological departments at Fisk University and Howard University worked in concert (if not always very closely) with these same institution's more reform-minded, social research-oriented departments.

In the case of North Carolina Central University, its spiritual errand (beginning in 1910 as the private National Religious Training School and Chautauqua for the Colored Race) was not fundamentally transformed when it became the state-supported "North Carolina College for Negroes" in 1925. Dr. James Edward Shepard, the school's founder, long-time president, and its literal "shepherd" as the institution transitioned from private to public, had a Moses-like aura in North Carolina's black community, often extolling the virtues of a Christian life, and frequently exhorting to the North Carolina State General Assembly and the public alike that "religion and work go hand and hand." Although Shepard died in 1947, his message of moral leadership, community service, and his spiritual presence as a symbol of African American accomplishment continued to be felt, perhaps most explicitly in a larger-than-life, bronze commemorative statue of Shepard that stands in front of North Carolina Central University's administration building. Created in 1956 by the renowned American sculptor William Zorach (a pioneer in the direct-carving movement in the United States), Shepard's statue—calm and classical in its overall impact yet moderately expressionistic in small details—was, curiously, not commissioned by the state of North Carolina. Rather, it was privately commissioned and dedicated in 1957 by the North Carolina branch of the Prince Hall Grand Lodge, a prominent African American fraternal order and mutual aid association that included Shepard among its most distinguished members.[23]

Another important work of art in the collection of North Carolina Central University, Minnie Evans's mixed media painting *Jesus Christ* (1963), provided similar moral and ethical lessons through a visual route. Discovered in the early 1960s while she was employed as a domestic and a gatekeeper for a garden estate near Wilmington, North Carolina and lauded for her visionary drawings in crayon, pencil, ink, and oil, Minnie Evans has, perhaps, depicted the most incredible spiritually instructive compositions of the modern artists who are usually represented in

Minnie Evans
*Jesus Christ,* 1963
Oil, ink, and graphite on paper, 16½ x 19¼ in.
Collection of North Carolina Central University
Art Museum
checklist 90

black college and university art collections. Evans's images of white-robed angels, winged devils, all-seeing eyes, flowers in full bloom, and other apparitions—all rendered in paisley print patterns with Rorschach symmetry—suggest that, in addition to the mainstream black religious orthodoxy, other spiritual views from black America were present and acknowledged in these institutional settings.[24] The ease with which Evans painted Jesus Christ Caucasian—oblivious to black nationalist arguments to the contrary—tells audiences that God's image, rather than subscribing to someone else's notions of the heavenly (or, for that matter, the earthly), is in the eye and mind of the believer. *Jesus Christ,* amazingly reminiscent of the dream imagery and conversion accounts of former slaves that Fisk University researchers gathered in the 1930s, illustrates how in spiritual matters African Americans often formed an impassioned yet idiosyncratic group of interpreters. From Aaron Douglas's modernist ode to the Negro spiritual, to Evans's portrait of a fantastic, metaphoric divinity, these images reflected the sentiments and counternarratives of the institutions that housed them yet, admittedly, begged the question of their efficacy as visual tutorials within these same institutions.[25]

Arthur P. Bedou
*Booker T. Washington with ribboned men,* n.d.
Collodion printing out paper mounted on board, 9³⁄₈ x 7⁷⁄₁₆ (image); 9⁷⁄₁₆ x 7⁹⁄₁₆ in. (sheet); 10¹⁄₁₆ x 8 in. (mount)
Collection of Tuskegee University
checklist 35

### The American Portrait Gallery

What was unquestionable in providing exemplars of success and teaching self-worth at historically black colleges and universities was the very *image* of an African American ideal. As already seen in the bronze statue of the North Carolina College's founder, Dr. James Edward Shepard, these palpable, physical markers of black accomplishment took on a symbolism that raised the art of historical portraiture at these institutions to a lofty, almost celestial level.

Without question, the biggest star in this galaxy of African American luminaries was Booker T. Washington. From his thirty-four-year tenure as Tuskegee Institute's president, to his almost mythic stature as a political strategist in the post-Reconstructed South, a trusted advisor on racial matters to several U.S. presidents, and an extraordinarily effective fundraiser for Tuskegee and other African American causes, Washington—the celebrated author of the autobiography *Up From Slavery* (1901)—literally embodied the classic African American success story. And, as seen in the many posthumous memorials, commemorative postage stamps, and other visual representations of Booker T. Washington (including portraits by modern artists like Henry Ossawa Tanner, Charles White, and William H. Johnson), his renown extended far beyond his death in 1915.

That much of this adoration was the result of Washington's own, carefully orchestrated presentation of selected words, narratives, and images is attested to

Carl Van Vechten
*Lena Horne,* 1940
Gelatin silver print, 9⅞ x 7⅞ in.
Fisk University
checklist 245

John Wilson
*Negro Woman*, 1952
Oil on fiberboard, 22 x 18½ in.
Collection of Clark Atlanta University Art Galleries
© John Wilson/Licensed by VAGA, New York, NY
checklist 258

Edward Bruce
*Portrait of William Friday*, 1934
Oil on canvas, 30⅞ x 25½ in.
Collection of Howard University Gallery of Art
checklist 48

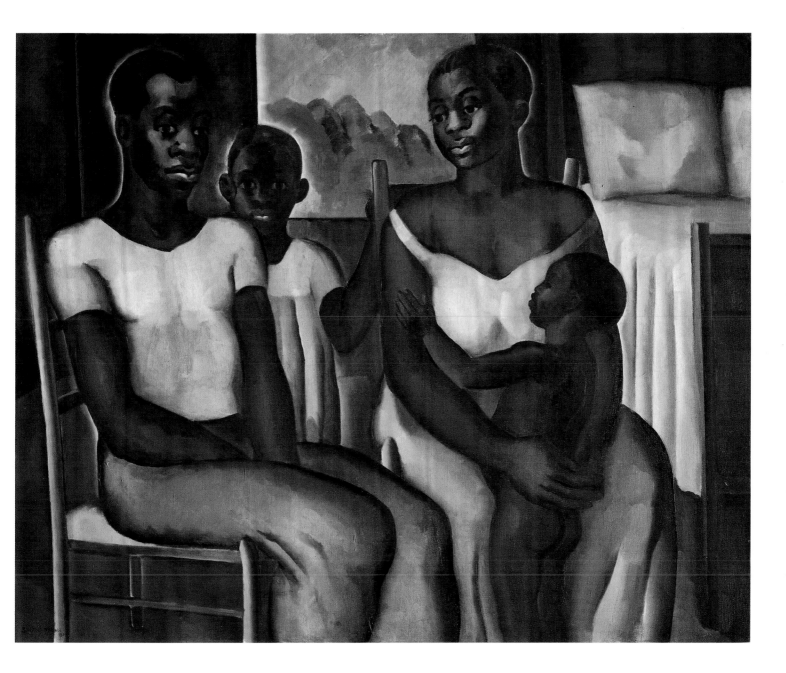

William Sherwood McCall
*An American Family*, 1935
Oil on canvas, 40 x 50 in.
Collection of Howard University Gallery of Art
checklist 169

in the volumes of positive publicity that Washington and Tuskegee Institute garnered during and after his presidency, and in the thousands of photographs that recorded almost all of Washington's official gatherings, success stories, encounters with greatness, and every picturesque "photo-op" of Tuskegee and the rest of Washington's wide sphere of power. A turn-of-the-century photograph of Washington conveys much about his charismatic personality, aura of black achievement, and self-mastery. Photographed in front of a mammoth plinth and surrounded by a group of similarly attired men (probably on the occasion of one of his many conventions), Washington flaunts an immovable, imposing figure. By posing Washington just beneath an elaborately ornamented, Second Empire baroque classical order, the photographer has crowned and enthroned the "Tuskegee Titan" and, thus, has subliminally heralded Washington's irrefutable status, c. 1900, as the most powerful and influential black man in the world.[26]

Some forty years later, New York art patron and celebrity photographer Carl Van Vechten attempted a comparable documentation project to "show young people of all races how many distinguished Negroes there are in the world." This ambitious goal of Van Vechten's (which actually began with his acquiring a Leica camera in 1932) resulted in hundreds of photographic portrait studies of famous African Americans. Most of these photographs were not taken much farther afield "in the world" than Van Vechten's makeshift studio in his midtown Manhattan apartment: an almost required New York City stopover for *all* prominent African Americans (from 1932 until the early 1960s), especially those in the literary, visual, and performing arts.[27]

A 1940 Van Vechten photograph of one of these "distinguished Negroes"—the stage and (soon to be) screen legend, singer and actress Lena Horne—is especially revealing. This study counters all expectations for the typical celebrity photograph, not to mention for Van Vechten's customary studio-based portraits. Photographed outdoors and without Van Vechten's usual props or special effects, Horne imparts such an informality and honesty here that, barring prior knowledge of her show business background, one might assume that this beautiful young woman was the "girl next door," or perhaps a wide-eyed coed. Which is not to say that this native New Yorker and former Cotton Club singer did *not* normally exude a genuine, youthful innocence both on and off the stage. Rather, what is present here (and what operates in countless other photographic portraits by Van Vechten) is his uncanny ability to deftly capture the public personae *and* the inner life of his sitters, with or (in the case of *Lena Horne)* without the expected, theatrical accoutrements. Van Vechten (who was frequently viewed as an artistic decadent, a voyeur, and a "Negrophile") departs dramatically from these perceived roles in this candid, almost naive portrait, and contributes his special documenting talents to the then formidable task of bringing images of famous African Americans into a proverbial "American Portrait Gallery." By making a number of educational institutions (most notably Fisk University and Yale University) major repositories for these photographic portraits, Van Vechten essentially ensured the realization of his stated goal of presenting this gallery of black notables to young people *across* the racial spectrum, as institutional vehicles for learning and social instruments for living.[28]

## American Expressionism

Atlanta University was at the forefront of colleges and universities that, at mid-century, embraced African American images and works of art as integral to learning. This institution inaugurated in 1942 an annual art exhibition, with a nationally juried competition for black artists and a regular program of awards and purchase prizes in various artistic media and genres. Although the Art Annual at Atlanta University ended in 1970, in the 28 years that the competitions were held they accomplished much to develop a greater awareness for the visual arts within black communities, and to cultivate individual and institutional black patronage. More importantly, the annual exhibitions also helped instill in black and white audiences a greater appreciation for African American subjects in art.[29]

In order to understand just how unusual (and often vexing) it was for the white art establishment and public to first *visualize* and then *revere* black subject matter, one need only return to those early years of the Art Annual, and read the reviews and commentaries on these "all-Negro" art shows. Disparaging statements that described Atlanta University's African American art students as "chocolaty," their subject matter as having a "primitive" quality, and their themes as largely concerned with "racial consciousness and antagonism" were not infrequent, and illustrated just how radical the annual exhibitions were. Boston artist John Wilson— who was included in more annuals than any other African American artist— described works like his *Negro Woman* (which received Atlanta University's 1955 Portrait/ Figure Award) as "African American versions" of an art that was popularized by the more socially conscious Mexican painters. According to Wilson, Mexican painters like José Clemente Orozco dealt with "images of people who were left out or unimportant," and with "the realities" that racism and capitalism often imposed on the world's darker peoples and the poor. This particular approach to a figurative art—exemplified in the furtive glance and defiant "nonwhiteness" of Wilson's *Negro Woman*—forced white viewers of the annual exhibitions to acknowledge "an almost frightening racial strength" and, conversely, black viewers to recognize themselves in the art and to visually savor the experience.[30]

After the first three exhibitions, the originator of the Atlanta University annuals, the widely traveled artist and broad-based teacher Hale Woodruff, felt that there would come a time when the art exhibitions would become integrated and, thereafter, appreciated *across* the historic racial and cultural divides in America, c. 1945. Woodruff's call for the loosening of the "all-Negro" emphasis of the annual exhibitions was rejected by Atlanta University President Rufus E. Clement, who felt that his institution's affirmation of the long depreciated black artist (not to mention his confidence in the larger mission of historically black colleges and universities) had *not* lost its imperative, despite all of the patriotic words and high hopes for racial reconciliation in the postwar years. One might interpret Woodruff's response to this statement of institutional "focus" (or "self-segregation") as two-tiered. First, he left Atlanta University (in 1946) to teach in New York University's art education department: one of the first, tenure-track appointments of an African American art educator by a predominately white university. And second, at the invitation of President Clement in 1950, he returned to Atlanta University to paint a six-paneled mural, *The Art of the Negro,* for the University's Trevor Arnett Library.[31]

This painterly "retort" of Woodruff's—a brilliant mixture of history, theory, figuration, abstraction, territoriality, and universality—culminated with a panel appropriately entitled *Muses*. In this panel Woodruff (in the tradition of Van Vechten and other chroniclers of celebrated blacks) portrays seventeen black artists of historical and contemporary significance. From the little known, pre-modern artisans of Africa, to the contemporary artists Charles Alston, Jacob Lawrence, Haitian intuitive painter Hector Hyppolite, and others, Woodruff enacted in *Muses* a visual "roll call" of black artistic greats, but framed within the entire mural cycle's painted history of acknowledged traditions, social disruptures, and cross-cultural interchanges. To a great extent, Woodruff's departing salvo to Atlanta University helped advance one of the original objectives for the Art Annual, providing "stimulus for development among black artists." What *The Art of the Negro* communicated to Atlanta University's audiences and competing artists was that not only were black *faces* beautiful and exhibition-worthy, but so were black *expressions, visions, dreams,* and *abstractions:* artistic avenues that were appealing,

Hale Woodruff
*Art of the Negro: Muses*, 1950–51
Oil on canvas, 144 x 145 in.
Collection of Clark Atlanta University Art Galleries

evocative, and historically grounded enough to stand alongside an entire community (and, ultimately, a *universe*) of contemporary art.[32]

Although most black audiences at mid-century could immediately relate to the figurative and largely realistic works of artist John Wilson (as evidenced by his popularity at the Atlanta University Art Annuals), many were confused by the less literal compositions of abstract artists like Hale Woodruff. Perhaps even more problematic for African Americans were the boldly distorted figures and expressive colors found in selected black artists's works. Paintings such as William H. Johnson's *Untitled (farm couple at work)* appeared "unintelligible" and "cryptic," even to the most conversant of the period's black art critics. Taking his cues from a variety of stylistic sources, the academically trained Johnson joined several other painters (e.g., Jacob Lawrence, Ellis Wilson, John Biggers, and Beauford Delaney) in the creation of an African American "branch" of the international art movement known as *Expressionism*. Like the more familiar Northern European archetypes in expressionist art, this African American offshoot reveled in flat, non-illusionistic painted spaces, palettes leaning towards the chromatically intense or anti-naturalistic, anatomically distorted figures, and in stylized, semiabstract renderings of an observable world.[33]

Along with links to international expressionism, works like Johnson's *Untitled (farm couple at work)* had ties to an art tradition of social commentary and protest. Works of this sort—many of which were produced during the 1930s and under the auspices of the Works Progress Administration's Federal Arts Projects (WPA/FAP) —conveyed a similar sense of emotionalism and connections to grassroot aspects of civilization, usually through moderately expressive renderings of form and socially conscious or politically charged subject matter. In *Lynching* (c. 1936), a wood sculpture by the white American artist Nat Werner, one also sees a *psychological* bridge between Johnson's fierce expressionism and Werner's visual indictment of a horrifying, racially motivated vigilantism. More naturalistic than expressionistic (with the exception of Werner's shocking integration of a visually jarring, broken tree branch tied to the victim's neck, and a tumbling, groping mass of attendants at the sculpture's base), *Lynching,* nonetheless, recalls the early twentieth-century German Expressionist sculptures of Käthe Kollwitz and Ernst Barlach: figural works that often evoked victimization and hopelessness, especially in the face of insurmountable, invisible forces.[34]

That these two works of art are also linked by an African American aversion to both the *expressive* and *nightmarish* in modern art is also telling. Following Tuskegee Institute and Howard University's respective acquisitions of the Johnson painting and Werner sculpture, neither was regularly exhibited at these institutions despite the powerful moods and messages that they related. For the Civil Rights-era patrons of the Howard University Gallery of Art, the physically contorted, black male nude corpse in Werner's *Lynching* may have been too much to bear. For potential audiences at Tuskegee Institute, the installation requirements for the Johnson painting may have simply precluded it from successfully hanging anywhere on the campus. Credit must be given to these universities and their curators for having had the foresight to acquire these two provocative works of artistic expressionism: objects that at the time were too emotionally searing to exhibit, but objects that the curators knew would *someday* be of art historical value, eventually placed on view, and critically examined.

## Modern Lives, Modern Impulses

In his 1957 book, *Black Bourgeoisie,* Howard University sociologist E. Franklin Frazier pointed out how one segment of African Americans—a mostly college-educated, middle-class elite—was resistant to the larger struggle within American society for social equality: a resistance that manifested itself in conspicuous con-

Anonymous Camera Club photographer
*The Old Time Cabin,* c. 1900
Gelatin silver print, 3¹⁄₁₆ x 5¼ in.
Collection of Hampton University Archives
checklist 14

Anonymous Camera Club photographer
*Barn on a 1-mule Farm,* c. 1900
Platinum print, 7³⁄₈ x 9½ in.
Collection of Hampton University Archives
checklist 12

William Henry Johnson
*Untitled (farm couple at work)*, c. 1941
Oil on plywood, 34 x 37¼ in.
Collection of Tuskegee University
checklist 132

sumption, economic exploitation of the black masses, and willful self-segregation. In close proximity to this "black bourgeoisie" (especially on the campuses of several black colleges and universities), one could also find black activists and intellectuals (like Frazier at Howard University), who were engaged in meaningful research on race, class, and culture, and black artists/ scholars (like Aaron Douglas at Fisk University and Hale Woodruff at Atlanta University) who pushed against the traditional boundaries of the imagination and challenged the racial status quo in creative ways. Although in the pre-Civil Rights era these institutions were largely isolated from the whirlwind of social, political, and racial upheavals that permeated the communities that immediately surrounded them, by the early 1960s there were indications that these institutions were also changing, and that the differences between those who called for a continued insularity and those who wanted to reach out beyond the institution's walls were less marked.[35]

Nat Werner
*Lynching,* n.d.
Wood, 48 x 20 x 24 in.
Collection of Howard University Gallery of Art
checklist 254

Pointing out the multiplicity of philosophies and the various approaches to higher education at these institutions, however, does not delete the fact that the teaching, collecting, and exhibiting of visual arts at historically black colleges and universities has been labor intensive and not entirely supported at any great length by these institutions. A former black university faculty member, cultural historian Richard A. Long observed that the arts at black colleges and universities have, by and large, been "fringe activities": sporadic cultural actions and institutional creations that have been promoted and developed by certain individuals at particular moments in an institution's life. Rather than part of a long-range agenda, or a strategically planned and sustained endeavor by administrators and trustees, the collecting and exhibiting of art at historically black colleges and universities has occurred when someone acted as a catalyst to make things happen. This was certainly the case for Howard University in 1930 when Professor James V. Herring successfully petitioned to create a permanent art gallery in the renovated basement of Howard's Rankin Chapel, the first art museum of its kind at a historically black college or university.[36]

A similar catalyst, resulting in the creation of a major collection of modern art, took place at Fisk University shortly after World War II. In 1949 artist Georgia O'Keeffe, on the encouragement of her friend, photographer and author Carl Van Vechten, donated 101 works of art to Fisk in memory of her recently deceased husband, the famed photographer and art dealer Alfred Stieglitz. Van Vechten was aware of the important advancements in higher education that were taking place at Fisk University and, no doubt, believed that the visual arts could play a special role in furthering the university's educational mission. His close friend, Fisk University President Charles S. Johnson, had been instrumental in attracting white and black leaders to the campus for meaningful discussions on race relations, and it was probably the university's growing national reputation as an "oasis" of tolerance in the segregated South that prompted Van Vechten to convince O'Keeffe to make such a significant contribution.[37]

Arthur G. Dove
*Swinging in the Park (there were colored people there)*, 1930
Oil on board, 23¾ x 32¾ in.
Fisk University
checklist 85

Paul Rudolph, *Interdenominational Chapel*, Tuskegee Alabama, 1960–69, Tuskegee University.
Photo by Ezra Stoller.

Included among the extraordinary African sculptures, the valuable modern art by Renoir, Toulouse-Lautrec, Cézanne, and Picasso, and other fine works given to Fisk University, were many paintings, sculptures, works on paper, and photographs by American artists (including O'Keeffe herself) who comprised Alfred Stieglitz's important circle of artists and friends. One of those works—Arthur Dove's *Swinging in the Park (there were colored people there)*—perfectly illustrated what O'Keeffe stated in 1949 was the rationale behind her benefaction:

> that it may show that there are many ways of seeing and thinking, and possibly, through showing that there are many ways, give some one confidence in his own way, which may be different, whatever its direction.[38]

Both a landscape painting and an abstraction, *Swinging in the Park (there were colored people there)* also illustrated Dove's belief in an art that had "a flexible form or formulation that was governed by some definite rhythmic sense beyond mere geometrical repetition." Dove's titular identification in this painting with a "rhythmic sense" that, rather than having been derived from "mere geometrical repetition," originated out of "swinging" (as in playground equipment *and* jazz) must have occurred to O'Keeffe as she selected this work for Fisk University. Like Woodruff's *The Art of the Negro* murals for Atlanta University, O'Keeffe clearly used this painting (as well as the other works of art in her donation) to push and prod audiences at Fisk to see and think differently, and to be confident in their differences of opinion and perception. O'Keeffe's gift and philosophical challenge were in perfect accord with the "new" Fisk University: a place where (because of President Johnson's unprecedented advancing of the social sciences and humanities) faculty and students were far more accepting of progressive ideas and modernist impulses than at other institutions in the South.[39]

On the other hand, the most identifiable visual markers of modernism at midcentury—action painting and geometric abstraction—slowly found their way into the art collections and visual landscapes of black colleges and universities. An especially conspicuous example of abstraction's presence in an African American academic setting was the Interdenominational Chapel at Tuskegee. Initially conceived and designed in 1960 (and completed in 1969) by the Harvard University-trained architect Paul Rudolph, the Chapel is quite unlike any other structure on that largely neoclassical and neo-Gothic campus. With its dramatic exterior and interior of soaring, asymmetrical brick screen walls, Rudolph revealed his debt to Le Corbusier's futuristic church in Ronchamp, France, and his basic understanding of the Tuskegee mystique. Indeed, the Interdenominational Chapel is no more than a short stroll from Keck's allegorical statue of Booker T. Washington, and both creations convey a formal dynamism that subliminally speaks to the institution's visionary and messianic sense of itself, past and present. Rudolph's reputation for idealized, expressive, and often unrelenting forms is perhaps on display at Tuskegee to its fullest degree. While most critics see the Interdenominational Chapel in sharp visual contrast to its African American (re: traditional) setting, a perceptive few see it as "a sublimely modern building, rooted in the culture which produced it." Or, in other words, a structure spiritually attuned to Tuskegee Institute, its history, and to its community who (at the close of the Civil Rights era) found themselves in a "rapidly changing relationship" with the world that surrounded them and, as a result, needed a new university space and sanctuary to help reconcile "the conflict of American life and the larger struggle of humanity beyond."[40]

At the same time that Tuskegee Institute was undergoing an architectural transformation, Fisk was also redefining its institutional and curricular relationship to the world of art. Under the leadership of artist David C. Driskell (chair of Fisk University's Department of Art and director of the university art galleries from 1966 until 1976), Fisk joined Atlanta University, Hampton Institute, and Howard

Alfred Stieglitz
*Equivalent*, 1926
Gelatin silver print, 5 x 4 in.
Fisk University
checklist 220

Alfred Stieglitz
*Equivalent*, c. 1924
Gelatin silver print, 5 x 4 in.
Fisk University
checklist 221

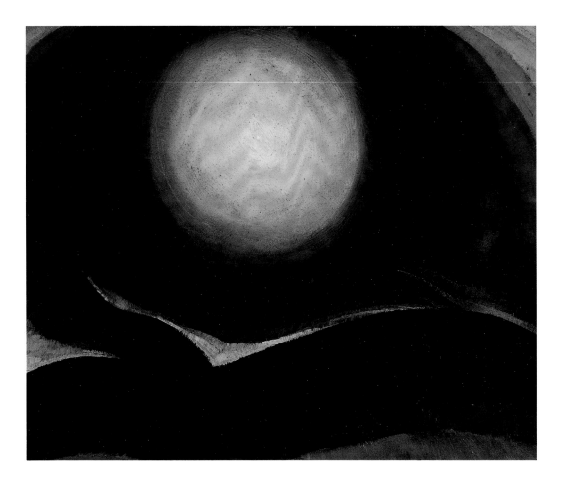

Arthur G. Dove
*Moon*, 1928
Oil on board, 8 x 10 in.
Fisk University
checklist 83

Alfred Stieglitz
*Equivalent*, 1925
Gelatin silver print, 5 x 4 in.
Fisk University
checklist 218

Alfred Stieglitz
*Equivalent*, 1925
Gelatin silver print, 4 x 5 in.
Fisk University
checklist 219

University as the leading black educational institutions with major art collections. One reason for the increased stature and growth of these collections in the late 1960s and early 1970s was the large and significant gifts of works by African American artists from the Harmon Foundation and the Smithsonian Institution. Another reason for Fisk University's prominence during this period was its ambitious acquisition policy, which (under Driskell's aegis) sought out a range of current African American art, especially works by black abstractionists.[41]

William T. Williams, one of the artists that David Driskell brought to Fisk and for whom a one-person exhibition was organized there in 1975, was described by Driskell as one of those younger African American artists in the late 1960s who "turned from those images . . . that literally commented upon black life or African antecedents relating to the black genre." "Williams's principal interest in painting," noted Driskell, "was the making of a highly reasoned form of art that was both poetically based and intellectually charged." "These works glowed with expressed energy imbued with clear and concise color motifs," Driskell continued and, despite their thematic distance from a recognizable African or African American subject, they joined African American art history through their improvisatory structures, color volatility, interplay of forms, and diverse cultural contexts.[42]

For example, Williams's *Do You Think A is B?* (in the Fisk University art collection) can be conceptually tied to one of its two companion canvases by Williams —*Elbert Jackson, L.A.M.F., Part II,* in the permanent collection of The Museum of Modern Art, and *Sophie Jackson, L.A.M.F.,* in his personal collection—and, therefore, critically seen as a postminimalist painting, primarily concerned with geometry, line, color, and perceptual intrigues. But precisely because of the painting's ties to these two other canvases (named after members of Williams's family), its implicit rhythms, compositional accents and interruptions (comparable to rhythmic strategies in jazz and blues), and the mock ridicule and signifying bravado in its title, *Do You Think A is B?* can also be linked to an African American sensibility: a consciousness underscored by Williams's interest in black cultural institutions, and by Fisk University's embracing of his particular artistic trajectory in abstract painting, which Driskell felt grew out of "the Black Visual experience in America."[43]

### Conclusion: Legacies for the Future

> *Ignored as significant repositories of art and marginalized as critical centers of discussion, HBCUs have been undervalued in the history of art and art production in our nation. If we commit ourselves to a fuller narrative documenting our common cultural heritage, reassessment and correction are appropriate measures now.*
> —Edmund Barry Gaither, "Towards a Truer History of American Art: The Contribution of Black Colleges and Universities" (1996)[44]

Interestingly it was around 1975 that the concept of "the Black Visual experience in America" became better known *beyond* the galleries and studios of black colleges and universities. Although institutions like Fisk University, Atlanta University, Hampton Institute, and Howard University continued to exhibit the works of such canonical figures in art as William Artis, Romare Bearden, Elizabeth Catlett, William H. Johnson, and Charles White (and acquiring works by these artists as well, usually as major gifts), by the mid-to-late 1970s works by a younger generation of African American artists (William T. Williams, Barkley L. Hendricks, Howardena Pindell, and others) were being exhibited at and acquired by predominately white institutions. Economics, of course, played a large role in what kinds of art black colleges and universities could realistically purchase. Yet, it is also clear that, from the late 1970s to the present, the curatorial focus of most black institutions was not directed towards contemporary, avant-garde, or postmodernist African American art.[45]

William T. Williams
*Do You Think A is B?*, 1969
Acrylic on canvas, 85¹/₈ x 61 in.
Fisk University
checklist 257

David C. Driskell
*Black Ghetto*, c. 1968–70
Oil on canvas with mixed media, 36½ x 25½ in.,
Fisk University
checklist 87

William Henry Johnson
*Untitled (seated man)*, c. 1939–40
Oil on panel, 30 x 25½ in.
Collection of Hampton University Museum
checklist 133

Also beginning in the 1970s important survey exhibitions like *Afro-American Artists: New York and Boston* (organized by the Museum of the National Center of Afro-American Artists in 1970), *The Barnett-Aden Collection* (organized by the Smithsonian Institution's Anacostia Neighborhood Museum in 1974) and *Two Centuries of Black American Art* (curated by David C. Driskell for the Los Angeles County Museum of Art in 1976) either traveled to major art museums across the United States or were discussed at length in the national press, introducing works that, for the most part, had been known primarily in black institutional art settings. The cultural custodianship and responsibility for documentation that black institutions historically had over the legacies of black artists were (as Woodruff predicted in the mid-1940s) increasingly shared with their white institutional counterparts. Major exhibitions by Romare Bearden, Jacob Lawrence, Sam Gilliam, and other African American artists were just as likely, if not *more* likely, to be seen at the Brooklyn Museum, or at black, non-university-affiliated museums like The Studio Museum in Harlem, than at black college or university art galleries. Ironically these post-Civil Rights-era shifts in the general perception and aesthetic appreciation of African American art and artists—resulting in a more diversified marketplace and less dependence upon black institutional support—made black colleges and universities mere players in conserving artistic legacies, rather than the primary historians, critics, and curators of African American art that they had been for almost a century.[46]

The role that these black educational institutions have played and continue to play in African American visual culture is vital. While the white cultural mainstream's curatorial embrace of artistic traditions from outside of a Euro-American cultural sphere is, of course, long overdue and welcomed, black colleges and universities provide something quite different from their white institutional counterparts in recounting, celebrating, and analyzing African American art. These differences, rather than having anything to do with vague, essentialist notions of race or ethnicity, are largely based on a distinct worldview: positions and perspectives that are generated from and informed by a unique set of historical circumstances, social phenomena, and cultural experiences. In other words, the experiential mosaic that makes up African American realities significantly shapes the structure, curriculum, and programming at black colleges and universities. While most American institutions of higher learning, regardless of their racial or ethnic makeup, enjoy many shared experiences, common values, and similar challenges, the idea that black colleges and universities might have their own particular view of the world (conditioned by racism and discrimination), their own way of educating students (many of whom come from educationally deprived backgrounds), and their own vision for the future (colored ironically by both apprehension and hope) is not, it seems, an unreasonable notion.[47]

As the primary educators of black people in America, what historically black colleges and universities instill in their audiences—especially in terms of arts education—is central to fostering visual literacy. From the sixty or so years of arts advocacy that Howard University's Gallery of Art has to its credit, to the twenty or so years that North Carolina Central University's Art Museum has provided an art education to the greater Research Triangle area, many black institutions of higher education have long used the visual arts to create lines of communication, both inside their respective institutions, and outward into their surrounding communities. In his book *American Negro Art* (1960) Cedric Dover optimistically wrote (in regard to black college and university art museums) that:

> With co-operative redistribution of their properties, and help from the foundations, these institutions could establish regional museums in which every American Negro artist of consequence would be represented, keeping for themselves teaching collections introducing world art, the art of the Americas, and American Negro art, with emphasis on local successes.

One might argue that this museum plan of Dover's for historically black colleges and universities has, in fact, been realized (as evidenced in the dozen or so extant black university art museums nationwide), but perhaps not to the degree that he originally envisioned in 1960.[48]

Howard University-based painter and art historian Floyd Coleman has often noted that the exhibitions, art appreciation classes, guest lectureships by visiting artists, and other arts-related programs that historically black colleges and universities sponsor are frequently the only sources for exposure to the visual arts in African American communities. As "sites of heroic resistance to misrepresentation, invisibility, and oppression," the art organizations and activities at black colleges and universities offer their constituencies a psychological buffer against visual and cultural assaults from the society-at-large, primarily via images that underscore the basic humanity, self-worth, and complexity of African Americans.[49]

It has already been noted that the most likely exhibition venues for African American artists—at least up to the mid-to-late 1960s—were art museums and galleries affiliated with black colleges and universities. The galleries at Atlanta University, Fisk University, Hampton Institute, Howard University, and, to a lesser extent, Tuskegee Institute and North Carolina Central University, all presented comprehensive exhibitions of African American art at a time when very few white art institutions were willing or even interested in doing so. Although black institutions now share and often compete with white institutions to present this same work, two historically black universities—Hampton University and Clark Atlanta University— now have state-of-the-art museums that join them to an already existing network of art venues nationwide, where a range of exhibitions can be seen and appreciated.

In addition to a first-rate university museum, Hampton is also the home of *The International Review of African American Art*: the only art journal devoted to African American visual culture. Founded in 1976 by art historian and artist Samella Lewis (under the name *Black Art: an international quarterly*), *The International Review of African American Art* (or *IRAAA*) and its affiliation with the Hampton University Museum (beginning in 1992) heralds an important step in black university art patronage: a level that moves beyond individual art acquisitions and public art commissions. In an era when many scholarly journals and magazines fold because they are unable to sustain themselves financially even with large numbers of subscribers, this journal's longevity speaks to the vision and tenacity of its founder, Samella Lewis. In a related vein, the *IRAAA*'s seven-year anchor at Hampton speaks volumes about that university's unparalled commitment to documenting, studying, and theorizing African American art: a commitment that extends back almost one hundred years to another pioneering, Hampton-based journal of cultural research and criticism, *The Southern Workman*.[50]

Finally, black colleges and universities provide an invaluable service to African American visual culture by making their libraries, special collections, and archives accessible to art historians, artists, critics, and other scholars. As repositories of not only important art works, but out-of-print books, the papers and correspondence of historic figures (for example, Alain Locke's papers at Howard, and Aaron Douglas's papers at Fisk), and other primary documents, they collectively represent a treasure trove of information. With their emphasis on the experiences and contributions of African Americans, they give those who study black Americana an ideal place to conduct research: sites abounding in primary and secondary research materials and in research data that encourages interdisciplinary and biographical cross-referencing. The photographic archives of many of these institutions alone (especially those of Hampton and Tuskegee) provide an incredibly rich and virtually untapped source for examining aspects of black visual culture (e.g., the landscape of race, images of class and caste, social portraiture, the ever changing notions of the physical ideal in black America, etc.).

Hale Woodruff
*Galaxy*, c. 1959
Oil on canvas, 47½ x 35½ in.
Collection of Clark Atlanta University Art Galleries
checklist 262

What does one do with this vast, artistic legacy from black colleges and universities? Is it enough to merely recount "the glory days" of the past (what some people uncritically refer to as the cultural and economic "advantages" that black institutions had during the era of segregation)? Or is it enough for us to simply point out the highlights and surprises of these art collections? Even within the framework of what art historian Edmund Barry Gaither has eloquently described as the important work of reinserting "the missing pages on black participation" in American art, one is still left with this huge *inheritance:* thousands of paintings, sculpture, photographs, drawings, and prints, all of which add immeasurably to the American art story, and much of which is in dire need of conservation. But "conservation" not just in the material sense of saving and preserving old objects. No, what these works need is a perceptual overhaul: reappraisals of their intrinsic value and reinvestments in their collective, cultural worth.[51]

*To Conserve a Legacy: American Art from Historically Black Colleges and Universities* takes stock of what has been saved (as well as what has literally survived) and, through a series of historical narratives on art, race, education, and collecting, offers up this legacy for reevaluation. Reflections on what "was lost, and is found" in black college and university art collections have already moved beyond inventory and documentation and, instead, towards critical analysis and interpretation: i.e., the place of African American history in visual culture, and the meaning of art in a black institutional context.[52]

A painting from Clark Atlanta University's art collection such as Hale Woodruff's *Galaxy* summarizes these questions about the subjects and settings of art. Woodruff's abstract explorations of the cosmos and artistic mapping—comprised of colored shards, fragments, and axial radii—force us to reassess this artistic endowment. Painted c. 1959, around the same time that the first human being was sent into outer space, when black students at the Agricultural and Technical College in Greensboro, North Carolina, inaugurated the first Civil Rights movement lunch counter sit-in, and when avant-garde jazz saxophonist Ornette Coleman recorded his first, free jazz masterpieces, *Galaxy* represents a "first" of another kind. Linking chaos, creativity, and universality, *Galaxy* pushes against the parochial attitudes of both art traditionalists and race essentialists and, in the context of the historically black university art collection, recalls the biblical adage that "wisdom is good with an inheritance; and by it there is profit to them that see the sun." Woodruff described this balancing act between celebrating black cultural experiences and aspiring to a wider and more universal realm of experience, in the following way: "I've got to see the universality of what you do and then understand the source from which it arrives." One hopes that after experiencing *To Conserve a Legacy: American Art from Historically Black Colleges and Universities* audiences will recognize the inherent universality in these art collections and, furthermore, will realize that this visual legacy is a cultural bequest not *just* for African Americans, but for *everyone.*[53]

1. Joshua C. Taylor, "Preface," in *America as Art* (Washington, D.C.: Smithsonian Institution Press, 1976), p. viii.

2. For the most part, the historical (rather than the contemporary) names of several of these black institutions of higher education will be used throughout this essay: e.g., "Hampton Institute" (which became Hampton University in 1984); "Tuskegee Institute" (which became Tuskegee University in 1985); and "Atlanta University" (which, following its merger with Clark College in 1988, became Clark Atlanta University). When the "National Religious Training School and Chautauqua for the Colored Race" came under the jurisdiction of the state of North Carolina, it became the Durham State Normal School (in 1923), the North Carolina College for Negroes (in 1925), and (since 1947) North Carolina Central University.

3. Three recent art historical studies of note that revise certain long-held paradigms of American art are: David C. Miller, ed., *American Iconology: New Approaches to Nineteenth Century Art and Literature* (New Haven: Yale University Press, 1993); Terry Smith, *Making the Modern: Industry, Art,*

*and Design in America* (Chicago: University of Chicago Press, 1993); and Mary Ann Calo, ed., *Critical Issues in American Art: A Book of Readings* (Boulder: Westview Press, 1998).

4. The reader will observe in this exhibition catalogue the side-by-side appearance of *Negro, black, African American,* and *person of color.* Rather than always referencing Americans of African descent according to contemporary nomenclature, this publication attempts the use of racial names that are consonant within the particular historical context under discussion. To some, the word *Negro* may be odious; however, history cannot be rewritten. There was never a national referendum to decide the ethnic designations of Americans of African descent so, as a consequence, all of the appellations that are used here are contextually based and, at times, interchangeable.

One recent study is especially attuned to using African American art and literature in a critical examination of American culture. See Eric J. Sundquist, *To Wake a Nation: Race in the Making of American Literature* (Cambridge: Belknap Press of Harvard University Press, 1993).

5. W.E.B. DuBois, *The Souls of Black Folk* (1903; reprint, New York: Avon Books, 1965), p. 291.

6. Booker T. Washington, *Up From Slavery: An Autobiography* (1901; reprint, New York: Avon Books, 1965), pp. 146–50.

7. DuBois, p. 267.

8. For an early recounting of the creations of several black colleges and universities, see Dwight Oliver Wendell Holmes, *The Evolution of the Negro College* (1934; reprint, New York: Arno Press and the *New York Times,* 1969). For artistic examples of emancipation and freedom, see Hugh Honour, *The Image of the Black in Western Art, Volume IV, From the American Revolution to World War I* (Cambridge: Harvard University Press, 1989).

9. Two noteworthy discussions of Edmonia Lewis can found in Albert Boime, *The Art of Exclusion: Representing Blacks in the Nineteenth Century* (Washington, D.C.: Smithsonian Institution Press, 1990), pp. 162–72; and Kirsten P. Buick, "The Ideal Works of Edmonia Lewis: Invoking and Inventing Autobiography," *American Art* 9 (summer 1995): 4–19.

10. DuBois, p. 284. For another thoughtful discussion about notions of freedom for African American artists, see Juanita Marie Holland, *Edward Mitchell Bannister, 1828–1901* (Stamford, Connecticut: Whitney Museum of American Art at Champion, 1992).

11. Lynda Roscoe Hartigan, *Sharing Traditions: Five Black Artists in Nineteenth-Century America* (Washington, D.C.: Smithsonian Institution, 1985), pp. 51–68; and Joseph D. Ketner, *The Emergence of the African American Artist: Robert S. Duncanson, 1821–1872* (Columbia: University of Missouri Press, 1993).

12. Francis Greenwood Peabody, *Education for Life: The Story of Hampton Institute* (Garden City, New York: Doubleday, Page, and Company, 1919), pp. 156, 164. For a more critical view of the "Hampton experiment," see William H. Robinson, "Indian Education at Hampton Institute," in Keith L. Schall, ed., *Stony the Road: Chapters in the History of Hampton Institute* (Charlottesville: University Press of Virginia, 1977), pp. 1–33.

13. For two very different views on Frances Benjamin Johnston's Hampton project, see Lincoln Kirstein, *The Hampton Album* (New York: The Museum of Modern Art, 1966); and Jeannene M. Przyblyski, "American Visions at the Paris Exposition, 1900: Another Look at Frances Benjamin Johnston's Hampton Photographs," *Art Journal* 57 (fall 1998): 60–68.

14. Peabody, pp. 157–58. Also see "An Indian Raid on Hampton Institute," *The Southern Workman* 7 (May 1878): 36.

15. "A Collection of Rare Baskets," *The Southern Workman* 34 (July 1905): 377.

16. Hampton's educational mission was published and distributed to interested people in the form of a small, maxim-filled pamphlet. Samuel Chapman Armstrong, *Education for Life* (Hampton, Virginia: Hampton Normal and Agricultural Institute, 1914).

17. William H. Holtzclaw, "A School Principal's Story," in Booker T. Washington, ed., *Tuskegee and its People: Their Ideals and Achievements* (New York: D. Appleton and Company, 1906), pp. 111–40.

18. Edith M. Dabbs, "About the Artist," in *Face of an Island: Leigh Richmond Miner's Photographs of Saint Helena Island* (New York: Grossman Publishers, 1971), n.p. For an essay that includes Miner in a discussion of turn-of-the-century pictorialist photographers, see: Barbara L. Michaels, "New Light on F. Holland Day's Photographs of African Americans," *History of Photography* 18 (winter 1994): 334–47.

19. The following is an example of a promotional, photo-illustrated brochure from Tuskegee Institute: *Tuskegee To Date* (Tuskegee, Alabama: Tuskegee Normal and Industrial Institute, 1915). For the quote from William J. Edwards (great-grandfather of noted filmmaker and black college alumnus Spike Lee), see: W.J. Edwards, "Uplifting the Submerged," in Washington, ed., pp. 224–252.

20. See "The Unveiling at Tuskegee," and William Anthony Aery, "The Booker T. Washington Monument," in *The Southern Workman* 51 (May 1922): 207–9, 217–26.

21. Amy Kirschke, *Aaron Douglas: Art, Race, and the Harlem Renaissance* (Jackson: University Press

Alvin Smith
*Neshoba Specter*, 1966
Oil on canvas with collage, 60 x 35½ in.
Collection of Clark Atlanta University Art Galleries
checklist 216

of Mississippi, 1995); and Alain Locke, ed., *The New Negro* (1925; reprint, New York: Atheneum Press, 1980), p. vii.

22. John Wesley Work, *Folk Song of the American Negro* (1915; reprint, New York: Negro Universities Press, 1969); and Kirschke, pp. 129–30.

23. Elizabeth Irene Seay, "A History of the North Carolina College for Negroes" (master's thesis, Duke University, 1941); and George W. Reid, ed., *A History of N.C. Central University: A Town and Gown Analysis* (Durham: North Carolina Central University, 1985).

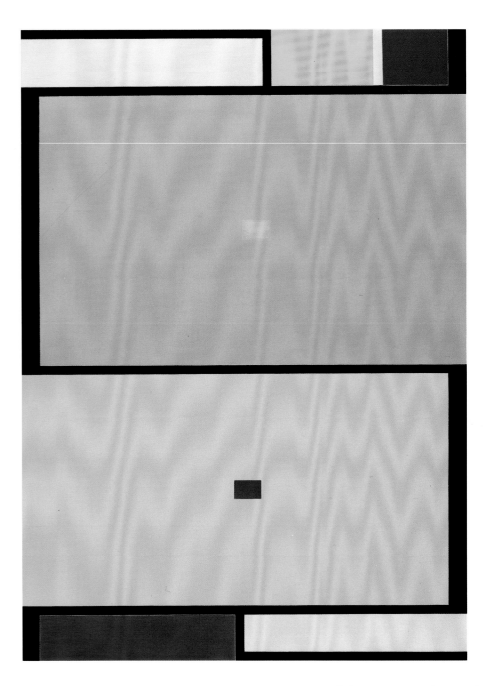

Felrath Hines
*Facade II*, 1988
Oil on canvas, 66½ x 48¾ in.
Collection of Howard University Gallery of Art
checklist 110

24. Mitchell D. Kahan, *Heavenly Visions: The Art of Minnie Evans* (Raleigh: North Carolina Museum of Art, 1986); and *Minnie Evans: Artist* (Greenville: East Carolina University, 1993).

25. Clifton H. Johnson, ed., *God Struck Me Dead: Religious Conversions Experiences and Autobiographies of Ex-Slaves* (Philadelphia: Pilgrim Press, 1969).

26. Lewis R. Harlan, *Booker T. Washington: The Wizard of Tuskegee, 1910–1915* (New York: Oxford University Press, 1983). Although this photograph of Booker T. Washington is unidentified and only tentatively attributed to the New Orleans photographer Arthur Bedou, the elaborate architectural setting, the summer clothing that Washington (and the other men) are wearing, and the Caribbean appearance of the surrounding men, lead one to speculate that this photograph may have been taken around July 1899 in London, England, while Washington was there with a group of other renowned men of color in a planning session for the upcoming Pan–African Conference of 1900. For evidence of Washington's presence in London at this time, see Lewis R. Harlan and Raymond W. Smock, eds., *The Booker T. Washington Papers, Vol. 5, 1899–1900* (Urbana: University of Illinois Press, 1976), pp. 154–67.

27. Rudolph P. Byrd, ed., *Generations in Black and White: Photographs of Carl Van Vechten* (Athens: University of Georgia Press, 1993), pp. xv–xxvii.

28. Bruce Kellner, *Carl Van Vechten and the irreverent decades* (Norman: University of Oklahoma Press, 1968).

29. Richard A. Long, "The Atlanta University Collection of Afro-American Art," in *Highlights from the Atlanta University Collection of Afro-American Art* (Atlanta: High Museum of Art, 1973), n.p.

30. "Black Beaux-Arts," *Time* 40 (September 21, 1942), p. 74; "Atlanta's Annual," *Time* 45 (April 9, 1945), p. 65; and "Racial Strength," *Time* 57 (April 9, 1951), p. 89. Also see Patricia Hills, "A Portrait of the Artist as an African-American: A Conversation with John Wilson," in *Dialogue: John Wilson/Joseph Norman* (Boston: Museum of the National Center of Afro-American Artists, 1995), pp. 24–33; and Lois Tarlow, "Profile: John Wilson," *Art New England* (August/September 1998): 22–23, 80.

31. Tina Dunkley, "The Atlanta University Art Annuals: Fostering a Tradition in Afro-American Art," *The International Review of African American Art* 11 (1994): 22–30.

32. Judith Wilson, "'Go Back and Retrieve It': Hale Woodruff, Afro-American Modernist," in *Selected Essays: Art and Artists from the Harlem Renaissance to the 1980s* (Atlanta: National Black Arts Festival, 1988), pp. 41–49.

33. James A. Porter, *Modern Negro Art* (1943; reprint, Washington, D.C.: Howard University Press,

1992), p. 115; and Richard J. Powell, "'In My Family of Primitiveness and Tradition': William H. Johnson's *Jesus and the Three Marys*," *American Art* 5 (fall 1991): 21–33.

34. J.L., "Sculpture by Nat Werner, An Artist of Unusual Versatility," *Art News* 36 (March 26, 1938): 13. In a photograph that accompanied another article about Nat Werner and his wife, artist Geri Pine, *Lynching* appears in the background of his crowded New York studio. See "Pine & Werner," *Art Digest* 17 (December 1, 1942): 13. For the cultural and artistic context behind a work like *Lynching*, see Marlene Park, "Lynching and Anti-lynching: Art and Politics in the 1930s," *Prospects* 18 (1993): 311–65. I am grateful to Karen C.C. Dalton, director, Image of the Black in Western Art Research Project and Photo Archive, Harvard University, for bringing Parks's article to my attention.

35. E. Franklin Frazier, *Black Bourgeoisie* (Glencoe, Illinois: Free Press, 1957).

36. M.J. Hewitt, "Major Art Collections in Historically African American Institutions: An Interview with Richard A. Long," *The International Review of African American Art* 11 (1994): 8–13. For more information on the role that James V. Herring played at Howard University and in the city of Washington, D.C., see Keith Morrison, *Art in Washington and its Afro-American Presence: 1940–1970* (Washington, D.C.: Washington Project for the Arts, 1985).

37. *The Alfred Stieglitz Collection for Fisk University* (1949; reprint, Nashville: Fisk University, 1984).

38. Ibid.

39. Arthur Dove, as quoted by Frederick S. Wight in *Arthur Dove* (Berkeley: University of California Press, 1958), p. 64. Also see: Stanley H. Smith, "Sociological Research and Fisk University: A Case Study," in James E. Blackwell and Morris Janowitz, eds., *Black Sociologists: Historical and Contemporary Perspectives* (Chicago: University of Chicago Press, 1974), pp. 164–90.

40. Kenneth Severens, *Southern Architecture* (New York: E.P. Dutton, 1981), pp. 174–76; and Carl Black, Jr., "The Space of Human Spirit: Interdenominational Chapel, Tuskegee, Paul Rudolph," in *Global Architecture 20* (Tokyo: A.D.A. Edita, 1973), n.p.

41. For an examination of David C. Driskell's contributions to African American art, see *Narratives of African American Art and Identity: The David C. Driskell Collection* (San Francisco: Pomegranate, 1998).

42. David C. Driskell, ". . . an unending visual odyssey," in *William T. Williams: An Exhibition of Paintings from 1974–1985* (Winston-Salem: Southeastern Center for Contemporary Art, 1985), n.p.

43. Ibid.

44. Edmund Barry Gaither, "Toward a Truer History of American Art: The Contribution of Black Colleges and Universities," in *Revisiting American Art: Works from the Collections of Historically Black Colleges and Universities* (Katonah, New York: Katonah Museum of Art, 1996), p. 5.

45. Robert M. Doty, *Contemporary Black Artists in America* (New York: Whitney Museum of American Art, 1971).

46. *Afro-American Artists: New York and Boston* (Boston: Museum of the National Center of Afro-American Artists); *The Barnett-Aden Collection* (Washington, D.C.: Smithsonian Institution Press, 1974); and David C. Driskell, *Two Centuries of Black American Art* (New York: Alfred A. Knopf, 1976).

47. For an examination of how race plays a role in basic, perceptual, and conceptual processes, see Naomi Zacks, "Race, Life, Death, Identity, Tragedy and Good Faith," in Lewis R. Gordon, ed., *Existence in Black: An Anthology of Black Existential Philosophy* (New York: Routledge, 1997), pp. 99–109.

48. Frank Bowles and Frank A. DeCosta, *Between Two Worlds: A Profile of Negro Higher Education* (New York: McGraw Hill Book Company, 1971); "Identity and Institutions in the Black Community," in Gerald David Jaynes and Robin M. Williams, Jr., eds., *A Common Destiny: Blacks and American Society* (Washington, D.C.: National Academy Press, 1989), pp. 161–204; and Cedric Dover, *American Negro Art* (Greenwich, Connecticut: New York Graphic Society, 1960), p. 38.

49. Floyd Coleman, "Black Colleges: The Development of an African American Visual Tradition," *The International Review of African American Art* 11 (1994): 30–38.

50. Jeanne Zeidler, "Reflections on 20 Years of IRAAA: A Conversation with Samella Lewis," *The International Review of African American Art* 13 (1996): 4–12.

51. Edmund Barry Gaither, pp. 5–18.

52. *Luke* 15:32.

53. *Ecclesiastes* 7:11. Also see "Hale Woodruff: An Interview with Albert Murray," in *Hale Woodruff: 50 Years of his Art* (New York: The Studio Museum in Harlem, 1979), p. 85. In the late 1950s, Mr. and Mrs. Chauncey Waddell, two long-time supporters of Atlanta University, instituted a small endowment to help support future acquisitions of contemporary art. Among the contemporary works that entered Atlanta University's collection through the Waddell's largesse was Woodruff's *Galaxy*. See Clarence A. Bacote, *The Story of Atlanta University* (Atlanta: Atlanta University, 1969).

# Conservation
# and Photographic
# Archives

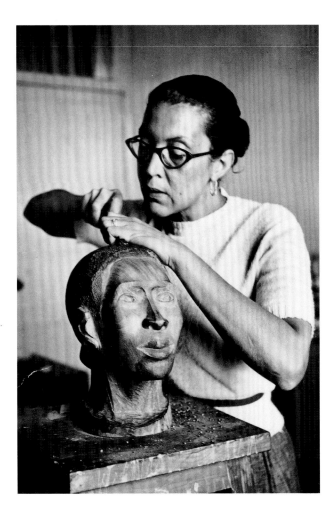 

left: Elizabeth Catlett working on *Negro Woman*,
c. 1956.

right: Elizabeth Catlett
*Negro Woman*, c. 1956
Wood and onyx, 11½ x 6½ x 9 in.
Collection of Clark Atlanta University Art Galleries
© Elizabeth Catlett/Licensed by VAGA, New York, NY
before treatment
checklist 50

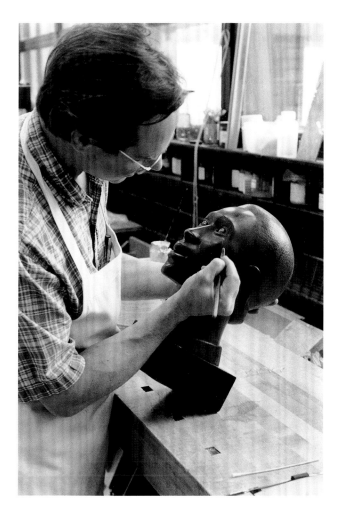

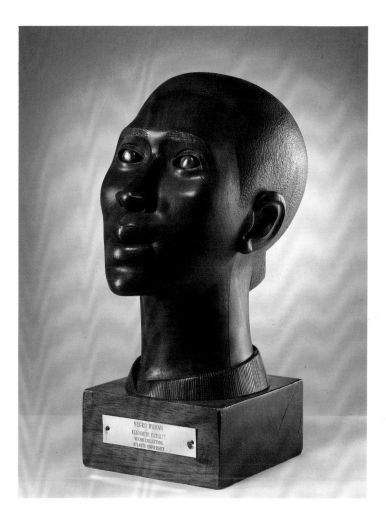

left: Alex Carlisle conserving *Negro Woman* at
the Williamstown Art Conservation Center,
1998.

right: Elizabeth Catlett
*Negro Woman*, c. 1956
after treatment

# Painters Painting,
# Conservators
# Conserving:
# The Laying On
# Of Many Hands

Thomas J. Branchick

The moment an artist completes a painting it slowly proceeds to change its visual appearance. Drying of mediums affects the gloss or reflectance. The canvas, board, or panel supports change color and can impact the overall tone. Interlayer drying cracks combined with physical breaks in the paint and ground layers all interrupt the once uniform surface. The artist's technique in paint application: thick or thin, smooth or heavily impastoed, lean or medium rich, palette knife or brush, all contribute to the aging process. Yellowed varnishes and ambient grime obscure the tone of a picture. In *To Conserve a Legacy,* the painting conservators at the Williamstown Art Conservation Center encountered some challenging works on which to practice the science and craft of conservation. The two oil on canvas paintings by John Biggers, *Old Man* and *Old Coffee Drinker*, Hampton University Museum collection, were received rolled. They were painted early in the artist's career, dating to 1945. While they were in their rolled state, the canvases were flexed and pressure cracks occurred, resulting in horizontal elevated lines through-

John Biggers
*Old Coffee Drinker*, 1945
Oil on canvas, 51³/₈ x 35³/₈ in.
Collection of Hampton University Museum
before treatment
checklist 40

out the compositions. The paint application was thin and these lines were extremely disruptive to the original artist's intent. Kirsten Younger, advanced painting intern, performed two remarkable treatments. Relaxing the canvas with moisture, together with consolidating the paint film with a heat-sensitive resin, returned the pictures to their proper plane. Additional structural support was provided by attaching a lining fabric to the reverse of the original canvas. The cosmetic process of inpainting the losses caused by the cracks was delicately and painstakingly performed. Proper level, color, texture, and reflectance must be considered to integrate an area of damage into the original context.

A similar problem was encountered on the James Weeks, *Jazz Musician*, 1960, Howard University Gallery of Art collection. Assistant Conservator Montserrat Le Mense skillfully relaxed the thick, heavy, cupped paint film into its proper plane. This work, only twenty-eight years old, began to crack due to the thickness of the paint. The canvas was also mounted to a nonkeyable wood strainer. A strainer does not allow tension to the canvas. It was bowed from the physical weight of the paint film. This had to be taken into account in the choice of a new solid secondary support panel which was shaped to conform to the bowed strainer. Heat, moisture, and adhesive secured the painting to the panel.

A significant "find" in the group of paintings was provided by Associate Conservator Michael Heslip's treatment of an originally inventoried "artist unknown" portrait of a Negro butler. This oil on canvas was grime laden, and suffered from a large tear to the center of the composition, discolored varnish layers, previous applications of overpaint and abrasion to the paint film from overcleaning. Upon close examination and cleaning, a signature appeared on the base of the column at the right: "T.W. Wood 1858." Inscribed on the stretcher reverse was "Christian Fleetwood's father – gift." Title and artist now known, this recorded Thomas Waterman Wood can now rejoin the body of this artist's work. Michael's task was to undo the not-so-skillful endeavors of the past. He could also demonstrate the sensitive attention to the surface of a painting required in repairing the large tear. A silicone rubber mold was taken from the weave of the painting and pressed into the fill material of the tear. This provided the proper topography for reconstruction during the inpainting process.

Associate Conservator Cynthia Luk was faced with a similar problem in a painting by Edward Bruce, *Portrait of William Friday*, 1934, Hampton University Museum collection. This work was also severely compromised by past damage and previous repair. The thin, smooth surface of the painting made disguising a complicated tear a challenge. Surface dirt, grime, and overpaint were removed, revealing the proper tone of the picture.

Several works by William H. Johnson were treated for the exhibition. Sandra Webber was challenged by *Spring Blossom*, Collection of Tuskegee University. This painting had been wax infused in the past to remedy the severe cracking and cupping that existed in the paint film. Johnson used a bast fiber burlap-like support for this picture. The embrittled fabric combined with the thick impasto of his palette knife application of pigment were the two factors that rendered this an extremely fragile work of art. Any physical flexing of the fabric would crack the paint. The crack would break the surface tension and allow air flow, temperature, and humidity to curl the paint film. The previous wax infusion did little to correct the structural problem, but it did serve to embalm the picture in an effort to prevent further loss. Sandy removed the wax and, with gentle heat and pressure, relaxed the paint film to the proper plane. The introduction of a consolidating resin added further penetration to secure the paint to the support, and the additional lining fabric supplemented and strengthened the weakened burlap. The cleaning process revealed the original color palette, rendering this painting (previously lacking acceptable exhibition quality) an excellent example of this period of the artist's work.

Another work by Johnson, *Untitled (farm couple at work)* from Tuskegee University collection was painted on 1/4 inch plywood. The choice of support contributed to the deterioration of this work. The plywood had warped and the laminate plys were separating. The grain of the wood was cracking and splitting, and all four corners were rounded off and missing color. At some point, a commercial flat molding had been nailed to the plywood. This cropped the composition by 2 inches in both the vertical and horizontal dimensions. The "inherent vice" from the choice of support had to be integrated into the course of treatment. Thomas Branchick, conservator of paintings, secured the delaminating plywood with adhesive and supplemented the missing corners with brace plates of a resin fiberglass sheet. The removal of dirt and grime brought the color to its proper presentation, and filling, texturing, and inpainting followed.

John Biggers
*Old Coffee Drinker*, 1945
Oil on canvas, 51³/₈ x 35³/₈ in.
Collection of Hampton University Museum
after treatment
checklist 40

Branchick also treated the Charles White, *Progress of the American Negro*, 1939–40, Howard University Gallery of Art collection. This work, dating from 1939, was also rolled and suffered from numerous cracks and losses in the paint film from the process. The cotton duck fabric was very strong and supple. After cleaning, the fabric was infused with a consolidating resin and the paint film was brought into plane on the vacuum hot table, using heat and pressure. The painting was then mounted to a custom wood stretcher and keyed out to tension. Interns Rayna Gardner (Tuskegee University), Hollie Hollowell (Fisk University), and Ahmad Ward (Hampton University) all provided assistance in applying the missing gesso ground to the losses, which elevated these linear scars to the proper level for reconstruction. Inpainting was executed in acrylic emulsion colors.

Intern Rodney Bennett (North Carolina Central University) assisted in surface cleaning the oil on canvas by Robert S. Duncanson, *Cottage at Pass Opposite Ben Lomond*, North Carolina Central University collection, and intern Elee Elijah Stewart (Clark Atlanta University) surface cleaned the John Wilson, *Negro Woman*, 1952, Clark Atlanta University Art Galleries collection. Pride in the process was demonstrated in their verbal presentation and will be their personal connection to the exhibition.

The conservation profession has often been compared to the medical profession. We diagnose and prescribe treatment for each individual ailing patient. *To Conserve a Legacy* provided a "waiting room" full of candidates that were waiting their cure, allowing them to strut once again.

Charles White
*Progress of the American Negro*, 1939–40,
*[Five Great American Negroes]*
Oil on canvas, 60 x 120 x 11 in.
Collection of Howard University Gallery of Art
top: before treatment; bottom: after treatment
checklist 256

William Henry Johnson
*Untitled (farm couple at work)*, c. 1941
Oil on plywood, 34 x 37¼ in.
Collection of Tuskegee University
top: before treatment; bottom: after treatment
checklist 132

# Lux, Lies, and Compromise: The Politics of Light Exposure

Leslie Paisley

Light is destructive to artwork, yet without light, there is no art. Each artwork (especially art on paper) has a limited physical lifespan and the endpoint (when unacceptable change makes the artwork no longer worthy of exhibition) is a finite number of years, not always centuries away. Finding the delicate balance between exhibition and preservation is an ongoing challenge and rationing of light exposure over the lifetime of the artwork and becomes the responsibility of a long line of directors, curators, and conservators. The key concept is the "lifetime" of the artwork. Unless the endpoint is known no exact recipe for "safe" light exposure can be prescribed. Contemporary art, some argue, should expend its first decade in the fast lane—brighter galleries, more frequent exhibitions—while it has the most to say. Save the rationing for its retirement years. This argument illustrates the type of problems at the center of preservation politics. A one-size-fits-all exhibition policy does not consider the museum's intention or the artist's preference for a "short effective life to a long shadowy one."[1] Often conservators will accept a fading rate with periodic peaks that expedite color change, as long as the entire lifeline is considered consciously at the front end, before the fading occurs. As more art is made with fugitive materials, museums may feel they have only two choices: not to collect it at all, or to use it before they lose it. Some curators of nineteenth-century photographs may tend their collections like the finest vintage Bordeaux wines which must be "put down" to be preserved; however, they may simultaneously feel that their chromogenic photographs (that will fade even in dark storage) are like a Beaujolais Nouveau, "you can't keep it, so enjoy it now."[2] Curators are reluctant to set the expiration date for a work of art and many prefer to place the restrictions upon the next generation or at least on the next curator. The most successful conservators know their job is to recommend, not to enforce lighting restrictions. These must be recommendations that can be readily implemented, otherwise they will likely be ignored. Conservators have also learned how not to say no to curators, but how to say yes (with conditions) and to pick their battles carefully. This kind of compromise ensures that the opinions of the conservator will be solicited in the future and that decisions will be made consciously rather than by default.

Understanding the rules of reciprocity for light exposure assists with rationing and balancing light exposure with storage in the dark. The degree of light damage is a direct result of three conditions: the amount of light (its intensity in lux), the energy of that light (whether it is filtered for the most destructive wavelengths—UV), and the duration of exposure (number of hours per year). One must understand that all effects are cumulative and that an increase in one component is directly reciprocal to another. Therefore, long periods of low intensity light exposure can cause change in artwork that is equivalent to brief periods of high intensity illumination, assuming that the light source is the same. For example, a typical exhibition of four months or 24,000 hours of exhibition at 100 lux is equivalent to eight months or 48,000 hours at 50 lux.

Sensible exhibition decisions are complicated. The average young human eye needs a minimum light level of 50 lux in order to perceive a work of art; however, the amount of light required to really see the artwork "well" varies with the colors in its palette and the age of the viewer. For example: a young eye may need 100–150 lux to view a dark image, while an older eye may need as much as 200–300 lux to see the same detail.[3] This is in direct conflict with many museum exhibition requirements of no more than 50 lux for light-sensitive works of art. And, while the expense of mounting an exhibition limits the *number* of annual exhibitions a museum can afford, the *duration* of those exhibitions often does not have the same institutional limits. Conservators struggle to make exhibition recommendations that protect the artwork and address these concerns in a way that can be readily embraced by the museum.

top: the surrogate of a non-collection test cyanotype; bottom: the original cyanotype.

Generally, recommendations regarding light levels and duration of exhibitions for art on paper are determined after works are placed into one of three categories of light sensitivity: durable, moderate, or sensitive. These categories are based on testing done by the International Standards Organization and can be applied to artwork once the materials and pigments in a work are identified analytically.[4] (The catch here is that artwork is not routinely analyzed for identification to determine exhibition restrictions, and visual identification alone has proven unreliable.)[5] It is important to note that while a pigment may fall into one of three categories of durability, the amount of light to induce the first noticeable fading on an oil painting with a fugitive pigment may exceed that necessary to fade a watercolor with the same pigment. Thin glazes in a watercolor wash are up to five times as sensitive as the full-strength color. Therefore, the pigment's binder, the type of coating on the painting, and/or the type of support, rather than the pigment itself, may affect lightfastness.[6] Also, the previous exhibition history may alter its classification.

The photographs selected for this exhibition were categorized using guidelines being developed by the Photographic Materials Group of the American Institute for Conservation. These guidelines helped establish recommendations for the maximum annual light exposure (time and intensity) for each photograph placed into one of three categories. Classification of the light sensitivity of a photograph is based upon the inherent stability of the specific photographic process (requiring proper identification by an expert),[7] the chemistry used to produce the final print, and any coatings applied to it. Other factors that affect appropriate light exposure include the photograph's condition as well as the state of preservation of its case or other mounting materials.

### The Challenge

The exhibition *To Conserve a Legacy: American Art from Historically Black Colleges and Universities* incorporates prints, watercolors, drawings, photographs, paintings, frames, and sculpture. The organizers and funders of this exhibition insisted that it reach the widest possible audience, resulting in an eight-venue exhibition traveling over a three-and-one-half-year period. Selections for this exhibition were difficult because some treasures from these university collections are also the most vulnerable to light. Curatorial interpretation required exhibition of some of the most light-sensitive photographs directly adjacent to more brightly lit, more lightfast paintings. Responsible lighting recommendations for a traveling exhibition are often complicated by the lack of exhibition histories or condition reports, and insufficient information about each site's ability to implement the recommendations. Illuminating the exhibition was also complicated by the variety of light sensitivities even within artistic disciplines. For example, within the selection of exhibited photographs, the cyanotypes are categorized as sensitive, those poorly processed and on printing out papers are moderately sensitive while the silver gelatin, well-processed developed out papers are durable. Further complicating the decisions was the fact that some photographs did not fit neatly into established categories. For example, while a faded albumen print can generally be categorized as moderately sensitive, the pristine albumen prints from the Francis C. Briggs's *Dakota Album* are very light sensitive and Doris Ulmann's platinum print *The Mourner's Bench* has moderately stable image material but a somewhat yellowed coating applied by the photographer, making it more light sensitive than an identical uncoated photograph. A description of some joint decisions and the conservators recommendations for exhibition of artwork in each category of sensitivity follows.

### Sensitive

Cyanotypes have proven to be very reactive to light, consequently they were categorized as sensitive. Many of Hampton University's Camera Club cyanotype proof prints requested for this exhibition have never before been exhibited. After consideration of all the factors involved, we decided to substitute surrogates for the original photographs. High quality surrogates of photographs (using high resolution digital scanning and inkjet printing technology) or vintage process prints (photographic copies from a negative using the same photo chemistry) allows a copy in the same or visually similar medium as the original. This decision satisfied several requirements for this exhibition without the risk of overexposure to light. First, these images were desired for inclusion in all venues; second, they were to be exhibited less as photographic artifacts and more for their context with certain paintings; and third, it was possible to produce high quality surrogates in-house. (For a description of the method used to produce these surrogates, refer to the article in this catalogue entitled: "Preserving the Cyanotype: Unlimited Access and Exhibition Through Digital Image Surrogates." A one-time exposure to the scanner (roughly equivalent to 60 lux for 2 seconds) was rationalized as a compromise which would not use up the limited exhibition life of the original, would provide a research copy, and reduce the insurance and conservation costs, allowing a redistribution of exhibition funds. Connoisseurs argue that unless you display the original you are not teaching the eye to appreciate the nuances of the original photograph. Preservationists, however, argue that these nuances are not readily visible through the glass in gallery lighting and that they may be lost altogether unless protected from exhibition. Surrogates may allow more images a wider audience in the future without risk to the original photograph. Few museums can afford the expense of a single venue exhibition. Surrogates of historic photographs, when labeled as such, may help the educational mission without sacrifice of the preservation of photographic collections, as long as a percentage of the fundings is spent on the care and repair of the original artwork.

### Moderate

While surrogates may approximate the visual appearance of certain art media, they can never replace originals. Good examples are the still life watercolors of Charles Demuth. Unfaded watercolors with an unknown palette should be treated as sensitive; however, these Demuths have been on permanent exhibition for the last fifteen years. More than likely, many of the pigments in these watercolors have already undergone a fading half-life, suggesting that they may have to experience an equivalent exposure before the next perceivable color change can be documented.[8] Therefore, these watercolors can no longer be considered fugitive. *To Conserve a Legacy* includes each watercolor in a limited number of venues with periods of darkness (between exhibitions) so, in fact, they will see less light during the same period than would occur at the home institution.

### Durable

The most durable works on paper in the exhibition are the relief and intaglio prints in black oil-based printing ink on artist's paper. Many of these images required extensive treatment to remove inferior matting materials and to reduce the damages caused by their use. The aquatints by Dox Thrash, after washing to neutralize the pH of the paper, can withstand controlled light levels at all venues of the exhibition without perceivable change. All works of art on paper as well as photographs received archival mats and were framed with ultraviolet absorbing glazing. Frame packages were vapor sealed to protect against environmental fluctuations during transportation and while at the various venues.

### Conclusions

There are several difficult questions surrounding the use of light-sensitive artwork. For instance, there are watercolor/gouache drawings on view which may, during this exhibition, be exposed to the largest audience they will ever have. We know this one exhibition will not cause visible change but can we better justify movement toward that change if it occurs while hundreds are watching versus the fading that might occur on the walls of the home institution with only dozens of witnesses? When a watercolor has faded, how does one determine when its exhibition value has been depleted? Museums continue to exhibit watercolors which are either accepted into the collection faded or have changed over the decades but retain considerable integrity even after fading. Who can make the decision that a faded watercolor has lost more than it can give to its viewers?

This essay attempts to describe the complexity of developing a well-reasoned response to questions regarding light exposure and how it affects works of art on paper in particular. Even rational guidelines become very difficult to consistently put into practice. As the number of annual loan requests increases, the decisions and conditions for loan become more complex. The "definitive" exhibition of a genre or an artist's work is redefined every ten years. We are in the midst of a media explosion. Digital computer technology offers instant accessibility to thousands of images, and promises more, faster, and better. With it comes the desire to "have it all." The entire equation, or what this means for collections, cannot be fathomed without examining all facets of the problems unique to each institution for each exhibition. Over the next millennium, museums must rely on creative solutions that balance the concerns of viewers (who pay for the right to see the collections) with the mandate for education and the preservation of the collections.[9] Sadly, it may take the increase in "lost" and aging masterpieces to instill in us a sense of privilege in the brief encounters with our national treasures and to learn to venerate the rarest arts of our heritage without having to see these icons so often or for so long. Through conscious and careful compromise, artists, conservators, and curators together will succeed in prolonging the exhibition lifespan of its artwork. For just as art requires light, without art there is no life.

1. Stephan Michalski, "Towards Specific Lighting Guidelines," ICOM 1990, p. 586.

2. Comment by John Szarkowski (curator emeritus, department of photography, The Museum of Modern Art) at a panel discussion at the Clark Art Institute, March 7, 1998, entitled "The Museum and the Photograph: Collecting Then/Collecting Now."

3. Stephan Michalski, p. 585.

4. Karen Colby, "A Standard Exhibition/Exposure Policy for Works of Art on Paper," *Journal of the International Institute for Conservation—Canadian Group*, vol. 17 (1992). This article provides very specific guidelines with a summary chart of the exhibition policy adopted by the National Gallery of Canada.

5. Notes from an unpublished research seminar CHEM 010 for students at Williams College entitled "An Investigation of Visual Methods for Identification of Fugitive Watercolors" conducted at the WACC by James Martin, January 1995.

6. Stephan Michalski, "Time's Effects on Paintings," *Shared Responsibility*. Proceedings of a Seminar for Curators and Conservators, National Gallery of Canada, 1989.

7. Photograph conservator Barbara Lemmen conducted the process identification of all the photographs in the exhibition. Conservators of Photographic Materials Gary Albright, Lyzanne Gann, Deborah Hess Norris, Nora Kennedy, Connie McCabe, Peter Mustardo, Doug Severson, and photographer Doug Munson were consulted on various aspects of exhibition and conservation.

8. Conversation with Stephan Michalski, fall 1995.

9. One example: as the greatest number of museum visitors reaches retirement age, museums may institute "Seniors Day" when light levels are turned up (twice a month?) to allow better visibility by the aging "baby boomers." Of course, the duration of the exhibition must be reduced to "pay" for these higher light levels.

# Preserving the Cyanotype: Unlimited Access and Exhibition Through Digital Image Surrogates

MK Lalor
James Martin
Nicholas J. Zammuto

## Introduction

Cyanotypes are easily identified by their blue image color and matte print surface. If unfamiliar with the cyanotype, the reader is probably aware of its kin, the blueprint. John Herschel developed the cyanotype process in 1842. The blue color that radiates an ephemeral quality kept cyanotypes from wide marketability as a photographic print material despite their commercial viability. With the introduction of inexpensive cyanotype paper in the 1890s, the cyanotype gained popularity with amateur photographers, and remained an important photographic process for some twenty years.

The blue image material is composed of Prussian blue (ferric ferrocyanide) and Turnbull's blue (ferrous ferricyanide). The absence of an image binder leaves the pigment more vulnerable to light-induced fading and the paper support more susceptible to light-induced embrittlement. Recent research by Dr. Michael Ware, for Britain's National Museum of Photography, indicates that "the most likely origin of light-sensitivity in cyanotypes is the incorporation of impurities deriving from the sensitizer."[1] While this light-induced fading reaction appears to be reversible in the dark, James Reilly, of Rochester's Image Permanence Institute, states that "the conservator must always seek to limit photochemical deterioration by carefully controlling the illumination of cyanotypes while in storage or on display."[2]

Thirteen cyanotypes were selected for the traveling exhibition, *To Conserve a Legacy*. Judging that months of light exposure could result in uncertain damage to some or all of the cyanotypes, a method was sought to produce surrogate images that would convey the cyanotypes's imagery and unique image qualities, and allow the cyanotypes to remain in protected, dark storage, hence, the experimentation with digital image surrogates.

## Making the surrogate images

Surrogate images were made using a multistep digital imaging process. First, images of original works were imported into a computer[3] with a scanner[4] capable of recording the subtle color variations characteristic of the original image. Care was taken to minimize the scan time to avoid unnecessary light exposure.[5] Using image editing software,[6] the high-resolution scanned images were carefully color matched to the originals by direct visual comparison with the on-screen image.[7] A color inkjet printer[8] capable of printing at extremely high resolution was then used to translate the digital image back to an image on paper[9] to be exhibited.

Most of the complexity of the color matching process came from calibrating the printer to the computer's monitor to ensure that the on-screen image matched the printed image, ultimately resulting in an accurate surrogate. Due to the difficulty of matching the on-screen image to the original, it was often necessary to print several versions of the surrogate, and closely compare the printed images with the original, in order to hone in on the best representation. Over several trials, the hue, contrast, and brightness of the printed surrogates were carefully adjusted so that the printed surrogates contained as much of the visual weight and impact of the original as was possible using these technologies. The result is a surrogate image suitable for long-term exhibition, that, from a comfortable viewing distance, is hard to distinguish from the original, but upon close inspection reveals its inkjet origin.

## Conclusions

This study explored the use of current digital scanning technology and high-resolution color inkjet printing to produce convincing surrogates of historic cyanotypes. This objective was achieved using a low-cost digital scanner and inkjet printer. The digital images have been archived to a single CD-ROM, which permits rapid retrieval for future reproduction, on-line use, and electronic transfer over the Internet. As these and other technologies evolve, so will the quality of resultant surrogate images of cyanotypes and other print media in collections.

The original cyanotypes? Spared a long-term exhibition and much handling and shipping, they rest protected in dark storage, where they await more occasional special opportunities to reveal their ephemeral beauty to scholars and students.

1. Michael J. Ware, *Cyanotypes: The History, Science and Art of Printing in Prussian Blue* (London: National Museum of Photography, n.d.).

2. James M. Reilly, *Care and Identification of 19th-Century Photographic Prints* (Rochester: Eastman Kodak Company, 1986), p. 25.

3. Dell XPSD233 Pentium II processor with 128mb SDRAM, 8mb video RAM.

4. UMAX Astra 1200S scanner (UMAX Technologies, Inc., Fremont, California 94538). Optical resolution: 600 x 1200 dpi. Color scanning method: single pass with a color CCD. Image color depth: 30/24 bit.

5. An optical resolution of 600 dpi was used in RGB mode. Light intensity readings directly over the moving lamp showed an approximate intensity of 60 lux, at a travel rate of approximately 2 seconds per linear centimeter. This resolution provided the necessary image resolution to achieve the highest print resolution, and was determined experimentally using a historic non-collection cyanotype.

6. Adobe PhotoShop, version 4.0 (Adobe Systems Incorporated, San Jose, California 95110)

7. Dell D1226H 19-inch Color Monitor, 0.26 dot pitch, 1600 x 1200 resolution at 75 Hz.

8. Epson Color Stylus 800 inkjet printer (Epson America, Inc., Torrance, California 90509), maximum printing resolution: 1440 x 720 dpi.

9. Prints were made on Epson Photo Quality inkjet paper, Product code S041062.

top: Anonymous Camera Club photographer
*Untitled cabin exterior*, c. 1900
Cyanotype, 4¹¹⁄₁₆ x 6¹¹⁄₁₆ in.
Collection of Hampton University Archives
checklist 15

bottom: Digital reproduction from original cyanotype

# Laurel and Hardship: The Tale of Two Picture Frames

Hugh Glover

Two unrelated nineteenth-century American picture frames in the exhibition, *To Conserve a Legacy,* are compared for their style, present condition, and the different approaches taken in their conservation and restoration treatments. The materials from which such frames are made and the common influences that affect their condition are also outlined.

For the purposes of this article, the Hampton University Museum frame has been referred to as LAUREL for its bold laurel leaf decoration, and the Howard University Gallery of Art frame as HARDSHIP, in reference to the marked decline of its condition since it was made. Both are American made, gilded with gold leaf, and both are original to the pictures that they serve to frame. When the frames are separated from their paintings, neither of them looks especially important, and there is no evidence to suggest that the two painters were involved in their making or design, though it is possible that they participated in the selection of the frames. Our current interest derives from the fact that the frames are good quality examples of manufactured nineteenth-century decorative arts. Furthermore, they are representative examples of their period and frame-making technology, and they provide insight into the original relationship between frame and painting.

In addition to broadening the corpus of knowledge concerning period taste and artistic decision-making, original frames allow us to better understand the evolution of picture frames themselves. Both of the frames addressed here were determined to be original to the paintings on account of their period style, together with collaborating details apparent on their backs. The original wood stretchers (onto which the canvas of the paintings is attached) match the frames for wood type and degree of oxidation. Furthermore, corresponding nail marks on both the frames and the stretchers give a detailed chronology of each time the paintings were removed from their frames, thus corroborating the provenance of both paintings and frames.

Picture frames are sensitive to the harm caused by the environment and normal wear and tear resulting from their subsidiary role as protective devices. Most nineteenth-century American picture frames are composed of joined wood support structures, together with added layers of ornament and decoration made up of relief designs in molded composition (compo) or plaster, gesso, bole, and metal leaf. The response of these assembled materials to fluctuating levels of relative humidity is dimensional change, and the movement results in separations between the various layers. This common predicament is exacerbated by the effects of handling, which causes detachment and loss of the loosened decorative layers. Picture frames collect dust and pollutants on upward facing surfaces, together with damage from impact and abrasion. Chemical reactions occur between the pollutants and the gilded surface, and the accumulation of grime causes a darkened appearance that cannot usually be cleaned without causing some damage to the gold leaf. Gold leaf is extremely thin (modern gold leaf is between 0.3 µm and 0.8 µm thick) and inherently soft, which renders it susceptible to damage from abrasion. The high purity of most gold used for leaf (usually at least 22K) ensures that the color of the leaf itself is consistent and not prone to tarnishing.

There are many gilded picture frames that survive in excellent condition, and, in fact, they are enhanced by the subtle signs of age. The term patina is sometimes used to describe surfaces that have developed slight darkening due to grime combined with oxidation (darkening) of the thin glue size coating originally applied to the new gold as a tone. Most of the gilding on the frame for *The Young Chief* (LAUREL) has a well-preserved gold color, although there are also occasional areas where the gold has been abraded during cleaning attempts, and the underlying gray and white preparation layers of bole and gesso are clearly visible. There is no gold colored paint that replicates the brilliance of burnished gold leaf, so new leaf will be applied with oil gilding over passages of loss to approximate the rich and bright surface of the original. Originally, the gilder added a final step of burnishing the highlights on the fresh layers of gesso, bole, and gold with a polished stone to achieve the rich surface. The process will not be repeated in the present treatment as the necessary new preparation layers would compromise the modeling of the decorative surface.

The bold design of laurel leaves and berries on LAUREL was achieved by attaching lengths of molded plaster to a substrate of softwood. In keeping with the fashion of the day, surfaces are richly gilded with abundant water gilding, followed by burnishing. The choice of laurel as a decorative motif serves a dual purpose. Since Greco-Roman times laurel (or bay) has been symbolic of victory, glory, and honor and in this context they underscore the impression of the sitter as "noble savage." In addition, the broad surfaces of the laurel leaves have a decorative value in that they complement and echo the forms of the subject's headdress and necklace. Casting plaster from molds was a fast and repeatable method of production that had become a popular means of rendering ornament in the later nineteenth century and early twentieth century. The section of plaster had to be massive to provide sufficient bulk for strength and this generally resulted in large plaster ornamentation without a lot of detail. The relatively minimal damage to the frame is largely due to a surviving shadow box of thin varnished wood that surrounds and protects it. In addition, one can assume minimal wear and tear, as this is one of the few American picture frames that survives with documentary evidence of its maker intact. A printed label pasted on the back reads: "*H.S. Jones • Artistic Picture Frames • 40–42 West 22nd St. • Bet. Fifth and Sixth Aves. • New York • Regilding of every description.*"

Leigh Richmond Miner
*The Young Chief,* 1902
Oil on canvas, 23 x 28 in.
Collection of Hampton University Museum
checklist 183

The conservation treatment of this frame will concentrate on replacing the abraded gold leaf with new leaf of similar color and matched tone. Instead of using the original method of water gilding, however, the new leaf will be applied with mordant gilding, so as to distinguish it from the original. Loose elements will be secured and small losses of gilded plaster will be restored with fills. The more significant concentrations of dark grime will be carefully removed and the maker's label will be protected with a cover of Mylar.

The second frame under consideration, HARDSHIP, for the portrait *Charles Wilson Fleetwood Jr.,* is shaped with a fashionable half-round arch at the top, although the stretcher of the painting is rectangular. The frame predates the plaster frame (LAUREL) by fifty years, and its ornament is made with molded composition, prepared from a mixture of resin, oil, hide glue, water, and powdered chalk. Composition ornament was introduced in the late eighteenth century, and it came to replace carved wood as an efficient means of ornamenting picture frames, since it could be mass-produced, with many ornaments coming from the same mold. It was also more durable than carved and gilded wood, which tended to lose its gilt decoration in the variable American climate. The mixed dough was pressed into reverse carved molds of the intended design and then applied to the wood substrate with glue. After drying to form a hard decorative surface, it was suitable for gilding with gesso, bole, and metal leaf, etc. Most frames, including this example, have a variety of composition moldings arranged in bands over the wood base to achieve a coherent relief design. Different moldings commonly occur at the back edge (close to the wall), on the forward projection (top molding), inside the cove or ogee and toward the sight edge. Composition was originally used as an efficient, less laborious means of achieving the sculptural quality of carved wood, but since the mold could not achieve the deep undercutting of the chisel, composition was obliged to evolve a decorative vocabulary of its own. The compo decoration of HARDSHIP is an example that indeed draws on the traditional carver's motifs, but has translated them into a shallower, more stylized scheme, more suited to the idiosyncrasies of the casting process.

HARDSHIP has survived in very poor condition, with splintered wood, abraded leaf, and extensive loss of ornament. Earlier restoration efforts attempted to conceal the damage with applications of bronze (copper alloy) overpaint, but the paint's fugitive color and resistance to safe removal make it a present-day conservation problem. The overpaint has darkened with oxidation resulting in an irregular color that has little resemblance to the original gold leaf. The gilding below the overpaint is so fragmented that only an entire regilding would restore the frame to its original intention. The loss of ornament presents another challenge. There is no trace of the bands of ornament from the top molding and back edge molding. Replacement of these two bands of missing ornament depends on finding a comparable frame to serve as a model, which is likely to entail an extensive search. Altogether, this is a very time-consuming task and at the present time adequate funding for the project is not available. A compromise has been devised that will satisfy the immediate exhibition requirements and the foreseeable future. Restoring and consolidating the damaged wood edges will improve the appearance of the frame, and once again gold colored paint will be applied to cover the gilding losses and old gold paint; however, the modern paint will be color stable and easily reversible.

When faced with a seriously deteriorated frame such as HARDSHIP, there is a temptation to simply replace the original with a better-preserved secondhand frame of the same age and size. However, two factors argue against such a solution. For several years now, the market in used frames has been flourishing and the current level of interest has made buying a secondhand frame sometimes as expensive (or more) as restoring the original. Secondly, we have seen how the relationship between frame and picture can be aesthetically complementary and can broaden our insight into period taste and connoisseurship. In replacing the frame we would lose this relationship and, thereby, lose a comprehensive understanding of the original conception.

Thomas Waterman Wood
*Charles Wilson Fleetwood Jr.,* 1858
Oil on canvas, 24 x 16 in.
Collection of Howard University Gallery of Art
checklist 259

# The Hampton Camera Club

Mary Lou Hultgren

A keen interest in the art of photography on the part of faculty and staff at Hampton Normal and Agricultural Institute at the end of the nineteenth century manifested itself in the formation of the Camera Club. Officially called the Kiquotan Kamera Klub, the group was organized in October of 1893, its mission "the cultivation and promotion of photography" among interested amateurs.[1]

One of the founding members of the Camera Club, Francis Chickering Briggs (1833–1908), was an avid and accomplished amateur photographer who created an important body of documentary photography prior to the club's organization. Briggs, an 1849 graduate of Phillips Academy, was Hampton's business agent from 1879 until his death. In the late fall of 1887, he traveled to Dakota Territory on behalf of the school, visiting a number of former American Indian students who had returned to their reservation communities of Standing Rock and Cheyenne River and touring several schools recently established to educate Lakota students. Briggs's photographs in the *Dakota* albums contain some of the school's earliest visual records of this region.[2]

The Camera Club, which began with a nucleus of fourteen members, undertook a number of successful, revenue-generating activities over the years. "The Hampton Calendar," a nationally circulated annual calendar featuring historical scenes of Hampton's campus, was well received. In 1895 the group took up the challenge of illustrating poems. Members did readings of poems using lantern slides to project the accompanying illustration.[3] Two years later, the club chose the poetry of Paul Laurence Dunbar as the subject of their interpretative illustration. Their artistic achievement was so successful that by 1899 the club was preparing a set of illustrations for a small volume of Dunbar's poetry, *Poems of Cabin and Field*. A report on the work noted:

Francis Chickering Briggs
*Dakota Album: Government School under Mr. AC Wells 4 miles from the Cannonball*, 1887
Albumen print, 6 x 8¹⁄₁₆ in. (image/sheet); 9¹⁄₁₆ x 11¹⁄₄ in. (mount)
Collection of Hampton University Archives
checklist 46

> The Camera Club is pushing to completion its work of illustrating Mr. Dunbar's poems for the publishers, Messrs. Dodd, Mead & Co., of New York. There are eight of these poems, most of which have already appeared elsewhere . . . with about fifty illustrations from negatives which the club is making for this purpose. This club has . . . made a more or less valuable collection of pictures of the school and its surroundings, including many studies of Negro cabins. . . . But the study of the old-time life of colored people which is involved in the composition of these illustrations is by far the most interesting if not valuable work which it has undertaken, and the enthusiasm of the members for it is unbounded.[4]

A committee that included Commandant of Cadets Robert Russa Moton (Class of 1890), one of the club's few African American members, was formed to oversee the arrangement of the book. Input on the final selection of photographs came from the Camera Club as a whole, the poet, and the publisher.[5] The committee format worked so well that the club utilized this for the next project, illustrating Dunbar's 1901 *Candle-Lightin' Time*. A review of this illustrated volume of poetry praised the artistic photography, stating, "no studied 'composition' by the engraver or etcher could surpass some of these glimpses of picturesque nature, or the poses of the human figures."[6] In 1903 sixty-nine photographs by club members appeared as illustrations in Dunbar's *When Malindy Sings* (1903).[7]

The turn of the century was also an exhilarating time for the club with the accomplished photographer Frances Benjamin Johnston on assignment on the campus in 1899. During this time, members, numbering twenty-five, were presented with "a rare opportunity for seeing some of the finest work of the day in photography."[8] Johnston mounted an exhibition of her own photographic work as well as that of other prominent photographers including Gertrude Käsebier, F. Holland Day, and Alfred Stieglitz.[9] The chance to observe different photographic prints could also have interested club members who worked chiefly in cyanotypes that were inexpensive and simple to process.

Only one member of the club, Leigh Richmond Miner (1864–1935), advanced to the ranks of a professional photographer. Miner launched his career at Hampton on December 1, 1898, as an instructor of drawing and joined the Camera Club just as the group commenced work on Dunbar's first poetry volume. By 1904 Miner was the sole club member selected to illustrate all of the poems in Dunbar's works *Li'l Gal*. That same year, Miner resigned from Hampton to operate a photography studio in New York City, where he illustrated the final two volumes of Dunbar's poetry *Howdy, Honey, Howdy!* (1905) and *Joggin' Erlong* (1905).

In anticipation of the school's participation in the 1907 Jamestown Exposition, Principal Hollis B. Frissell hired Miner to return to Hampton in 1906 to photograph buildings, groups, and individual students at work. Miner subsequently rejoined the faculty as the school's director of applied art, official school photographer, cinematographer, and landscape designer until his retirement in 1933.

A native of Cornwall, Connecticut, Miner matched the profile of the majority of Hampton's early faculty in that he was white, originally from New England, well educated, and long tenured. He was a graduate of the National Academy of Design in New York with a major in applied arts. It is not known if Miner had any formal training in photography, but his sensitivity in capturing the experiences of Hampton students and the campus environment is evident in the large body of work he produced. Miner also interacted with Frances Benjamin Johnston during her photography sessions at the school that resulted in *The Hampton Albums*, thus learning from a master of documentary photography.[10] When Frissell wrote Miner concerning the photographs he was to take of the school for the Jamestown Exposition, he stated, "You know the work that Miss Johnston did; something of the same sort would be needed now."[11]

After a period of more than thirty-three years and the involvement of more than one hundred members, the Camera Club ended its activities in 1926, leaving behind more than one thousand photographs as a record of the group's creative energy.[12] A second camera club sprang up during the early 1940s among students and provided a stimulating environment that produced Hampton's best known photographer Reuben Burrell (Hampton's Class of 1947). For half a century,

Christopher Ethelbert Cheyne
*Major Robert Russa Moton Commandant—*
*Hampton Institute,* c. 1890
Gelatin silver print mounted on board
5½ x 3¹³⁄₁₆ in. (image/sheet);
5½ x 3⅞ in. (mount)
Collection of Tuskegee University
checklist 58

Leigh Richmond Miner
*Portia in drawing room,* 1907
Digital reproduction from original cyanotype
6¹⁄₂ x 4⁹⁄₁₆ in.
Collection of Hampton University Archives
checklist 176

Leigh Richmond Miner
*Study hour,* 1907
Digital reproduction from original cyanotype
6⁵⁄₈ x 4⁵⁄₈ in.
Collection of Hampton University Archives
checklist 182

Burrell has been the official photographer, continuing the tradition of photographic excellence established by the historic Camera Club of Hampton University.

1. Minutes of the Kiquotan Kamera Klub, 21 October 1893, Camera Club Files, Hampton University Archives.

2. Briggs also documented the trip through letters sent back to Hampton in which he noted that some of the photographs were taken under conditions "with the thermometer near zero." *The Southern Workman* 16 (December 1887): 129. Briggs's *Dakota Albums* are included in the exhibition *To Conserve a Legacy: American Art from Historically Black Colleges and Universities*.

3. Minutes of the Kiquotan Kamera Klub, 27 October 1895.

4. *The Southern Workman* 28 (February 1899): 229.

5. The dummy for *Poems of Cabin and Field*, housed in the Hampton University Archives, contains handwritten notes indicating input from various persons and identifies some of the photographs by the initials of the photographer.

6. *The Southern Workman* 31 (January 1902): 40.

7. For a discussion of Dunbar's poetry see Nancy McGhee, "Portraits in Black: Illustrated Poems of Paul Laurence Dunbar" in *Stony the Road: Chapters in the History of Hampton Institute*, ed. Keith L. Schall (Charlottesville: University Press of Virginia, 1977), pp. 63–104.

8. *The Southern Workman* 29 (January 1900): 49.

9. The club had additional contact with F. Holland Day in 1905 when he visited Hampton and in 1906 when he was sent club photographs from which he selected the prize winners for a group exhibition. The club also received a photograph from Day which hung in the club house. Kiquotan Kamera Klub Minutes, 14 May 1906.

10. Miner appears in several of Johnston's photographs including *A Sketching class at work* and *Field work in sketching*.

11. Letter from H. B. Frissell to Leigh R. Miner, 24 October 1906, Hampton University Archives.

12. Ray Saperstein, Hampton Camera Club Master Name List, Camera Club Files, Hampton University Archives.

Prentiss H. "P.H." Polk
*"Bill Pipes" and his Melody Barons*, c. 1935
Gelatin silver print, 3¹⁵/₁₆ x 8¹³/₁₆ in.
Collection of Tuskegee University
checklist 196

# Chronicling Tuskegee in Photographs: A Simple Version

Cynthia Beavers Wilson

Photographs at Tuskegee University have always been important. The photographers of some of the earliest photographs are difficult to document. The limited sources offer conflicting information. Often there is no identification of the individuals in the photograph, the time of the photograph, or the occasion being photographed. Without the presence of Booker T. Washington, George Washington Carver, or an easily identifiable individual, one might not even attribute a photograph to Tuskegee. Documentation of all kinds was and still is important at Tuskegee, and almost anything and everything that happened at this institution has a corresponding piece of paper somewhere. The challenge is finding and matching the pieces.

Photographs appear in the annual catalogues as early as 1893. In the 1895–96 edition of the catalogue, photographs are credited to *Harper's Weekly*. Booker T. Washington's famous autobiography *Up From Slavery* contains only one photograph, which does not give credit to the photographer. In 1904 Doubleday and Co. published *The Story of My Life and Work* by Washington. Correspondence between Cornelius Marion Battey, a New York photographer, and Booker T. Washington indicates that Battey is most likely the photographer of pictures in *The Story of My Life and Work*. The correspondence is located in the Library of Congress Registry of the Booker T. Washington papers and among the edited version of his papers by Louis Harlan. In a letter to his secretary, Emmett J. Scott, Washington expressed concern that one photograph was not appropriate for the book. That photograph did not appear in *The Story of My Life and Work*.

Lack of photography credit designations presents an interesting and confusing issue. A great many of the book's photographs and others of a similar style have been credited to Frances Benjamin Johnston by some sources.

Johnston, the photographer of *The Hampton Albums* made a trip in 1903 to Tuskegee but none of the photographs in the collection at Tuskegee bear any stamp or signature indicating that she took them, nor is there any indication of correspondence between her and Booker T. Washington during that time period. This is not to say that some photographs of Tuskegee credited to Johnston are incorrect, but short of cross-referencing her archives in the Library of Congress, it is impossible to say with certainty who the photographer was. A New

Leonard C. Hyman
*Untitled (man with cabbage)*, c. 1930
Gelatin silver print, 10 x 8 in.
Collection of Tuskegee University
checklist 115

Arthur P. Bedou
*Agriculture, Fruits picked at School's Farm*, n.d.,
Gelatin silver print, 7½ x 9½ in. (image);
7¹¹⁄₁₆ x 9¾ in. (sheet)
Collection of Tuskegee University
checklist 32

Orleans photographer, Arthur P. Bedou, further confused the crediting issue. Bedou is noted by some sources as Booker T. Washington's personal photographer. Bedou visited Tuskegee on several occasions and photographed Booker T. Washington and Emmett J. Scott. Bedou also accompanied Washington on fundraising tours. Somewhere in the archival material generated at Tuskegee, in the Library of Congress, and other archives (for example, the Emmett J. Scott papers held by Morgan State University) possibly lies the answer.

In a letter to George Eastman in 1905, Booker T. Washington wrote about his desire to add photography to the school's curriculum. He felt strongly that even with prejudice ". . . A colored man would have almost as good an opportunity to succeed as a white man . . . " in the field of photography.[1] The genesis of the photography program came with the administration of Robert R. Moton. Selected to succeed Booker T. Washington, Robert Moton began his work at Tuskegee in September 1916. The annual catalogue for that year shows the name of Robert R. Moton as principal, C. M. Battey, photography, and Prentiss H. (P.H.) Polk, student.

Cornelius M. Battey was born in Georgia in 1873. He worked in New York City as superintendent of the Bradley Studio and as a partner in Battey and Warren. In 1916 Battey moved to Tuskegee with his wife, who assisted him with his work at the Institute. He served as head of the department until his death in 1927. Battey's duties included not only classroom instruction but also chronicling in photographs the campus life at Tuskegee. Photographs from his tenure included classroom settings, views of the Booker T. Washington monument with Battey in the photograph, the preparing of grounds for the monument, and the dedication ceremony.

Arthur P. Bedou
*Booker T. Washington in New Orleans,* n.d.
Gelatin silver print
6½ x 4½ in. (image); 7 x 5⅟₁₆ in. (sheet)
Collection of Tuskegee University
checklist 34

Leonard C. Hyman followed Battey as official institute photographer but left no biographical information. His photographs, however, continued the style set by Battey. The change in style came with Battey's student, Prentiss H. Polk. He was "Mr. Polk" to those individuals who grew up in the community seeing him scurry through homecoming crowds with a camera around his neck to match the one in his hand. To the world around Tuskegee, he was P.H. Polk, the artist. Using his camera not only as a tool for documentation but as a means of creating works of art, he sought to reproduce images he felt within himself.

For sixty years or more, P.H. Polk was the primary photographer in and around Tuskegee. Arriving from Bessemer, Alabama, he originally entered Tuskegee with hopes of being a painter. House painting was the available offering at the time, so he chose photography. After leaving Tuskegee, Polk worked in a shipyard in Alabama, moving to Chicago in the early 1920s, where he worked as an apprentice photographer. He returned to Tuskegee in 1927 and subsequently joined the staff of the Photography Department at Tuskegee Institute. Later, he was named head of the department and served for five years before moving to Atlanta where he operated a studio for two years. He returned to Tuskegee where he remained until his death in 1984. Polk's patrons included not only blacks but whites as well. With hundreds of his prints and negatives held by the Tuskegee University archives, Polk's oral record of George Washington Carver, a subject of his in many photographs, is also a prized possession.

Chronicling Tuskegee University does not end with photography of Arthur P. Bedou, Cornelius M. Battey, Frances Benjamin Johnston, Leonard C. Hyman, or Prentiss H. Polk. The tradition lives on in those photographers who strive toward documentary and artistic excellence at Tuskegee.

1. Booker T. Washington to George Eastman, 28 November 1905. *Booker T. Washington Papers; Volume 8, 1904–1906.* Edited by Louis R. Harlan and Raymond W. Smock. Urbana: University of Illinois Press, 1979, pp. 451–52

# Conservation Directions for Sculpture: Cleaning and Compensation of Edmonia Lewis's *The Old Arrow Maker and His Daughter*

Katherine A. Holbrow

Conservators value traditional hand skills highly, but new scientific tools and techniques allow art to be understood and cared for in increasingly sensitive ways. Edmonia Lewis's *The Old Arrow Maker and His Daughter* demonstrates how typical sculpture problems—embedded dirt and missing elements—are met with a combination of art historical research, chemistry, and artistic skills. The result is both historically appropriate and aesthetically satisfying, yet remains reversible and inert for the long-term protection of the sculpture.

Improper storage, mishandling and long neglect left *The Old Arrow Maker and His Daughter* with deeply embedded grime, paint, and stains, as well as nicks and chips. Substantial losses included the left front leg of the deer, the tool held in the arrow maker's right hand, and a section of fur on his robe.

The sculpture was cleaned in stages, using a series of poultices made from cleaning agents suspended in a cellulosic gel.[1] This gentle cleaning technique pulls dirt upward through capillary action as the gel dries. Dirt and poultice are peeled together, thus minimizing scrubbing and the risk of abrasion. To avoid acid dissolution, the pH was adjusted to match the natural alkalinity of calcium carbonate.

When replacing missing sculptural elements, historic photographs, related works, or contemporary descriptions must be used as models. Otherwise, replacement parts will be inappropriate products of the restorer's imagination. Art historical research produced images of the *The Old Arrow Maker and His Daughter* with the fur robe and the deer's leg intact.[2] Because no documentary evidence could be found of the broken tool, it was not replaced.

Replacement parts were modelled from a modern resin, designed to simulate the translucent nature of marble.[3] A combination of polyvinyl acetate and acrylic acid copolymers, the resin can be tinted to simulate warm, creamy Carrara marble, then carved, filed, and polished to blend with Lewis's work.

Edmonia Lewis
*The Old Arrow Maker and His Daughter,*
modeled 1866, carved 1872
Marble, 23½ x 15 x 17 in.
Collection of Tuskegee University
checklist 161
right: Summer 1997 student interns Rodney Bennett, Tamara Holmes, and Kelli Hall clean the sculpture.

1. Lisa A. Goldberg, "A fresh face for Samuel Gompers: methyl cellulose poultice cleaning," *Journal of the American Institute for Conservation* 28 (1989): 19–29.

2. Thanks to Drs. Marilyn Richardson and George Gurney for generously sharing their files on Edmonia Lewis and to intern James V. Herring of Howard University for his research.

3. Susanne Gansicke and John W. Hirx, "A translucent wax-resin fill material for the compensation of losses in objects," *Journal of the American Institute for Conservation* 36 (1997): 17–29. Thanks to Rodney Bennet for his assistance.

# Contributors
## to the
## Checklist and
## Exhibition
## Catalogue

Scott Allan
Scott W. Baker
Andrea D. Barnwell
Tritobia Hayes Benjamin, Ph.D.
Monica DiLisio Berry
Thomas J. Branchick
Teresia Bush
Alexander X. Byrd
Floyd W. Coleman
Brett A. Crenshaw
David C. Driskell
Kathryn Dungy
Ernest Dunkley
Tina Dunkley
Jacqueline Francis
Frank Getlein
Hugh Glover
Helen A. Harrison
David C. Hart
Salah M. Hassan
Chester Higgins, Jr.
Katherine A. Holbrow

Camara Dia Holloway
Mary Lou Hultgren
Bruce Kellner
Amy Kirschke
MK Lalor
Barbara Lemmen
Julie Levin
James Martin
M. Akua McDaniel, Ph.D.
Valerie J. Mercer
Lori Mirazita
Kirsten Mullen
Leslie Paisley
Richard J. Powell
Kenneth G. Rodgers
Helen M. Shannon
Louise Stone
Cynthia Beavers Wilson
Nicholas J. Zammuto
Jeanne Zeidler

# Exhibition
# Checklist

The following is the complete checklist of artworks appearing at one or more venues on the national exhibition tour. All measurements are in inches, unless otherwise noted. Height precedes width precedes depth. One measurement is given for photographs and prints when, if known, image and sheet measurements are the same. Due to their fragility and sensitivity to light, all cyanotypes are replaced with digital reproductions for the exhibition. Biographical information is provided for each artist. However, in some cases there is little information available.

1

2

## Josef Albers
### (1888–1976)
**Painter, designer, printmaker**
One of a generation of German émigré artists who contributed to the growth of modern art in America through their work and teaching, Albers is best known for his series of hundreds of paintings and lithographs based on the square that utilize subtle chromatic harmonies. The squares were made to demonstrate that identical colors are perceived differently by observers depending also upon place and time. A student at the Bauhaus, Albers was consistently experimenting in his work but concentrated on the manipulation of color after his move to the United States. In addition to his painting career, he taught at Yale University.

1. *Forest's Carpet*, 1959
Oil on board
30 x 30
Collection of Hampton University Museum, 00.3175a, gift of the artist

2. *Remote*, 1957
Oil on board
20 x 20
Collection of Hampton University Museum, 67.45.1, gift of the artist

3. Study for *Homage to the Square*, 1957
Oil on board
20 x 20
Collection of Hampton University Museum, 67.45.2, gift of the artist

Upon hearing the name of artist Josef Albers, one immediately and inevitably thinks of the phrase "interaction of color." Albers himself once stated that the introduction of this term was his single greatest contribution to modern painting. Indeed, the exploration of color as a principal pictorial theme occupied the artist for much of his life, ultimately leading him to embark on the lyric *Homage to the Square* series.[1]

In 1913 Albers enrolled in Berlin's Royal Art School. After two years, Albers returned to the city of his birth, Bottrop, where he developed his skills as a printmaker, producing figurative works in the style common at that time. While studying with artists Franz von Stuck and Max Doerner in Munich, he learned of a new school called the Bauhaus and quickly enrolled. Albers later asserted that this was the best thing he ever did; his studies there impressed upon him the value of comprehensive visual training and the importance of craftsmanship and materials, leading the artist to his dictum that "In the beginning there is *only* the material."[2]

Albers thrived at the Bauhaus, both personally and professionally. From 1920 to 1925, he attended the preliminary course (*Vorkurs*), learning to work in stained glass, furniture, metal, and typography. In 1925, he was appointed a master at the school, one of the first students to be afforded this honor. Albers subsequently became one of the most successful and beloved teachers at the Bauhaus; students clamored to enroll in his classes and praised him for "releasing their latent artistic and spiritual capabilities." In 1933 the Nazis denounced the Bauhaus as a "germ-cell of bolshevism" and asserted pressure on the faculty to close the school. Director Mies van der Rohe and his faculty soon complied, leaving Albers without a job.[3]

Albers was almost immediately invited to join the faculty of the newly founded Black Mountain College in North Carolina. He accepted, and he and his wife Anni moved to the United States. They remained at the college until 1949, when Albers decided it was time for a change. For a short time, the artist taught courses at the Cincinnati Art Academy and the Pratt Institute in Brooklyn, then in 1950 he was appointed chair of Yale University's Department of Design, a position he held until his retirement in 1958.[4]

Albers's appointment at Yale coincided with a major transitional period in his artistic development. The same year that he became chair of the design department, he began his *Homage to the Square* series, the group of paintings and prints for which he is best known. Employing simple groups of three to four nested squares, precisely drawn and neatly rendered, Albers demonstrated the dynamic nature of color. "We discover that there is always a discrepancy between physical fact and psychic effect—that color is the most relative medium in art . . . ," said Albers. Through his thoughtful juxtapositions of color, he also revealed the evocative nature of the medium. Said one student of Albers, "[He] stripped the blinders from my prejudiced eyes and succeeded in flinging open the doors to a wondrous universe of color. . . ."[5]

To use color successfully, Albers maintained, one had to always remember that seeing was a very personal experience and that a single color evoked a different response in each viewer. "In order to use color effectively it is necessary to recognize that color deceives continually," he noted. The purpose of studying color, therefore, was to cultivate one's eye for the medium; "this means, specifically," said Albers, "seeing color action as well as color relatedness." This belief in the importance of seeing complemented Albers's overarching belief that the content of art was a visualization of our reaction to life and the aim of art "revelation and evocation of vision." In 1963 Albers recorded all of his views on color and the art of seeing in his famous treatise, *Interaction of Color*; this book was subsequently translated into eight languages and used throughout the world as a major component of art instruction.[6]

The Hampton University Museum owns three images from Albers's *Homage* series. Study for *Homage to the Square* and *Remote*, both painted in 1957, and *Forest's Carpet* (1959). The paintings, all oil on board, were given to the museum by the artist in 1967. Examination of these images reveals them to be vintage Albers in their execution. Each image is composed on a board primed with at least two coats of flat white paint; in the case of *Forest's Carpet*, Albers applied six coats of white "Liquitex." The artist then proceeded to describe a series of nested squares by laying down bold expanses of green, yellow, and blue paint straight from the tube. The colors are applied in one primary coat with no mixing. The results are luminous, revealing a color's ability to transmute based on such factors as the color abutting it, the light illuminating it, and the visual knowledge of the seer. "We are able to hear a single tone," observed Albers. "But we almost never . . . see a single color unconnected and unrelated to other colors."[7]

—Lori Mirazita

1. Emile de Antonio and Mitch Tuchman, *Painters Painting* (New York: Abbeville Press, 1984), p. 145.

2. Nicholas Fox Weber, "Josef Albers at Yale," in *Yale Collects Yale*, ed. Sasha M. Newman and Lesley K. Baier (New Haven: Yale University Art Gallery, 1993), pp. 49–51.

3. Walter Gropius founded the Bauhaus in 1919 with the aim of establishing an institution whose primary goal was to create "the unified work of art." Gropius and his followers sought to introduce a new approach to art and the world in which it existed. The focus was on creating an architecture that unified the building's structural and decorative components, thereby creating a marriage of art and technique. Jane Turner, ed. *The Dictionary of Art* (New York: Grove's Dictionaries, 1996), pp. 548–49; *Painters of the Bauhaus, March–April 1962* (London: Marlborough Fine Art Limited, 1962), pp. 5, 14; and Weber p. 52.

4. Although Albers retired in 1958, he remained at Yale as a visiting professor until 1960. Turner, p. 549.

5. Newman and Baier, p. 21; and Weber, p. 56.

6. Josef Albers, *Interaction of Color* (New Haven & London: Yale University Press, 1963), p. 10; and Josef Albers, *Search Versus Research: Three Lectures by Josef Albers at Trinity College, April 1965* (Hartford: Trinity College Press, 1969), p. 10.

7. The author spoke with Dr. Richard A. Long, director of Hampton University Museum at the time the Albers paintings were acquired. Although Dr. Long did not know why Albers chose to give three paintings to Hampton, he informed me that Albers may well have become familiar with Hampton through their mutual friend and Albers's former Yale student James E. Lewis. At the time Hampton acquired the Albers images, Lewis was an instructor in the art department at Morgan State College in Baltimore. Albers gave a number of paintings to Morgan State during Lewis's tenure there. When Hampton acquired the Albers paintings, Long turned to his friend and colleague Lewis for assistance in appraising the works. Telephone interview with Dr. Richard A. Long, Institute of the Liberal Arts, Emory University, Atlanta, 23 June 1998. Also see Kirsten Younger, Examination Record for Study for *Homage to the Square*, *Remote*, and *Forest's Carpet*, Williamstown Art Conservation Center, Inc., 11 May 1998, and Albers, *Interaction of Color*, p. 15.

## Anonymous

*4. Fruit from Farm being shipped away*,
c. 1920s
Gelatin silver print
7⅝ x 9½ (image); 8¹⁄₁₆ x 10 (sheet)
Collection of Tuskegee University

## Anonymous

*5. George Washington Carver*, n.d.
Gelatin silver print
7¹³⁄₁₆ x 4¹⁵⁄₁₆
Collection of Tuskegee University

## Anonymous

*6. Red Shirt, Ogalala Dakota*, n.d.
Albumen print
15⅛ x 12¾ (image); 24 x 20 (mount)
Collection of Hampton University
Museum, 00.4305

8

9

**Anonymous**

7. *Rollo Browning, Navajo, Fort Lewis Indian School*, n.d.
Gelatin silver print
8½ x 7
Collection of Hampton University Museum, 991.28.23.m, gift of Dr. Samella Sanders Lewis

**Anonymous**

8. *School and Church in Warrior Stand, Alabama*, n.d.
Silver print on collodion printing out paper
7⁹⁄₁₆ x 9½ (image); 7¹³⁄₁₆ x 9¾ (sheet)
Collection of Tuskegee University

**Anonymous**

9. *School Farm, Students at Work*, c. 1920s
Gelatin silver print
7¾ x 9¹³⁄₁₆
Collection of Tuskegee University

**Anonymous**

10. *Untitled (stacking hay)*, c. 1920s
Gelatin silver print
7¹¹⁄₁₆ x 9½ (image); 8 x 10 (sheet)
Collection of Tuskegee University

6

**Anonymous**

11. *Untitled (woman at a gate holding cat)*, c. 1890s
Gelatin silver print
8⅞ x 7¼
Collection of Tuskegee University

**Anonymous Camera Club photographer**

12. *Barn on a 1-mule Farm*, c. 1900
Platinum print
7³⁄₈ x 9½ (image); 9½ x 11½ (sheet)
Collection of Hampton University Archives

**Anonymous Camera Club photographer**

13. *The Old Folks at Home, (Cabin Interior–Sheppards at dinner)*, 1900
Digital reproduction from original cyanotype
7³⁄₈ x 9⁵⁄₁₆
Collection of Hampton University Archives

**Anonymous Camera Club photographer**

14. *The Old Time Cabin*, c. 1900
Gelatin silver print
3¹⁄₁₆ x 5¼
Collection of Hampton University Archives

**Anonymous Camera Club photographer**

15. *Untitled cabin exterior*, c. 1900
Digital reproduction from original cyanotype
4¹¹⁄₁₆ x 6¹¹⁄₁₆
Collection of Hampton University Archives

**Anonymous Camera Club photographer**

16. *Untitled (man and woman repairing cabin)*, c. 1900
Gelatin silver print
4⁵⁄₈ x 6¹¹⁄₁₆
Collection of Hampton University Archives

**Anonymous (Lakota artist)**

17. *Dance wand*, c. 1880
Porcupine quills, native tanned hide, tin, brass beads, glass beads, horsehair, silk ribbon, sinew, and wood
47 x 2⁵⁄₈ x 2³⁄₁₆
Collection of Hampton University Museum, 85.1345

**Anonymous (Lakota artist)**

18. *Pipe bag*, acquired before 1900
Native tanned hide and glass beads
41 x 6³⁄₈ x½
Collection of Hampton University Museum, 00.1497

Hampton University Museum's Native American Collection is an outgrowth of the school's historic American Indian education program, which educated over 1,300 students representing sixty-five tribal groups between 1878 and 1923. The program was the forerunner of the late-nineteenth-century federal off-reservation boarding school system. Acquired primarily during the forty-five-year period of this historic program, the collection contains some 1,700 objects representing more than ninety tribal groups. Excellent examples of beadwork, quillwork, basketry, and textiles are included in the collection.[1]

The Native American Collection was described in 1905 as containing "material to illustrate Indian civilization from the mound builders to modern times—costumes, weapons, ceremonial paraphernalia and games. United States history classes can get much from intelligent study of these both with and without instruction." As curator reports from the early twentieth century indicate, the museum and its multicultural holdings were "quite unlike that of the ordinary museum . . . in broadening the education of pupils, and in the case of the Indian and African exhibits, stimulating race pride and understanding." Photographs document that objects from the collection were used in classroom settings as teaching tools and worn by students to add authenticity to plays and tableaux having native themes. Frances Benjamin Johnston's 1900 photograph from *The Hampton Albums* entitled *Class in American History* shows Lakota Louis Firetail (Crow Creek Sioux) wearing the traditional regalia of a Lakota warrior from the museum collection and serving as an object lesson for his fellow classmates.[2]

17

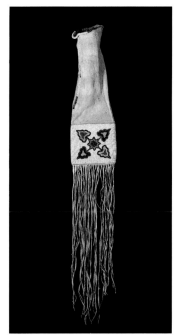

18

Unique to the Native American Collection is a group of objects created by students while they were at the school. The first artwork created within the boarding school environment continued the tradition of late nineteenth-century Plains pictorial hide painting. Hampton's first American Indian students included seventeen Southern Plains men who were former hostages from Fort Marion in Florida, where they had been part of a well-documented artists's colony. At Hampton they continued to create detailed and colorful scenes of camp life, including warriors and horses wearing traditional attire. Rather than painting on hide, however, the school produced works were executed on paper, wooden blocks, and commercially produced pottery.[3]

One of this group was Kiowa artist Etahdleuh Doanmoe (1856–88), who was enrolled at Hampton between 1878 and 1879. Among Etahdleuh's creations was a cylindrical jar featuring a standing warrior, a tipi, and a mounted Kiowa warrior carrying an eagle feather fan included in this exhibition. Painted in Hampton's Industrial Sewing Room, this type of work was done for sale or as gifts to the school's financial benefactors. Early teacher Cora Mae Folsom recalled that "the articles decorated became quite a fad and the demand was always more than equal to any possible supply." This preservation of Native American painting was fostered by Samuel Chapman Armstrong, the school's founder and principal. In the 1879 school report he stated, "the Indian has the only American art, I believe it to be a duty to preserve and in a wise and natural way to develop." By the mid-1880s, Euro-American style

artwork supplanted the pictorial style of native students from the Plains.[4]

In the early 1900s Hampton once again sought to foster native art and received support from reform organizations such as the Women's National Indian Association and the Sequoyah League, whose members were inspired by the American Arts and Crafts movement's interest in craft revival. The museum's acquisitions at this time included baskets donated by prominent patrons, such as advocate for basketry revival Neltje Doubleday (wife of Frank N. Doubleday, the New York publisher). In 1901 after a visit by Doubleday to Hampton, where she "encouraged" students to pursue basket making, recent graduate Arizona Swayney returned to her North Carolina home on the Eastern Band of Cherokee reservation to learn "from some of the old women of the tribe the secret of the 'double weave' used in the beautiful Cherokee baskets."[5]

When Swayney joined Hampton's faculty in 1902, the school became one of the first in the country to employ a Native American as instructor of native arts and to encourage female students to learn the craft as a means of self support. Swayney and her students used the museum's expanding basketry collection as an important resource in teaching native basketry techniques and patterns. Included in this collection are a group of seventy-two Chitimacha baskets acquired in 1905 that were part of a craft revival and exhibited in the government building at St. Louis's 1904 Louisiana Purchase Exposition.[6]

The school's announcement of the gift indicated that the collection "is believed to include one basket of every shape and pattern made" by Chitimacha basket weavers, including the expert double-weave basketmaker Clara Darden. The baskets were to serve a two-fold purpose at Hampton. First, placing the baskets in Hampton's museum would make them "accessible to all students" with an ethnological interest in the collection, and second, but "hardly less important," was placing the baskets where "Indian pupils may have access to them" with the hope of "the stimulating of an interest in the revival of the craft among the youth of the race." The museum's basketry collection eventually grew to include over two hundred examples of basketry from twenty-six different tribal groups.[7]

For more than a decade and a half, the museum has undertaken a series of exhibitions, publications, lectures, and programs involving Hampton's traditional Native American collection as well as contemporary Native American art. The result has been a renewal of contacts with descendants of some of Hampton's early native students as well as the acquisition of carefully selected contemporary art objects that show both continuity and change in Native American art.

—Mary Lou Hultgren

1. For more information on the historic program, see Mary Lou Hultgren and Paulette Fairbanks Molin, *To Lead and To Serve: American Indian Education at Hampton Institute 1897–1923* (Virginia Beach: Virginia Foundation for the Humanities, 1989), and for more information on the collection see Mary Lou Hultgren, "American Indian Collections of the Hampton University Museum," *American Indian Art* (winter 1987): 32–39.

2. Cora Mae Folsom, "The Museum" (1905), p. 1, Hampton University Archives. Miss Folsom was primarily responsible for overseeing the development of the museum's Native American collection. Her 42 years of close contact with Indian students, plus her 12 trips west, provided her with excellent opportunities for building the collection. A curator of the museum, Folsom developed detailed collection notes which provide excellent documentation. Also see Cora Mae Folsom, "Historical notes on the museum" (n.d.), p. 2, Hampton University Archives, and Frances Benjamin Johnston, *The Hampton Albums: I*, p. 31.

3. The artistic accomplishments of these Southern Cheyenne, Arapaho, and Kiowa men, incarcerated from 1875 to 1878, have been the subject of numerous studies. See Karen Daniel Petersen, *Plains Indian Art from Fort Marion* (Norman: University of Oklahoma Press, 1971) and Joyce Szabo, *Howling Wolf and the History of Ledger Art* (Albuquerque: University of New Mexico Press, 1994).

4. Cora Mae Folsom, "Indian Days at Hampton" (May 1918), p. 18, Hampton University Archives, and Samuel Chapman Armstrong, *Report of officers of the Hampton Normal and Agricultural Institute* (Hampton: Hampton Normal School Press, 1879), p. 13.

5. For additional information on Neltje Doubleday's role as an advocate of basketry revival, see Erik Krenzen Trump "The Indian Industries League and its Support of American Indian Arts, 1893–1922" (Ph.D. diss., Boston University, 1996), pp. 177–253, and *The Southern Workman* 55 (February 1902 and May 1902): 278.

6. Swayney graduated from Hampton in 1899 and returned to complete the post-graduate course in 1901. She taught basket weaving classes at Hampton until 1906. For a discussion of Swayney's career, see Sarah H. Hill, *Weaving New Worlds: Southeastern Cherokee Women and Their Basketry* (Chapel Hill: University of North Carolina Press, 1997), pp. 216–21, and *The Southern Workman* 34 (July 1905): 377.

7. Ibid. Many of these baskets were purchased by the school from field matrons working to revive basket weaving on western reservations.

20

## Anonymous (possibly Harry Roseland)

19. *Guest at Dinner*, c. 1869
Oil on canvas
33½ x 43½
Collection of Howard University Gallery of Art

## Edmund Minor Archer
### (b. 1904–1986)
**Painter**

After studying painting at the University of Virginia, Cape Cod School of Art, and Art Students League (with Kenneth Hayes Miller and Boardman Robinson), Edmund Archer continued his training abroad (in France and Italy). During the 1930s and 1940s Archer exhibited his sympathetic portraits of black Americans at the Corcoran Gallery of Art, Carnegie Institute, and Virginia Museum of Fine Arts, among other art institutions. In addition to teaching art for many years at the Corcoran School of Art and George Washington University, Archer was a curator for a brief period at the Whitney Museum of American Art in New York.

20. *Susan*, c. 1930
Oil on canvas
35 x 23¼
Fisk University, Nashville, Tennessee

## William E. Artis
### (1914–1977)
**Sculptor**

An award-winning, nationally recognized artist in clay, Artis depicted his black subjects (largely in the portrait bust format) with both sensitivity and architectonic balance. A former student of the acclaimed sculptor Ivan Mestrovich as well as the renowned Harlem art teacher Augusta Savage, Artis had a long and distinguished teaching career, working at state universities in Nebraska, Minnesota, and briefly at Tuskegee Institute. In addition to Howard and Hampton, his works are in the permanent collections of the Walker Art Center, Joselyn Art Museum, and North Carolina Museum of Art.

21. *Bust of Miss Coleman*, 1946
Terra-cotta with wood base
14 x 8 x 9
Collection of Howard University Gallery of Art

William Ellsworth Artis was awarded a Harmon Foundation fellowship in 1946 to demonstrate his ceramic sculpting techniques at six southern black colleges.[1] The terra-cotta *Bust of Miss Coleman* was created during this year. The sitter, then a student at Howard University, can be seen modeling for this portrait in a documentary photograph by Addison Scurlock (see checklist nos. 213 and 214). The artist is shown in the process of finishing the sculpture prior to firing. Direct evidence of the artist's hand becomes apparent upon close examination of the surface, where thumbprints, fingernail impressions, and the imprint of a finely woven textile are preserved in the fired clay. A texture of superficial scratch marks made by a blunt, rake-like tool unifies and enlivens the sculpture.

The upper section of the head was broken off at some point during the life of this terra-cotta, and the two sections were rejoined with shellac. The small losses along the break had not been filled, and residual drips of brown adhesive indicated an incomplete and somewhat careless repair.[2] In preparation for the current exhibition, conservation treatment was carried out to improve the stability and visual integrity of the sculpture. The treatment included reversing the shellac join, removing dark adhesive residue, and filling and toning the losses around the break. The regularity of the crack indicated an intentional cut through the top of the head. Why would such a clean cut exist, particularly when the Scurlock photograph clearly illustrates the sculpture in a nearly finished state? The damage seemed puzzling.

As the treatment progressed, the answers were exposed. When the two sections were separated and the adhesive residues dissolved, deliberate gouges were found along the exposed wall, and extruded ceramic was visible along the interior of the break. It became apparent that Artis had cut the head open using a thin wire in order to hollow the interior of the bust before firing.[3] The wire cut was probably made when the exterior clay had reached a firm, leather-hard stage, yet the interior clay was still soft enough to scoop away. Once the bust was hollowed, gouges were made along the exposed wall to increase surface area, and a clay slip was applied to fill the voids and cement the two sections together. Artis could then refinish the exterior surface around the join. Once fired, the join would not be readily discernable.

Subsequent examination of several other terra-cotta busts by William Artis, including Hampton University's *Head of a Girl* (1940) and Fisk University's *Male Head* (1945), revealed a consistent working method of removing the upper section of the head to permit hollowing of the interior. In both cases, extruded clay is visible

from the interior, and the exterior has been finished to disguise the cut. A hint of irregularity can be detected in raking light on *Male Head*, and the inherent weakness of the slip join is illustrated in *Head of a Girl* by a hairline crack outlining the cut. It would not be surprising that even a minor blow to the *Bust of Miss Coleman* may have caused the weak slip join to fail.

—Monica DiLisio Berry

1. Gary A. Reynolds and Beryl J. Wright, *Against the Odds: African-American Artists and the Harmon Foundation* (Newark: The Newark Museum, 1989), p. 150.

2. No curatorial records were located at Howard University to indicate how or when the break occurred, or who carried out the repair.

3. A hollowed interior minimizes the chances of cracking due to uneven contraction of the clay in the heat of the kiln.

22. *Eddie*, n.d.
Plaster
13¾ x 5½ x 7½
Collection of Hampton University Museum, 67.760, gift of the Harmon Foundation

23. *Head of a Girl*, n.d.
Terra-cotta
13½ x 5½ x 7½
Collection of Hampton University Museum, 67.759, gift of the Harmon Foundation

22

23

# Henry Wilmer (Mike) Bannarn
## (1910–1965)
### Sculptor, painter

After leaving the Minneapolis School of Art, Bannarn chose Harlem, the Art Students League, and the Beaux Arts to continue his learning and creative life. "306" (306 West 141st Street), Bannarn's studio shared with painter Charles Alston, was a major gathering place for Harlem artists in the 1930s. Quietly prolific and inspired by ordinary life, he drew heavily upon the aesthetics of expressionism in art.

24. *Daywork*, c. 1940
*[Woman Scrubbing], [Scrubwoman]*
Limestone
15 x 8½ x 7¾
First Award in Sculpture, Atlanta University Art Annuals, 1955. Collection of Clark Atlanta University Art Galleries

Henry Wilmer (Mike) Bannarn's exhibition record during the Atlanta University Art Annuals reveals a skilled and multitalented artist. Between 1943 and 1957, Bannarn

1960s are the most prominent works of this genre in American art history. Bearden was no doubt influenced by them. But his greatest and most sustained influence came from the accumulative assemblage techniques common in African sculpture, the patchwork quilt, the "newspapered" interiors of black homes in his native North Carolina, and the inspiration of the blues and jazz music, from which he created works of great power and authority. It is from these roots that Bearden sought and found "ownership," mastery of the images that filled his collage compositions of 1964 and forward.[2]

Bearden's family migrated north, first to Pittsburgh and subsequently to Harlem. He studied mathematics at New York University and produced political cartoons before enrolling in the Art Students League in 1936–37 to study with George Grosz. Bearden's trips to North Carolina kept him connected to the culture of the South, the stories—their complex, interwoven structures, and superimposed patterns—that would inspire the *Mecklenburg County* series and numerous other works.

Jazz and the blues were constant sources of inspiration for Bearden. His *Folk Musicians* (1943), and his interest in and pursuit of song writing (c. 1950–54) reflect his abiding love of music. Of the 1964 pieces that focused on jazz, his *Jazz: (Chicago) Grand Terrace Ballroom—1930s* and *Jazz (N.Y.) Savoy—1930s* are seminal works that inspired Bearden to make multiple photomontages of them. The collage *Jazz: (Chicago) Grand Terrace Ballroom—1930s* has the power and presence of a Kongo Nkisi figure: forms emanating from a composite of the subconscious and improvisational brilliance; a reconstruction of a remembered reality, one that produced absorbing, confrontational imagery that at once internalized and reflected the angst and the celebratory dimensions of black urban life. Bearden's collages struck the essence of the mood of black America in 1964. Responding to persistent discrimination and blatant racism, youths led riots in cities across the United States, shaking the confidence of the nation. Bearden's work embodied this rebelliousness and was perhaps as revolutionary as the most politically radical actions that occurred in the streets.

—Floyd Coleman

1. Spiral was formed in Bearden's Canal Street studio in 1963 in response to the March on Washington and the intensification of the Civil Rights struggle. Although a short-lived group that mounted only one public exhibition at their Christopher Street Gallery in 1965, the artists of Spiral continued to work, teach, and encourage young artists—for instance, Bearden and Lewis, along with their friend Ernest Crichlow, who founded the Cinque Gallery in New York City. See Myron Schwartzman, *Romare Bearden: His Life and His Art* (New York: Harry Abrams, Inc., 1990), p. 208.

2. Art historian Raymond Dobard, twentieth-century modernist scholar and expert on quilts, has contended that the space and structure of Bearden's collages and photomontages follow the organizational principles of African American quilts and to a far lesser degree to cubism, as is most often maintained.

## Arthur P. Bedou
### (1886–1966)
### Photographer

A photographer in New Orleans for over sixty years, Bedou is best known for his portraits which document the public and private life of Booker T. Washington. He is also recognized for landscape photographs of the Mississippi and Louisiana countrysides.

32. *Agriculture, Fruits picked at School's Farm*, n.d.
Gelatin silver print
7½ x 9½ (image); 7¹¹⁄₁₆ x 9¾ (sheet)
Collection of Tuskegee University

33. *Booker T. Washington in his study*, n.d.
Digital reproduction from original gelatin silver print
9½ x 7¾
Collection of Tuskegee University

The photograph of Booker T. Washington on exhibition is a contemporary color print made from a digitally retouched copy of the original. Digital restoration was used in partnership with traditional photograph conservation techniques to both meet the demand for repeated use of this historically important image and help ensure the long-term preservation of the original print.

Through repeated handling, attempts at unmounting, and other misadventures, the original photographic print had become severely damaged. All four corners had been lost, the gelatin image layer was gone in several peripheral areas, and there was a hole in the print through Washington's right foot. As a first step in its preservation, traditional conservation treatment methods were applied to stabilize the object and fill the hole in the paper support. At this point in the treatment, to

31

30

ready the photograph for display, a conservator might visually restore the image by inpainting the losses with media selected for long-term stability and compatibility with the materials in the original. In this case, however, it is preferable that the original print not be exhibited. It is physically very fragile and chemically deteriorated, probably through a combination of residual processing chemicals left in the paper and storage in poor environmental conditions at some point in the past. For these reasons, and to reduce the risk of further deterioration through exposure to light, some other means of producing a display quality image had to be used—in this case digital restoration.

The stabilized and conserved photograph was scanned at high resolution into a computer and the resulting digital image was retouched. Damaged areas were filled by copying and blending sections of the image from regions with similar tonal quality or details. Unevenness in tone, caused by chemical deterioration of the silver image, was also corrected to some extent. Once this process was complete, the computer file was used to create a high-resolution color negative. Although the original image is technically "black and white," only a full-color reproduction process could capture the richness and warmth of the original image. That negative was then used to make the surrogate print on display in the show. In addition, this negative (and additional copies) can be used to make further prints so that this historic image can be made available for reference, research, and publication without putting the valuable original at risk.

—Barbara Lemmen

34. *Booker T. Washington in New Orleans*, n.d.
Gelatin silver print
6½ x 4½ (image); 7 x 5¹/₁₆ (sheet)
Collection of Tuskegee University

35. *Booker T. Washington with ribboned men*, n.d.
Collodion printing out paper mounted on board
9³/₈ x 7⁷/₁₆ (image); 9⁷/₁₆ x 7⁹/₁₆ (sheet); 10¹/₁₆ x 8 (mount)
Collection of Tuskegee University

36. *Church on a Hill, East of Tuskegee Institute*, 1909
Gelatin silver print
7⁷/₈ x 10⁵/₈ (image); 7¹⁵/₁₆ x 9⁷/₈ (sheet)
Collection of Tuskegee University

38

37. *George Washington Carver in the chemistry lab*, n.d.
Collodion chloride on printing out paper
2⁷/₁₆ x 3⁵/₈ (image/sheet); 3⁷/₈ x 5¼ (mount)
Collection of Tuskegee University

38. *The class in shoe-making*, n.d.
Silver print on collodion printing out paper
7¹³/₁₆ x 9⁹/₁₆
Collection of Tuskegee University

## John Thomas Biggers
### (b. 1924)
**Muralist, painter, sculptor**
Biggers's murals are filled with subtle and bold symbols of Africa, its spiritual mysteries, and the rich heritage of African American culture. His murals have a beauty and power that enable African Americans to proudly see themselves. Much of his work has fierce social commentary. Biggers received his B.S., M.S., and Ph.D. from Pennsylvania State University and he founded and chaired the art department at Texas Southern University. "Sacred geometry" describes his work during and after the 1980s.

39. *Aunt Dicy*, 1954
Terra-cotta
20 x 11½ x 8½
Collection of Hampton University Museum, 989.18.72, gift of the artist

40. *Old Coffee Drinker*, 1945
Oil on canvas
51³/₈ x 35³/₈
Collection of Hampton University Museum, 989.8.38, gift of the artist

41. *Old Man*, 1945
Oil on canvas
58½ x 34¾
Collection of Hampton University Museum, 989.8.37, gift of the artist

John Biggers is a powerful storyteller. Through his skillful paintings, drawings, and sculpture, he conveys an understanding of community, the environment, struggle and achievement, and the cycle of life. Inspired by African American culture and its African origins, he chose to live in the South close to his roots. During a career of almost six decades, he has developed a visual vocabulary of symbols drawn from everyday life and African art to communicate ideas and concepts about the human condition.

Biggers was the youngest of seven children raised in a close family environment that valued education and hard work; his mother supported her family working as a laundress after the death of her husband. In 1941 Biggers enrolled at Hampton Institute (now Hampton University) intent on becoming a plumber. An evening art class with Viktor Lowenfeld compelled him to change his major to art. Lowenfeld, an Austrian of Jewish heritage, was a psychologist and an artist who fled the Nazi persecution. His widely published ideas on art education promoted the creative process as a means for self-expression, and his teaching at Hampton successfully engaged the minds and talents of his students. John Biggers became the student most closely associated with Lowenfeld. In 1946 when Lowenfeld accepted a job at Pennsylvania State University, Biggers transferred to that school, where he completed his B.S., M.S., and Ph.D. degrees.

Biggers's education at Hampton was interrupted by service in the United States Navy during World War II. Stationed at Hampton Institute, he illustrated educational materials for the naval training program at the school. This provided him the opportunity to continue his development as an artist, working in the art department's studio evenings and weekends. It was during this period that he created the painting *Old Coffee Drinker*.

From Viktor Lowenfeld, Biggers learned to create art from his own experience. His early paintings established themes that remained central to the artist's work throughout his career. His first painting, *Crossing the Bridge* (1942), is about people moving in search of a better life; the second painting, *Crucifixion* (1942), is a strong political and social statement on the oppression of blacks in the South; the third painting, *Mother and Child* (1943), is a tender portrayal of the centrality of women in the universe; and *Gleaners* (1943), celebrates the dignity of ordinary people.

*Old Coffee Drinker* also reflects Biggers's developing view of the world, but it was painted at a time when the artist was creating a group of related works to capture the meaning of a range of characters he had known. Transient homeless people were a common sight in Gastonia, North Carolina as Biggers was growing up. The memory of these individuals was ignited when he saw an old man in a café near the Hampton campus. The resulting painting was a composite of the many people he had seen walking from town to town in search of food. The artist portrayed the difficult, endless journey through the well-worn shoes, downcast eyes, and unshaven face of the man perched uncomfortably on a stool. He sought to depict a life that many of his fellow students had never witnessed.

Other works which Biggers created during this period are *Old Man* (1945), *Preacher Man* (1945), *Blind Boy and Monkey* (1948), *Pregnant Prostitute* (1943), *The Garbage Man* (1944), and *Victim of the City Streets* (1946). Striving to illustrate a cross section of life, his goal was an exhibition of these contrasting character studies to reveal the powerful and complex nature of individuals that may be revered, forgotten, scorned, or ignored by the larger society. Removed from the stretcher and rolled with other canvases when Biggers left Hampton in 1946, *Old Coffee Drinker* and *Old Man* were stored in a barn in Gastonia for several years until the artist moved to Houston. They remained rolled in a storage loft in his studio until they were acquired by Hampton in 1989.

John Biggers has made major contributions both as an artist and an educator. In 1949 he founded the art department at Texas Southern University in Houston. As head of the department until his retirement in 1983, he built a widely respected program. Moreover, he is highly regarded as an inspirational teacher and forceful lecturer. His art work incorporated more African symbols and imagery after his pioneering trip to West Africa in 1957. He also began to use a brighter color palette and to convey more motion as his work became progressively more abstract and complex. Mural painting has been a hallmark of Biggers's career and he has completed more than twenty-three. For him, murals provide a useful storytelling format, for they enable him to present multiple concepts in a fashion that is very accessible to a large number of people.

—Jeanne Zeidler

# Robert Blackburn
## (b. 1920)
### Printmaker

Blackburn has maintained a place in the center of the black art world since he attended the Art Students League. Blackburn studied under Rex Gorleigh, Henry Bannarn, Charles Alston, and Riva Helfond and was a master printer and teacher for many years. Blackburn is also well known as the founder and director of the Printmaking Workshop in New York.

42. *Refugees*, 1938
Lithograph on paper
15 x 19¾
Collection of North Carolina Central University Art Museum, gift of Mr. Christopher Massey

39

42

# Alexander "Skunder" Boghossian

**(b. 1937)**

**Painter**

Boghossian is recognized as one of the progenitors of contemporary Ethiopian art. His paintings reflect a strong basis in the ancient culture and symbolism of his homeland. Boghossian's work was exhibited at the Biennale de Sao Paulo, Brazil and the London Contemporary Arts Society, among other venues. He was the first Ethiopian whose paintings were bought by The Museum of Modern Art, New York, and the first African to have work in the Musée d'Art Moderne in Paris. A professor at Howard University, he has influenced a generation of painters.

43. *Ghosts of the Atlantic Ocean*, 1964
Mixed media (including opaque watercolor, acrylic, and ink) on paper board
27⅝ x 40¼
Collection of Hampton University Museum, 67.369, gift of the Harmon Foundation

43

*Ghosts of the Atlantic Ocean* (1964) is most significant as a representation of an important period in the art of Skunder Boghossian. The period marks his transition from the figurative paintings of the 1950s to the new style that was to define Skunder as one of the most influential Ethiopian artists today, and as a revolutionary force in African art. The painting belongs to a series of works Skunder produced between 1963 and 1964 with gouache and tempera on paper, and with a new visual vocabulary of meaning and symbolism. It was part of the big breakthrough in Skunder's work that came with his series *Nourishers*. This series, which included *Explosion of the World Egg* (1963), *Fertility Goddess* (1963), and *Cosmological Explosion* (1964), demonstrated Skunder's early preoccupation with the themes of birth, life, fertility, and the creative process. The series was executed at a time when Skunder was experimenting with surrealism. His compositions were preoccupied with insect-like forms, skeletal structures, and delicate almost embryonic shapes in a palette of subdued colors. It was an effective style that expressed his growing interest in what he calls "Afro-Metaphysics" and in concepts such as the "eternal cycle" and other symbolic aspects of various West African cosmologies.

*Ghosts of the Atlantic Ocean* belonged to a group of works which Skunder brought to New York in 1964 on his second visit to the United States. The trip, sponsored by the Harmon Foundation, came in the wake of his first and highly successful one-man show in 1962, sponsored by the Harmon Foundation at the Madison Avenue gallery in New York of Merton D. Simpson. These new works established young Skunder's reputation as a new, talented artist from Africa. Evelyn Brown of the Harmon Foundation found these new paintings "thought provoking, expressing his inner feelings and far removed from his previous work." They "weave tiny weird and haunting faces into complicated, lacy designs."[1]

*Ghosts of the Atlantic Ocean*, executed in the style that defines Skunder's Parisian period (late 1950s to the early 1960s), depicts distorted and tortured mask-like faces and doll-like figures adorned with bull horns against a wavy backdrop of deep sea blue. The figures are characterized by subdued shades of gray and ivory in which elemental forms and lines dominate the overall composition. The human and animal-like figures are rendered in geometric designs and interspersed with traditional patterns and decorative elements relieved by circles of brilliant yellow and orange. Here we observe Skunder's early experiments with the scroll-like patterns which have come to define his later works, and which are reminiscent of ancient Ethiopian manuscripts. The squares, circles, and other geometric patterns which permeate this composition are subjected to further fragmentation and improvisation in pursuit of their open-ended potentiality. Typical of the *Nourishers* series, *Ghosts of the Atlantic Ocean* conveys a sense of a slow, twisting motion created by a mass of coiling forms. The effect is one of startling, unsettling surrealism, and it is with a certain shock that the viewer realizes that the staring haunting eyes enclosed in narrow vertical frames, are the stylistic hallmark of traditional Ethiopian religious painting.

The title of the work, *Ghosts of the Atlantic Ocean*, is significant in revealing Skunder's intellectual journey and his Pan-Africanist leanings. Skunder's titles reflect his passion for traditional Ethiopian poetry, known by the metaphor of "wax" and "gold" for its deeper levels of meaning. The metaphor refers to the poetic convention of writing simultaneously on two different levels, the wax signifying the outer layer of meaning and gold the inner, hidden meaning. In the 1960s Skunder was closely associated with poets such as Solomon Derressa, who revolutionized modern Ethiopian poetry, and who was often involved in titling Skunder's work.[2] *Ghosts of the Atlantic Ocean* is a title that conceals as much as it reveals, and leaves much to the imagination. The title may be symbolic of Skunder's own crossing of the Atlantic, or may be intended as homage to the thousands of Africans who perished during the Middle Passage, and to those who suffered the horror of slavery. Unquestionably, the painting is indicative of Skunder's conscious effort to create a wider Pan-African identity.

Skunder's later works grew increasingly transparent and vibrant in color. They retained the rich symbols, motifs, forms, and shapes drawn from his own Ethiopian heritage and the larger African continent, as well as his contemporary surroundings. The best example of this synthesis is his painting *The Spirit is Landing* (1987–89), in which Skunder included his trademark painted scrolls on a vibrant background. Skunder, who works competently with oil, acrylic, gouache, crayon, and pen and ink, has also experimented with such material as wood relief, bark cloth, and goat skin. His *Time Cycle II* (1982) offers the finest example of Skunder's innovative techniques in a variety of media. Skunder's work is a synthesis of Ethiopian traditions and European techniques; a synthesis which draws creatively from his country's rich heritage in the decorative arts, murals, scroll painting, and illuminated manuscripts.

Skunder is associate professor of painting at Howard University, where he has taught since 1974. Previously, he studied at Saint Martins School, the Central School, and the Slade School of Fine Arts, London, and attended the École des Beaux Arts, Paris, subsequently teaching there and at the Academie de la Grande Chumière, Paris, until 1966. During a period of great intellectual ferment in Paris, Skunder associated with the Senegalese scholar and philosopher Sheikh Anta Diop, other major figures in the Pan-Africanist and Negritude movements and black artists from Africa, Latin America, and the United States. He was particularly influenced by Paul Klee, Andre Breton, George Braque, Max Ernst, the Afro-Cuban painter Wifredo Lam, and a group of West African artists. Like Max Ernst, Skunder begins a painting by deliberately creating accidental effects, splashing water on the canvas, and spraying over it with paint. Through this act, Skunder creates what Solomon Derressa calls the "possessed space."[3] As Derressa further explains, Skunder creates surfaces alive with molecular energy which allows him to release configurations from within rather than imposing figures from without. It is an act that perfectly embodies Skunder's repeated motto of letting "the painting paint itself!"

Skunder returned to Ethiopia in 1966, where he taught at the Fine Arts School of Addis Ababa and made a lasting impact on younger Ethiopian artists. After moving to the United States in 1969, Skunder continued to influence modern Ethiopian painting through Ethiopian artists such as Wosene and Germai Hewitt, who followed him to Howard University and studied with him there. For the last three decades Skunder's art has defined modern Ethiopian painting, attracting a circle of younger artists who are influenced by his charismatic personality and inspired by his art.

Skunder's impact goes beyond the modern African art movement to artists of African descent in the African diaspora. Arriving in the United States in the aftermath of the Civil Rights movement, Skunder witnessed the rise of the Black Power movement. The emergence of liberation and decolonization movements in Africa during the 1950s and 1960s became a tremendous source of inspiration and solidarity among artists of African descent. The search for a new visual vocabulary rooted in the African experience which accompanied these movements has its share of cross-influences among African American artists. Skunder has been an integral part of all this.

—Salah M. Hassan

1. Evelyn S. Brown, *Africa's Contemporary Art and Artists* (New York: The Harmon Foundation), p. 20.

2. The cultural atmosphere was invigorated by the occasional poetry readings that were held at the Ras Makonen Hall, the Creative Arts Center at the then Haile Selassie I University and at the homes of some of the poets. The poets and writers included poet laureate Tsegaye Gebra Medhin, art critic and poet Solomon Deressa, Tesfaye Gessese, Seifu Metaferia, Mengistu Lemma, Gabre Kristos Desta, and Yohannes Admassu.

3. Solomon Derressa, "Skunder Boghossian," *Ethiopian Observer*, 1966.

# Francis Chickering Briggs
## (1833–1908)
### Photographer

Briggs, a member of the Hampton Normal and Agricultural Institute staff for twenty-nine years, was also an active amateur photographer and, in 1893, became one of the founding members of the school's Camera Club. His photographic albums of Dakota Territory scenes, taken in 1887, are important documents of the tribal communities that were home to some of Hampton's American Indian students.

47

**44.** *Dakota Album*, 1887
Bound volume of one hundred thirteen
albumen prints
Each approximately 6 x 7¾ (image);
9 x 11⅜ (sheet)
Collection of Hampton University
Archives

**45.** *Dakota Album*, 1887
Bound volume of eighty-six albumen
prints
Each approximately 6 x 7¾ (image);
9 x 11⅜ (sheet)
Collection of Hampton University
Archives

**46.** *Dakota Album: Government School
under Mr. AC Wells 4 miles from the
Cannonball*, 1887
Albumen print
6 x 8¹/₁₆ (image/sheet); 9¹/₁₆ x 11¼ (mount)
Collection of Hampton University
Archives

**47.** *Dakota Album: Mrs. Van Solen's School
9 miles from the Cannonball River on the
River (Miss. River) road*, 1887
Albumen print
5⅛ x 7¾ (image/sheet); 9 x 11⅜ (mount)
Collection of Hampton University
Archives

57

# Edward Bruce
## (1879–1943)
**Painter**
Edward Bruce's art career began relatively
late in life, following many years as a lawyer
and publisher. Largely self-taught, Bruce
painted in a manner that closely resembled
the "precisionist" paintings of such
Depression-era artists as Charles Sheeler
and George Ault. Beyond his own work,
Bruce's other major contribution to the
world of art was conceiving and implement-
ing this nation's first federal art program,
the Public Works of Art Project. A close
associate of President Roosevelt's, Bruce
also headed up the federal art program
known as "The Section," which awarded
commissions to artists nationwide for
murals and sculptures in public buildings.

**48.** *Portrait of William Friday*, 1934
Oil on canvas
30⅞ x 25½
Collection of Howard University Gallery
of Art

# Elizabeth Catlett
## (b. 1915)
**Sculptor, painter, printmaker**
Catlett earned her B.A. from Howard (1936)
and an M.F.A. (1940) from the University
of Iowa. Catlett also studied at the Art
Institute of Chicago and headed the art
department at Dillard University. Her work
conveys pride and dignity regarding the
black figure. Catlett has lived in Mexico
since the 1940s and is married to a
Mexican graphic artist. Themes of women,
especially women of color, are found
throughout her art. Her work deals master-
fully with the struggles and triumphs
of people of color amid the western
hemisphere.

**49.** *Negro Woman (Sharecropper)*, c. 1952
Linocut on medium-weight wove paper
23¹/₁₆ x 19⅛
Second Award in Prints, Atlanta University
Art Annuals, 1952. Collection of Clark
Atlanta University Art Galleries

**50.** *Negro Woman*, c. 1956
Wood and onyx
11½ x 6½ x 9
Second Award in Sculpture, Atlanta
University Art Annuals, 1956. Collection
of Clark Atlanta University Art Galleries

**51.** *Black Women Series: I Am the Black
Woman*, 1946, printed later
Linocut on medium-weight wove paper
11½ x 10
Collection of Hampton University
Museum, 993.15.12, Museum Acquisition
Fund

**52.** *Negro Women Series: I am the Negro
Woman: In Sojourner Truth, I Fought for the
Rights of Women*, 1946
Linocut on medium-weight wove paper
5¹/₁₆ x 4
Collection of Howard University Gallery
of Art

**53.** *Negro Women Series: I Have Special
Houses*, 1946
Linocut on medium-weight wove paper
5¾ x 6½
Collection of Howard University Gallery
of Art

**54.** *Black Women Series: I Have Special
Reservations*, 1946, printed later
Linocut on medium-weight wove paper
11 x 10
Collection of Hampton University
Museum, 993.15.8, Museum Acquisition
Fund

55. *Negro Women Series: In Harriet Tubman, I Helped Hundreds to Freedom*, 1946
Linocut on medium-weight wove paper
5¹/₁₆ x 4
Collection of Howard University Gallery of Art

56. *Black Women Series: There are Bars Between Me and the Rest of the Land*, 1946, printed later
Linocut on medium-weight wove paper
11 x 10
Collection of Hampton University Museum, 993.15.9, Museum Acquisition Fund

Despite the two distinctly different designations, *Black Woman Series* and *Negro Woman Series*, entry nos. 51 through 56 are all part of the original *Negro Woman Series* that Elizabeth Catlett created in 1946–47. When entry nos. 51, 54, and 56 were acquired by the Hampton University Museum in 1993, these three linocuts—reprinted from the original linoleum blocks—were given a new serial name. In spite of the updated racial nomenclature on these three prints, what is consistent among all of Elizabeth Catlett's works is a steadfast interest across time and space in the realities, experiences, and struggles of women of African descent.

57. *Woman With Guitar*, 1947
Oil on canvas
38¾ x 31¾
Collection of North Carolina Central University Art Museum, gift of Professor James Vernon Herring

Among the first paintings of an African American woman accessioned by the North Carolina Central University Art Museum, Elizabeth Catlett's *Woman With Guitar* is one of the museum's most popular paintings. It was gifted by the founder of the Howard University Art Department and Gallery of Art, James V. Herring. This was one of the first paintings to treat what was to become a recurring theme in her work: the championing of the dignity, strength, and perseverance of black women. The unique qualities of this dignified woman are singular, but they are also the affirmation of an Afrofemcentric consciousness—a black woman artist focusing on the realities and experiences of a black woman as subject.[1]

49

Elizabeth Catlett's life and art have always been infused with a visceral, social vision. Her work has consistently addressed race, culture, and gender-based identity in the context of equity throughout the years. She has remained steadfast in her philosophy that "Art is important only to the extent that it helps in the liberation of our people. It is necessary only at this moment as an aid to our survival."[2] Catlett's artistic development coincided with a particularly volatile time for black American artists. Catlett trained at Howard University after being rejected from Carnegie Institute of Technology in Pittsburgh (now Carnegie Mellon University) because of her race, despite winning a competitive scholarship.[3] By 1940 Catlett had become the first student to complete requirements for a master of fine arts degree at the University of Iowa, where she was influenced by Grant Wood and Ossip Zadkine. While under Wood's tutelage, she was encouraged to find inspiration in her own people.[4]

*Woman With Guitar* was painted in 1947, during the second year of a Rosenwald Fund fellowship, won by Catlett for study in Mexico.[5] There she would meet the major Mexican artists, including the towering muralists David Alfaro Siqueiros, Diego Rivera, and José Clemente Orozco whose ideals she would embrace. The present work, and others from the mid-forties through the early sixties, was informed by Catlett's participation in the Taller de Gráfica Popular (Taller), a group committed to maintaining the social and political ideals of the Mexican Revolution.[6] The populist workshop's ideology was that art should be utilized to service the needs of the people. Artists working for schools, organizations, and movements created didactic posters that could communicate directly with everyone. This dictated a pictorial style that everyone could recognize. A stated position was that art "has always been characterized by the absence of abstract techniques, which would not be understood by the masses."[7] The stylistic evolution occurring in Catlett's graphic work and painting became more naturalistic because of this involvement and is quite apparent in *Woman With Guitar*.

The subject, a heroic and dignified black woman playing a guitar rekindles Catlett's own childhood desire to become a blues singer.[8] Dual themes of performance and perseverance are compellingly presented and demand immediate engagement. Part of the *Negro Woman* series, *Woman With Guitar* represents a figural style characterized by simple, massive planes and is seated with legs akimbo.

This posture increasingly surfaced in Catlett's work and would become an aspect of her sculptural signature. A conspicuous portrayal of a working-class woman with pronounced negroid features anticipates work to come. The high cheek bone structure, broad nose, and thickened lips affirmed a strong aesthetic rooted in the African continuum. Her melancholic facial expression reveals a hard life made easy by the realization that the blues is not only her musical muse, but her spiritual booster.

There is no explicit social commentary in *Woman With Guitar*; however, beneath the surface lies a universal identification with and allegiance to the downtrodden in society. A distinction between the literal strumming of the guitar, and the prevalence of triumphal nuances of overcoming oppression against overwhelming odds could be her mantra. The linearity of the rather ordinary dress, worn over a collarless blouse with sleeves pushed up, hints at a planar cognizance that would become the hallmark of Catlett's future sculptural stylistic oeuvre. A striated pattern emanates, somewhat halo like, from the upperhalf of the composition surrounding the head. A limited palette of richly impastoed blues, with contrasting pinks, animates the canvas with textural contrasts. The brushwork communicates a dynamism that at times appears to be an incisive graphic gesture.

*Woman With Guitar* represents a theme that would occupy Catlett for many years, and has proven a rich vein of gender subject matter. Subtle stylization of the entire body, but particularly the hands, foreshadows sculptural pieces of the 1950s through the 1990s. The predecessor to a long line of stalwart women printed in monochrome linocut or multihued serigraph, sculpted in wood and bronze, terracotta and marble, she is imbued with gritty determination.

—Kenneth G. Rodgers

1. Freida High Tesfagfiorgis, "Afrofemcentrism and Its Fruition in the Art of Elizabeth Catlett and Faith Ringgold," *Sage: A Scholarly Journal of Black Women*, vol. 4, no. 1 (spring 1987): 26, and Jontyle Theresa Robinson, "Bearing Witness," *Contemporary Works African American Women Artists* (Atlanta: Spelman College and Rizzoli International Publications, Inc., 1996), p. 102.

2. Samella S. Lewis and Ruth G. Waddy, eds., *Black Artists on Art*, vol. 2 (Los Angeles: Contemporary Crafts, 1971), p. 107.

3. Romare Bearden and Harry Henderson, *A History of African-American Artists: From 1972 to the Present* (New York: Pantheon Books, 1993), p. 419.

4. Regenia A. Perry, *Free Within Ourselves* (Washington, D.C.: Smithsonian Institution, National Museum of American Art, in association with Pomegranate Artbooks, San Francisco, 1992), p. 47.

5. See Mora J. Beauchamp-Byrd, *An Aesthetic of Survival: The Visionary Art of Elizabeth Catlett in Struggle and Serenity* (New York: The Franklin Williams Caribbean Cultural Center, 1996), p. 11.

6. Catlett credits the Taller de Gráfica Popular with the development of a collective aesthetic that placed art in the service of people. See Samella S. Lewis, *The Art of Elizabeth Catlett* (Claremont: Handcraft Studios, 1984), p. 21.

7. Michael Brenson cites an introduction to a book about the philosophy of the Taller de Gráfica Popular written by Bauhaus architect Hannes Meyer. Meyer also stressed that the Taller should create "an art that is true to the life of the people" and "inseparably bound to their destiny." See Michael Brenson, "Elizabeth Catlett's Sculptural Aesthetics," in *Elizabeth Catlett Sculpture: A Fifty-Year Retrospective* (Purchase, New York: Neuberger Museum of Art, 1998), p. 35.

8. Elizabeth Catlett, interview by Glory van Scott, 8 December 1981, in *Artists and Influence*, James V. Hatch and Leo Hamalian, eds., 1991, vol. X (New York: Hatch-Billops Collection, 1991), p. 1.

# Christopher Ethelbert Cheyne
## (1869–1928)
### Photographer

Cheyne began his photography work at the end of the nineteenth century and established Cheyne's Studio in Hampton, Virginia where Negroes and whites patronized the establishment despite segregation. After his death, the doors of Cheyne's Studio remained open for another generation of Hampton residents.

58. *Major Robert Russa Moton Commandant—Hampton Institute*, c. 1890
Gelatin silver print mounted on board
5½ x 3¹³⁄₁₆ (image/sheet);
5½ x 3⁷⁄₈ (mount)
Collection of Tuskegee University

# William Christenberry
## (b. 1936)
### Photographer, painter, sculptor

Christenberry was commissioned by the Art-in-Architecture program of the United States General Services Administration to create a wall work for the federal building in Jackson, Mississippi, in 1978. He was a Guggenheim and National Endowment for

59

the Arts fellow and is currently a professor at the Corcoran School of Art. As a multi-media artist, Christenberry has been exploring his Southern heritage for over three decades. He uses photography, sculpture, and found objects to examine the effects of time and aging around his native Hale County, Alabama.

59. *House, Stewart, AL*, 1962
Gelatin silver print
3 x 3 (image); 8 x 10 (sheet)
Collection of Hampton University Museum, gift of the artist

60. *Tingle House, Near Akron, AL*, 1962
Gelatin silver print
3⅜ x 5¹/₁₆ (image); 8 x 10 (sheet)
Collection of Hampton University Museum, gift of the artist

61

## Claude Clark, Sr.
### (b. 1915)
**Printmaker, painter**
After studies at the Philadelphia Museum School of Art and the Barnes Foundation (where he perfected his expressionistic approach to the figure), Clark joined Philadelphia's legendary WPA/FAP graphics division. Years later Clark moved to California, where he continued his studies at California State College at Sacramento and at the University of California at Berkeley. He has taught at Atlanta University, Fisk University, and Talladega College.

61. *Jumpin' Jive*, c. 1940
Color etching on heavy-weight wove paper
7½ x 9 (image); 9¾ x 11¹³/₁₆ (sheet)
Collection of Howard University Gallery of Art

## William Arthur Cooper
### (1895–1974)
**Painter**
Minister, educator, and graduate of North Carolina Central University, self-taught painter Cooper specialized in portraits which captured the spirit of the common man in lives of simplicity. He published a collection of essays and twenty-seven portraits in 1936.

62. *My Dad*, 1931
Oil on canvas
30⅛ x 24³/₁₆
Collection of North Carolina Central University Art Museum

A native North Carolinian and a graduate of the National Religious Training School (now North Carolina Central University) in Durham, William Arthur Cooper was a minister, teacher, and self-taught painter determined to make each of his callings serve the others. In the 1930s, working under the auspices of the North Carolina Interracial Commission, he realized this goal with a project combining portraiture, biography, and oration. Cooper believed that burlesque, sensationalized images of American Negroes, then so prevalent, were both cause and consequence of the South's poor race relations. A program of arts education combining realistic portraiture, sympathetic biography, and honest conversation, he argued, could ameliorate how Negroes and whites imagined one another and thus ultimately how they interacted.[1]

To these ends, during the Depression Cooper painted a series of portraits depicting Negro worthies and common people. Among his subjects were businessmen and cooks, preachers and shoe shine boys, farmers and educators, washerwomen and college students. Cooper's subjects were actual Carolinians, but in selecting his sitters and in preparing the paintings themselves, he strove to capture broader truths about contemporary Negro life. So rather than identify his subjects by name, Cooper appended to his portraits brief expositions on the representative significance of each character. A young woman in her Sunday best was *Ambition*. "She is very energetic and is liked by both the colored neighbors and the white people in whose service she works regularly."[2] Another Cooper portrait, *A Negro Woman in the Field of Elementary Education*, underlined the fact that "much of the sacrificial and constructive labor of the Negro leaders has been in the field of Elementary Education and has been carried on by the women of the race."[3] Cooper's *The Shoe Shine Boy* —kneeling at the ready with wide eyes and a welcoming smile—portrayed a work ethic the artist found in evidence among many Negro laborers: "the doing of the small things so well and with so much sunshine that promotion comes in due time because of duty well done. . . ."[4]

As can be gathered from the above, a kind of middle-class conservatism pervaded much of Cooper's work. Concerning the place and progress of Negroes in America, he painted and preached patience. In some cases, this didactic caution underpowered his work. Thus, in a depiction of black religious life—*A Negro's Conception of Christ in the Life of Today*—Cooper followed convention and painted Christ as white. Moreover, through portraiture and essay the artist made clear that the prime path to racial progress was for Negroes to imitate "the ideals and habits" of their white employers. In a political and social context dominated by the Scottsboro case and the resultant struggle then raging between socialists and liberals over the best means to achieve racial justice, Cooper's intentions were clear.[5] He and his art were on the side of capital. All the same, given the hyperbolic images of Negro men and women prevalent in advertising and popular culture, there can be no doubt that Cooper's conservatism carried with it, nonetheless, a subversive edge. By refusing to paint Negro southerners as gross caricatures and by rendering his friends, neighbors, and co-religionists at repose and as he saw them from day-to-day, Cooper achieved a realism that was radical inasmuch as it was documentary. He painted black faces *sans* blackface and the other disfiguring accretions then cleaving to popular images of the race.

Cooper's *My Dad* is among his most successful portraits—simultaneously revealing both the radical and reactionary poles of his artistic inclination. Wanting to project a sense of agrarian common sense and simplicity, the younger Cooper entreated the elder not to dress up for the portrait. Cooper painted his father in his work clothes, just as if he would have gone into the fields. *My Dad* is a sharecropper and day laborer—hard working and God-fearing. The sitter's life has been spartan. But if he has suffered more than some, he has also been blessed with more faith than most. He is satisfied with his lot in life though not complacent. He is careful, wise, but above all, patient and dexterous. He is, in a man, everything his race requires to survive and prosper: "the power of adjustment, tolerance and faith."[6]

Cooper lectured and exhibited throughout the 1930s. Regionally, he was a well-known artist, educator, and arts administrator. He won prizes in portraiture at competitions sponsored by the North Carolina State Fair, and he organized the state's first exhibition of black artists. Cooper showed nationally in exhibits organized through the Harmon Foundation. In 1936 he published a collection of brief essays and twenty-seven portraits, *A Portrayal of Negro Life*. The book embodied his ideas on how arts education might encourage interracial cooperation. Throughout his career as an artist Cooper maintained his position as a minister, pastoring the Clinton Metropolitan A.M.E. Zion Church in Charlotte, North Carolina.

—Alexander X. Byrd

62

1. For biographical details on William Arthur Cooper, see his *A Portrayal of Negro Life* (Durham, N.C.: The Seeman Printery, 1936).

2. Ibid., p. 34.

3. Ibid., p. 86.

4. Ibid., p. 22.

5. In the spring of 1931, nine young black men riding the rails in search of work were accused of rape by two white females jumping the same trains. Though the evidence against them was almost nonexistent, the young men were summarily tried, convicted, and sentenced to death during a trial in Scottsboro, Alabama. With the assistance of socialist legal activists, the young men began a marathon of appeals, retrials, and parole hearings lasting more than a decade. Socialist and left-leaning political groups were quick to the defense of the Scottsboro Boys, while mainline black organizations were more cautious. The resultant political maneuvering between socialist and liberals was a watershed moment in determining the character and pace of succeeding civil rights struggles. See Dan T. Carter, *Scottsboro: A Tragedy of the American South*, rev. ed. (Baton Rouge: Louisiana State University Press, 1979); and Robin D.G. Kelley, *Hammer and Hoe: Alabama Communists during the Great Depression* (Chapel Hill: The University of North Carolina Press, 1990).

6. Cooper, p. 2.

## Allan Rohan Crite
### (b. 1910)
**Painter, author, illustrator**

Crite and his artwork have always been intimately associated with Boston, where he has lived most of his life. The artist studied at the School of the Museum of Fine Arts, Boston, between 1929 and 1936, and received a B.A. from the Harvard University Extension School in 1968. In addition to depicting the daily lives of the black people of his community, Crite interpreted religious themes and texts using black figures and has created numerous liturgical artworks for black churches. Crite worked with the WPA/FAP and during the 1940s Harvard University Press published two volumes of his illustrations of Negro spirituals.

63. *Beneath the Cross of St. Augustine*, 1936
Oil on canvas
20 1/8 x 36
Collection of Howard University Gallery of Art

*Beneath the Cross of St. Augustine* is an early work from an extensive series of neighborhood paintings that Allan Rohan Crite produced during the 1930s and 1940s. In this scene, the artist captured the Shawmut Avenue stables near Lenox Street, in the lower Roxbury district of Boston. In front of the carefully rendered old brick buildings, horses, wagon drivers, and street vendors move about hurriedly as they begin another day of work in the city. In the upper portion of the painting, in line with the tree tops, the cross of St. Augustine's Episcopal Church hovers silently above the early morning activity. Crite has lived in the South End neighborhood of Boston since his family moved from New Jersey soon after he was born. At age eighty-eight, Crite continues to produce and exhibit his art work and maintains his home as a museum devoted to his long and prolific artistic career.

Crite painted *Beneath the Cross of St. Augustine* during his brief tenure with the WPA/FAP during the Depression. According to Crite, the financial support he received from the WPA/FAP came at a particularly important moment in his career, when he was developing a variety of themes in his art. In 1936 Crite was in his final year at the School of the Museum of Fine Arts, Boston and exhibiting his work professionally with the Boston Society of Independent Artists and the Harmon Foundation. While the young artist developed his artistic style, he established a philosophy that would guide his choice and presentation of subject matter for the next six decades. Crite's goal in the neighborhood paintings was to portray the people of his community "as ordinary human beings going about their business in a New England city, rather than as the exotic sharecropper of the South or jazz personality of Harlem, which were popular images being presented."[1] The vantage point the artist establishes for himself and for the viewer is not that of a voyeur but of a witness and a participant in the daily life of a community. Although Crite's paintings fit within the general style of American realism, the intimacy and directness of his representation of African Americans remains unique among the work of his fellow artists.

Crite describes himself as an "artist reporter," and a hallmark of his narrative paintings is the extreme care with which he portrays the details of the topography, architecture, and fashions of the time. Decades after painting *Beneath the Cross*, the artist reviewed the notes and sketches from his diaries of the 1930s and wrote these recollections:

> . . . as a young man, I remember the many mornings hurrying by the old stables to Saint Augustine's Church . . . to assist at the Mass. I recall over the door of the stables the sign 'Horses Boarded and For Sale' and over the door of the smaller shop the sign 'Endicott Blacksmith Shop. A. Shaffer Manager, General Blacksmith.'[2]

Many of the neighborhood paintings, focused as they are on documentation, now serve as valuable visual records of a lost era in the history of Boston. St. Augustine's Church is the only building from that period still extant in this area, and today the cross looks over new buildings and a vacant lot on Shawmut Avenue. Thus, the church buildings that often appear in the background of Crite's street scenes symbolize the importance of religion to the African American community and the stability of their ecclesiastical institutions amidst the chaos and desolation brought about by urban renewal.

Crite also felt it was important to document the spiritual life of his community, and some of the neighborhood paintings depict scenes of worship services and choir practices. The artist's own religiosity and his longtime fascination with Christian iconography emerges as well in his extensive body of art work dealing with traditional religious themes. During the thirties, Crite was interpreting religious texts and Negro spirituals in brush and ink drawings and creating altarpieces and stations of the cross, some of which he later would display in black churches. He frequently represents Christ and other biblical figures as people of color and places them in contemporary urban settings reminiscent of Boston. In this work, Crite's subtle depiction of the church as both buried within the neighborhood and presiding over it, brings nuance to the theme of religion and community in an original way.

—Julie Levin

1. Allan Rohan Crite, interview by Julie Levin, July 1998.

2. Allan Rohan Crite, "Walking Tour: Allan Rohan Crite's South End," *Glue Magazine* (Boston: September 1997): 18–19. Crite originally wrote these comments in 1975.

## Clara Darden
### (1800–1910)
**Fiber artist**

Darden, daughter of Jean Baptiste Alexandre Dardenne, Jr., the last lineage chief of the Chitimacha, was a medicine woman and community leader. Tribal history refers to her as the person "responsible for the bringing back the almost lost art of basketry." In 1899 Darden, who was the only tribal member remaining who knew the names and meanings of Chitimacha basket designs, undertook a project to teach the younger women in the tribe the techniques of traditional basketry. Contemporary Chitimacha artists continue to employ these techniques exclusively in their basketry.

63

65

64. *Covered baskets*, c. 1904
River cane, pigment
Sizes vary from 2⅞ to 6 inches in height,
width, and depth
Collection of Hampton University
Museum, 14.1969.2, 4, 5, 6–12, gift of
Mrs. N.J. Doubleday,

## Charles C. Davis
**(b. 1912)**
**Painter**
An easel painter with the Illinois Federal
Arts Project, Davis exhibited largely in the
Chicago area during the 1940s, in such
venues as the Art Institute of Chicago and
the Southside Community Arts Center.

65. *Newsboy (The Negro Boy)*, 1939
Oil on canvas
36 x 30
Collection of Howard University Gallery
of Art

## Jane Eliza Davis
**(c. 1857–1935)**
**Educator, administrator, photographer**
In various capacities that included editor-
ship of *The Southern Workman* and director
of the publications office, Vassar graduate
Davis served Hampton until her retirement
in 1926.

66. *Untitled, Family along fence*, c. 1900
Digital reproduction from original
cyanotype
3¾ x 6¹/₁₆
Collection of Hampton University
Archives

## Roy DeCarava
**(b. 1919)**
**Photographer, printmaker**
DeCarava's principal subjects are Harlem's
people and neighborhoods as well as jazz
musicians and black entertainers. He initially studied painting and printmaking and
was already a trained artist when he developed as a photographer. He received the
first Guggenheim grant awarded to a black
artist (1952). DeCarava became a freelance
photographer in 1958 and his photographs
appeared in *Sports Illustrated*, *Look*,
*Newsweek*, *Time*, and *Life*.

67

67. *Close up*, c. 1950
Color serigraph on medium-weight
wove paper
9½ x 11½ (image); 10¾ x 12⅞ (sheet)
Collection of North Carolina Central
University Art Museum, gift of Howard
Greenberg

68. *Pickets*, c. 1946
Color serigraph on paper
12 x 10½
Third Award in Prints, Atlanta University
Art Annual. Collection of Clark Atlanta
University Art Galleries

Born of Jamaican extraction in Harlem,
DeCarava demonstrated his facility to draw
large scale chalk renderings of cowboys
and Indians on his neighborhood pave-
ments and at the specialized Textile High
School in New York City. Denied a four-
year scholarship to Pratt Institute by his
high school, DeCarava entered Cooper
Union after passing a highly competitive
entrance exam.[1] Overwhelmed by glaring
cultural differences that affected his ability
to "fit in," DeCarava left after two years
upon discovering the Harlem Community
Art Center where he was nurtured and
emotionally supported by a distinguished
staff that included Augusta Savage, Aaron
Douglas, and Charles Alston.

The show-card lettering skills he developed in adolescence enabled him to learn
silk screening in the poster division of
WPA/FAP, facilitated by his mother's
employment there as a clerk.[2] Through
interaction with Harlem Renaissance
scholar Alain Locke—who championed the
notion of a black aesthetic—and with the
Harlem Art Center's staff, DeCarava's
themes consistently alluded to the individual in the context of his environment. In
tandem with many of his contemporaries
(most of whom were his seniors, e.g.,
Charles White, Romare Bearden, Ernest
Crichlow, and Jacob Lawrence), DeCarava
subscribed to the responsibility of black
artists serving as spokespersons for the
black community.

*Pickets* typifies this early preoccupation, which continued into his acclaimed
work as a photographer. Clad for cold climate, two monoxyl figures stand with a
resolute demeanor between blank signs
that engage the viewer to speculate on
the variables of social and economic injus-
tices to which the men are responding.
Executed around 1946, *Pickets* comes near
the period of DeCarava's transition from a
palette of pigment to a palette of light—
black and white photography.

68

73

During the Atlanta University Art Annuals (1942–70), DeCarava exhibited two paintings in 1944 and two prints in 1946, but became discouraged over winning third instead of first prize in printmaking.[3] Only recently did he discover that first prize went to his mentor, Charles White, with whom he studied painting and drawing at George Washington Carver Art Center in New York City (1944–45). Other artists who received purchase awards in that year included Joseph Delaney, Ellis Wilson, Elizabeth Catlett, and Richmond Barthé.

Known for his inexhaustible use of gray values in his photographs, the cool and neutral-chromatic colors in *Pickets* illustrates how serigraphy became the precursor to DeCarava's photography. Through the process of taking pictures of subjects in preparation for his silkscreens, thereby engaging live subjects, who inadvertently extricated DeCarava from professed timidity, his penchant for still photography soared.[4]

As evidenced in the exhibition, "Roy DeCarava: A Retrospective," organized by The Museum of Modern Art, DeCarava is recognized as one of America's leading fine art photographers. With the miniaturization of the 35mm camera and the development of low light, sensitive film, DeCarava was able to abandon the studio and replace it with the streets of New York as his workshop and backdrop, exchanging models for real people, doing real things. He developed a unique voice in photography. He pressed beyond documentary photography, coming closer perhaps to the influence of Henri Cartier-Bresson, yet refraining reportage. His body of work is a visual sonata in which he chooses moments from the river of life as it cascades and twists through the canyons and gullies of New York City.

DeCarava captures the world of the rejected, the revolutionary—those who have not found access to the palaces and board rooms. DeCarava's camera finds only the uplifting defeat of adverse conditions. Lewd and lascivious characters are not in his visual vocabulary. In compositions of people who are unstoppable in their quest for dignity and love, we see faces with eyes that look inward to crossroads without U-turns. There is a conspicuous absence of the rich, the powerful, and successful insiders. The aesthetics and music of jazz musicians reflect the style of DeCarava's body of work more than any paradigm of the Western fine art tradition. A master of the shadows, the tonal range of his gray scale is the substance of things felt and not seen. DeCarava does the work of a sorcerer, turning ordinary lives into golden moments, black and white pearls—peak moments woven together by a conjurer.

—Tina Dunkley
—Ernest Dunkley

1. Elton C. Fax, *Seventeen Black Artists* (New York: Dodd, Mead & Co., 1971), p. 171.

2. Peter Galassi, *Roy DeCarava: A Retrospective* (New York: The Museum of Modern Art, 1996), p. 13.

3. See exhibition records at Clark Atlanta University Art Galleries Archives; DeCarava's reflections and comments on his participation in the annuals while visiting the university art collections in Atlanta for the first time, 7 July 1998.

4. In response to the question of "What prompted DeCarava to leave printmaking for photography?" during a question and answer period following a lecture on his retrospective, DeCarava stated that he was very shy as a young man and that photography facilitated his ability to interact with people. Moreover, he found the act of painting/printmaking to be too solitary and preferred interfacing with his subject during his creative process. (Atlanta: High Museum of Art at Georgia Pacific, 26 June 1998).

## Charles Demuth
### (1883–1935)
### Painter

Demuth worked in oil, tempera, and watercolor and created about seven hundred and fifty paintings and three hundred and thirty drawings even though he was chronically ill most of his life. Demuth's art demonstrated his keen ability to manipulate intensities of color to create subtle emotional effects. His paintings varied from still lifes to abstractions.

69. *Calla Lilies*, 1927
Oil on composition board
42¹⁄₈ x 48
The Alfred Stieglitz Collection, Fisk University, Nashville, Tennessee, gift of Georgia O'Keeffe

70. *Cyclamen*, 1916
Watercolor on paper
13³⁄₈ x 9¾
The Alfred Stieglitz Collection, Fisk University, Nashville, Tennessee, gift of Georgia O'Keeffe

71. *Eggplant and Peppers*, 1922
Watercolor on paper
9¾ x 13¾
The Alfred Stieglitz Collection, Fisk University, Nashville, Tennessee, gift of Georgia O'Keeffe

72. *Oranges and Artichokes*, 1926
Watercolor on paper
13¾ x 19⅝
The Alfred Stieglitz Collection, Fisk
University, Nashville, Tennessee, gift of
Georgia O'Keeffe

73. *Red and Yellow Flowers*, 1926
Watercolor on paper
17⅞ x 11⅝
The Alfred Stieglitz Collection, Fisk
University, Nashville, Tennessee, gift of
Georgia O'Keeffe

## Etahdleuh Doanmoe
### (1856–1888)
**Painter**

Etahdlueh was among the first group of students who entered Hampton Normal and Agricultural Institute in 1878 to participate in the school's historic experiment in American Indian education. While at Hampton, he and other early American Indian students decorated commercially produced pottery with scenes of warriors and hunters and marketed them to campus visitors. In 1879 Etahdleuh left Hampton to recruit students for the Carlisle Indian School in Pennsylvania, which he also attended. Etahdleuh worked at the Smithsonian Institution in 1880 as an informant on Kiowa language.

74

74. *Untitled painted jar*, c. 1879
Painted terra-cotta
6⅜ x 4½ diameter
Collection of Hampton University
Museum, 00.1926

## Aaron Douglas
### (1899–1979)
**Painter, muralist, illustrator**

Douglas was the artist most associated with the Harlem Renaissance. His art focused on social engagement and the celebration of black culture in which African motifs and objects combined with the angular Art Deco style. Douglas's subject matter ranged from moments in black history to contemporary scenes of the jazz culture. His illustrations were carried in the *Crisis* and other publications and he was chair of the art department at Fisk University for twenty-nine years.

75

75. *Building More Stately Mansions*, 1944
Oil on canvas
54 x 42
Fisk University, Nashville, Tennessee

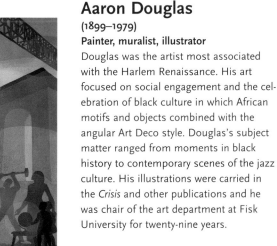

Aaron Douglas was the primary illustrator of the Harlem Renaissance.[1] Within weeks of his arrival in Harlem in 1925, Douglas was hired by W.E.B. DuBois and Charles S. Johnson to illustrate *Crisis* and *Opportunity*, magazines with a wide appeal and substantial readership. Douglas tried to create a new, positive image for his audience, which made a conscious and direct connection to Africa. He developed his own signature style, a technique he used primarily in his illustrations and large scale murals, combining the influences of Egyptian art (to represent Africa), West African art (in particular the art of the Ivory Coast), and cubism.

In 1939 Douglas was hired by Fisk University as chairman and founder of the art department. Until his retirement in 1966, Douglas taught Fisk students while creating art and illustrations for Fisk University. In 1944 Douglas was commissioned to paint *Building More Stately Mansions*, executed for the International Student Center at Fisk University, with references to World War II. The title might appear to be a biblical reference, but, in fact, Douglas stated that he took the title for this piece from *The Chambered Nautilus*, a poem by Oliver Wendell Holmes. He said the title was used to "create a starting point around which pertinent symbols might be collected, in the hope of giving greater illumination to the work."[2]

The panel was meant to represent the progression of cultures and civilizations from the dawn of recorded history to the present. Beginning on the upper left side of the panel, Egyptian civilization, and therefore Africa, is symbolized by a pyramid and a sphinx. The large profile of the sphinx which dominates the upper portion of the panel is a combination of Egyptian elements and the profile of a Dan mask of the Ivory Coast, a typical combination for Douglas. Douglas presents several towering columns, capped by the entablature of a temple, representing classical Greek civilization. On the far right is a triumphal arch, recalling the spirit of Roman civilization. The pagoda-like structure near the center of the composition is intended to symbolize all Asian cultures and civilizations. The cross, spires, and rose windows of the Gothic cathedral in the center of the panel symbolize the cultures of medieval and modern Europe. Lower down on the left side of the panel Douglas placed a skyscraper, which he considered to be America's unique contribution to the architecture of the Western world. The fire and smoke rising from the skyscraper is to remind us of the two world wars as well as the recent Asian confrontations the United States had experienced.

Douglas placed a small log cabin in front of the skyscraper, which he stated symbolized a shield guarding the spirit of liberty and progress for so many generations. The figures in the foreground of the composition show African Americans working in agriculture and construction, science (symbolized by the beaker of fluid and a cog), and industry. Douglas has led us to the final figures by the use of concentric circles of light, highlighting a mother or teacher with two young children and a globe. This was a technique common in Douglas's work, showing his knowledge of cubism and orphism. Shades of mauve and green dominate the composition. All of the figures, including the sphinx, are heavily influenced by Egyptian art. Douglas described his method of creating figures in a 1971 interview:

> The head was in perspective in a profile flat view, the body, shoulders down to the waist turned half way, the legs were done also from the side and the feet were also done in a broad . . . never toward you . . . perspective. I got it from the Egyptians.[3]

Douglas stated that he wished to:

> remind each new generation to look back on, face up to, and learn from the greatness, the weaknesses and failures of our past with the firm assurance that the strength and courage certain to arise from such an honest and dutiful approach to our problems will continue to carry us on to new and higher levels of achievement.[4]

Douglas is showing all people, all civilizations coming together after the ravages of World War II. He places African Americans in a prominent position, dominating the lower half of the composition, and providing a link with the ancient civilizations of Africa, via Egypt. The painting is unusual because it employs his signature style, rather than the more realistic, traditional style he usually reserved for his paintings (including his portraits and landscapes). While much of the symbolism contained in the panel can be found in some of Douglas's earlier illustrations and in his library murals at Fisk, the combination of elements here is unique.

—Amy Kirschke

1. For more information on the life of Aaron Douglas, see Amy Kirschke, *Aaron Douglas: Art, Race and the Harlem Renaissance* (Jackson: University of Mississippi Press, 1995).

2. Aaron Douglas, interview by Jacqueline Fonvielle-Bontemps, "The Life and Work of Aaron Douglas: A Teaching Aid for the Study of Black Art," (master's thesis, Fisk University, 1971), 53–55.

3. Aaron Douglas, interview by L. M. Collins, July 1971, Black Oral Histories, Fisk University Special Collections, Nashville, Tennessee

4. Aaron Douglas, interview by Jacqueline Fonvielle-Bontemps, "The Life and Work of Aaron Douglas: A Teaching Aid for the Study of Black Art," (master's thesis, Fisk University, 1971), 53–55.

76. *Meditation* and *Music*, c. 1925
Opaque watercolor with ink over graphite underdrawing on wove paper
Each image 2½ x 4; 12¹/₁₆ x 9 (sheet)
Collection of Howard University Gallery of Art

77. *Noah's Ark*, 1936
Oil on canvas
48 x 36
Fisk University, Nashville, Tennessee

78. *Rebirth*, c. 1925
Ink and graphite on wove paper
12¹/₁₆ x 9
Collection of Howard University Gallery of Art

79. *Rise Shine for Thy Light has Come*, 1927
Opaque watercolor and black ink on paper board
11¾ x 8¼
Collection of Howard University Gallery of Art

80. *Sahdji*, c. 1925
Ink and graphite on wove paper
12¹/₁₆ x 9
Collection of Howard University Gallery of Art

In the spring of 1925 when Aaron Douglas, living in Kansas City, Missouri, read the "Harlem" issue of *Survey Graphic* edited by Alain Locke, he had no idea that by autumn he would produce many of the illustrations for its conversion into the book *The New Negro*.[1] Douglas could have stayed in Missouri in a secure position teaching high school art, but galvanized by the spirit of the magazine, he decided to leave and move to Harlem, arriving in early summer. Within weeks, he met two men vital to his development as an artist: Winold Reiss, the German-born artist and designer who had been commissioned by Locke to create drawings for the *Survey Graphic* and Locke himself who requested Douglas's work for *The New Negro*.[2]

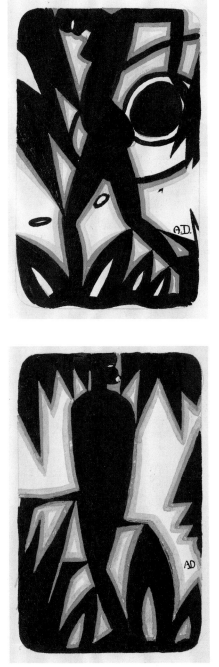

82

80

78

Soon after arriving, Douglas arranged to study with Reiss and, like any student's exposure to a more mature artist, his first efforts share similarities with his teacher. As one of the first visual artists of the Harlem Renaissance, a movement dominated by writers, Douglas was immediately and frequently called upon to illustrate books and magazines. He quickly needed to forge a style commensurate with the innovations of the New Negro movement. The drawings included in this exhibition are a window into the transformation of his style.

Reiss's own work offered exposure to French and German modernists, although Douglas certainly could have known their work from literature read while still in the Midwest. But Douglas explored directly a source that had inspired these movements—the sculpture of Africa. Again, he could have read articles on African art in the May 1924 *Opportunity* while still in Kansas City. Living in New York, he could have seen Picasso and other contemporary artists in galleries and African art at the Brooklyn Museum and the American Museum of Natural History.

In the 1920s blacks began to add West and Central Africa to the prevailing nineteenth-century idea that identified "Africa" primarily with Egypt and Ethiopia. It is the inclusion of Egyptian influences in their art that, among other things, distinguishes New Negro modernism. For European artists, African sculpture offered models for a reconfiguration of the body as a means of rejecting academic realism. For Douglas, African and Egyptian art possessed the diametrically different function of models for recuperating the integrity of the black body after the depredations of caricature and stereotype. Other artists such as James Lesesne Wells also looked to regions across the breadth of the continent for inspiration. (See checklist nos. 250 and 253.)

*Sahdji* and *Rebirth* reveal this confluence of West and Central African with Egyptian motifs. In the former, the pyramidal shapes and the three dancing women have direct Egyptian precedents in architecture and wall-painting. In the latter, two masks appear in the lower-right quadrant and the many oval shapes suggest the shields that were then ubiquitous in African collections. The kneeling figure in the lower left conforms to the Egyptian canon of proportion with his profile head, frontal torso, and profile legs.[3] Yet even here Douglas has mixed several aesthetic languages. The eye is not frontal, as would be expected in Egyptian art, but also in

profile. In the center of *Sahdji* stands a female figure in a twisting pose that gives the illusion of three-dimensionality, the product of a Western drawing technique.

One element of these drawings is unsettling—the use of the white lips common to the vocabulary of minstrelsy. Douglas's use of this stereotype may reveal one of the major premises of art history, that artists seeking new forms begin with a known image that is eventually transformed into a new pattern. In seeking a modernist, that is, non-naturalistic mode of representing the body, Douglas consciously or unconsciously used the existing convention of black-face, which in 1925 was still being worn by black performers on Broadway. If these drawings were the first that Douglas created to illustrate *The New Negro*, within a few weeks he had rejected this formulaic way of presenting black facial features. Included towards the middle of the anthology are two illustrations that do not employ this physiognomy. They reveal Douglas to be well on the way toward the sophisticated, uplifting style for which he is best known, represented by *Noah's Ark* and *Building More Stately Mansions*.

—Helen M. Shannon

1. *Survey Graphic* 53 (1 March 1925); Alain Locke, ed., *The New Negro: An Interpretation* (New York: Boni and Liveright, Inc., 1925); revised as *The New Negro*, edited by Alain Locke with an introduction by Arnold Rampersad (New York: Atheneum, 1992).

2. For a biography of the artist, see Amy Kirschke, *Aaron Douglas: Art, Race and the Harlem Renaissance* (Jackson: University of Mississippi Press, 1995).

3. Douglas discusses his use of Egyptian motifs in "Aaron Douglas Chats about the Harlem Renaissance," in David Levering Lewis, ed., *The Portable Harlem Renaissance Reader* (New York: Viking Penguin, 1994), p. 123.

81. *Still Life*, n.d.
Watercolor and graphite on laid paper
18⅝ x 20⅝
Fisk University, Nashville, Tennessee

82. *The Sun-God* and *Poet*, c. 1925
Opaque watercolor with ink over graphite underdrawing on wove paper
Each image 2½ x 4; 9 x 12¹/₁₆ (sheet)
Collection of Howard University Gallery of Art

# Arthur G. Dove

**(1880–1946)**

**Painter**

A first-generation modernist and pioneer in abstract art, his form was derived from nature and linked him to both earlier and later artists. He was a protégé of Alfred Stieglitz and the first American artist to develop a consistent non-representational style. He was determined to remain close to nature and the origins of his abstract forms in landscapes and plants can often be glimpsed.

83. *Moon*, 1928
Oil on board
8 x 10
The Alfred Stieglitz Collection, Fisk University, Nashville, Tennessee, gift of Georgia O'Keeffe

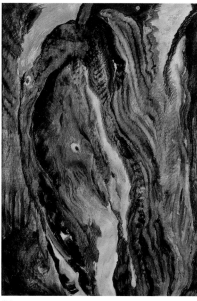

84

84. *Something Brown, Carmine, and Blue*, 1929
Oil on metal
27¾ x 19⅝
The Alfred Stieglitz Collection, Fisk University, Nashville, Tennessee, gift of Georgia O'Keeffe

85. *Swinging in the Park (there were colored people there)*, 1930
Oil on board
23¾ x 32¾
The Alfred Stieglitz Collection, Fisk University, Nashville, Tennessee, gift of Georgia O'Keeffe

86. *Yellow, Blue, and Violet*, 1928
Oil on canvas
22⅛ x 17⅞
The Alfred Stieglitz Collection, Fisk University, Nashville, Tennessee, gift of Georgia O'Keeffe

As one of the American modernists championed by Alfred Stieglitz, Arthur G. Dove occupies a secure position among the small band of innovators who pioneered abstract painting in this country prior to World War I. Indeed, it has been argued that Dove was among the earliest Western painters to create pure abstractions,[1] although he preferred to describe his process of developing nature-derived imagery as "extraction."

Dove's papers, preserved in the Smithsonian Institution's Archives of American Art, contain many theoretical statements—often transcribed by his wife and fellow painter Helen Torr—as well as correspondence and technical notes that shed light on his creative method. Several consistent threads run through this documentation, and one of the strongest is Dove's conviction that art must be more than either the transcription of observed phenomena or the invention of non-associative forms. To Dove, art's purpose was to express subjective responses to sensory stimuli, or as he put it, "the presenting of the thing felt. That is not using nature as a model glancing back and forth."[2]

Like the abstract expressionists who followed him, Dove viewed creativity as a direct, unmediated process and believed it was crucial for his images to function independently of their sources. Although he consistently relied on external stimuli—both tangible, like landscape elements, buildings or animals, and intangible, like sounds and physical sensations—he maintained that those sources did not translate into art unless they could be made to transcend their original context. It was Dove's contention that art was required to function as an independent identity. It had to be, in his words, "something that is real in itself, that does not remind anyone of any other thing, and that does not have to be explained."[3]

Notwithstanding such purist notions, Dove's art never entirely severed its connection to external reality. Virtually all of his "extractions" retain evident references to the phenomena that inspired them and bear titles that identify their sources. Sometimes, as in the small oil sketch *Moon* (1928), the reference is both explicit and literally abstract, despite Dove's dislike of the term. The muted, mysterious aura of lunar light, expressed in a generalized atmosphere that conjures the essence of moonglow, exemplifies abstraction in its basic sense, as a distillation of fundamentals.

Dove's larger, more complex composition, *Swinging in the Park (there were colored people there)* (1930), juxtaposes a familiar reference point—the tree—with dynamic lines that suggest the sweeping movement of a swing suspended from its branches. There may be, however, another level of interpretation for this painting, based on Dove's use of intangibles. He often listened to the radio while working, and, therefore, may also have intended his title to refer to the rhythms of swing music, which he analogized in slightly earlier works inspired by George Gershwin and Irving Berlin tunes. As Debra Balken has pointed out, the undulating black lines in those 1927 compositions correspond to "the tempo of a musical score."[4] Thus, *Swinging in the Park* can be seen as a visual double entendre, referring simultaneously to physical movement and rhythmic beat.

In *Yellow, Blue, and Violet* (1928) and *Something in Brown, Carmine, and Blue* (1929), nature provided Dove with what he called "form motives." He collected and assembled these elements in composites that fulfilled his ambition to create entities divorced, or at least estranged, from their origins. His use of the word "something" in one title is revealing, indicating that the artist declined to specify what he pictured. The viewer is forced to make inferences, based on experience or insight, about what the colors and forms suggest.

Often, however, it seems pointless to guess whether Dove is referring to water, rock formations, the texture of tree bark, or the radiance of a back-lighted cloud. Whether nature is invoked directly or essentialized beyond recognition is less germane than the fact that Dove's images transcend their sources and attain the independent status he sought for them.

—Helen A. Harrison

1. For a summary of critical responses to Dove's early work, see Debra Bricker Balken, "Continuities and Digressions in the Work of Arthur Dove from 1907 to 1933," in *Arthur Dove: A Retrospective* (Andover: Addison Gallery of American Art; Cambridge: The MIT Press, 1997), pp. 22–27.

2. Arthur Dove, undated typescript, Arthur Dove and Helen Torr Papers, Archives of American Art, Smithsonian Institution, microfilm reel 4682, frame 80.

3. Arthur G. Dove, statement for "Arthur G. Dove Paintings—1942–43," exhibition checklist, An American Place, New York, 11 February–17 March 1943.

4. Balken, p. 33.

86

87

# David C. Driskell

## (b. 1931)

### Painter

Driskell's work combines abstraction with social considerations and figurative elements. His paintings and prints project African American imagery in colorful imaginative patterns. In addition, his teaching, curatorial, consultant, and gallery director experiences are extensive and varied. In his art and related work he concentrates on the role of black artists in American society and traditional African art as it influences African American art. A Howard University graduate, Driskell has taught in and chaired the art departments at Talladega College, Howard University, Fisk University, and the University of Maryland.

87. *Black Ghetto*, c. 1968–70
Oil on canvas with mixed media
36½ x 25½
Fisk University, Nashville, Tennessee, 1991.2047, gift of the artist

The introduction of found objects into the art created by African American academic painters is mainly an invention borrowed from black folk art. Long before the concept of the assemblage was commonly seen among American artists such as Joseph Cornell and Robert Rauschenberg, black folk artists defied the usual rules of conventional painting by adding objects and curio items they thought befit the subjects they created. I saw many such "assemblages" and "constructions" being made by artists when I was a child growing up in Eatonton, Georgia and later in Appalachia in western North Carolina. My father, Reverend G.W. Driskell, was among those I saw drawing and assembling these special objects, objects that were often nailed to the walls of a barn or smokehouse. But no one thought of these pieces as art, similarly as my grandfather's ancestors in West Africa seldom characterized the visual objects they made for festivals and shrines as art.

In an important way, many of these unusually curious-looking drawings, paintings, and three-dimensional objects have remained with me over the years as memories from a distant past. It is in the context of memory that a number of the works I created in the 1960s, and even today, have been highly informed by my remembrance of growing up in the rural South, more particularly in the Appalachian Mountains. In the 1930s and 1940s, everyone living in these remote parts of the nation had to be self-sufficient in matters pertaining to cultural and economic survival. It was important in those post-Depression years for one to learn to be frugal in all things. We saved everything: the old discarded bedposts, books, magazines, household gadgets, old clothing, and the like. My mother converted the old clothing into strip quilts. In an atmosphere where this kind of cultural rat-packing prevailed, a creative child could have a field day sorting out things, knowing that we were lucky to receive one toy at Christmas.

Many of the compositions I created in the 1960s drew heavily upon my memory of collecting furniture parts, memorabilia, and found objects of curious shapes at an earlier time. *Black Ghetto* is one such work. The composition is an autobiographical reflection of my own childhood, one in which I look out into the larger world from beyond my narrowly confined abode. In the main, the wonders of a youthful life are what drive this motionless gaze. The figure of the young boy is all but hemmed in and orderly, contained by the rectangular format of the painting. Found objects such as a decorative segment of a carved piece of furniture, perhaps a dresser or a night stand, an old book, and a number encasement from a dial telephone are strategically placed throughout the composition. They touch upon the temporal elements of my life, emphasizing the move from the peace and quiet of my rural past, as viewed from within the city, to the black ghetto. In those days, I often painted classical columns in my work as a signature of my own familial lineage, indicating my father's and grandfather's knowledge of the building trade.

*Black Ghetto* also addresses the issue of having to confront life in America along the lines of color and race. By 1968, after the assassination of Dr. Martin Luther King, Jr., and the devastating riots that brought about urban blight to many American cities, African Americans began to revisit the issues of social justice and racism with totally different mindsets. The lingering dream of the Great Society that presidents John F. Kennedy and Lyndon B. Johnson promoted suddenly became a vision without a future. The year 1968 was important in our assessment of the pros and cons of the Vietnam War. That same year, I created a composition entitled *Of Thee I Weep* as a companion work to *Black Ghetto*. Both works were an attempt to respond visually to the uneven gait in life at which Americans of African ancestry pace themselves to avoid being symbolically ghettoized.

—David C. Driskell

# Robert S. Duncanson
## (1821–1872)
### Painter

Duncanson was the first major landscape painter of color and one of the most unique and noteworthy artists of the nineteenth century. His success grew steadily throughout the 1850s and his works were purchased by Cincinnati and Detroit socialites. He was the first black artist to achieve national and international prominence and to exhibit his work with other American artists. Duncanson's lyric romanticism in his landscape work endeared him to collectors and patrons. Despite the lack of formal training, he was very knowledgeable about literary works of that period and inspired by writers.

89

88. *Classical Landscape (Time's Temple)*, 1854
Oil on canvas
34 x 39
Collection of Howard University Gallery of Art

89. *Cottage at Pass Opposite Ben Lomond*, 1866
Oil on canvas
12³⁄8 x 20³⁄8
Collection of North Carolina Central University Art Museum, purchased with funds given by Friends of the Museum, Gordon Hanes, The Mary Duke Biddle Foundation, and Mary Ran

The first African American landscapist to receive national and international acclaim, Robert Scott Duncanson is one of the earliest mid-nineteenth-century artists to enter the North Carolina Central University Art Museum's collection. Essentially self-taught, Duncanson began his career painting landscapes and abolitionist portraits. Noted abolitionists James G. Birney, Lewis Cass, Richard S. Rust, and Nicholas Longworth had their portraits painted by Duncanson.[1] Influenced by the Hudson River School philosophy, Romantic literature, and Ruskinian aesthetic theory, he secured a respected reputation at home and outside the United States.

In 1866 Duncanson painted *Cottage at Pass Opposite Ben Lomond*. That year proved to be a watershed in his life and art. He returned to the United States after touring Canada, Scotland, and England with a new vision that was less grandiose than before. He became known as one of the Ohio River Valley's leading landscape painters as he neared his forty-fifth birthday. *Land of the Lotus Eaters* (1861), a landscape that became the subject of considerable attention, was an immediate popular and critical success. Critics on both sides of the Atlantic applauded Duncanson's achievements. Writing in the *London Art Journal* in 1866, a critic wrote:

> America has long maintained supremacy in landscape art, perhaps its landscape artists surpass those of England. Certainly we have no painter who can equal [Frederic] Church . . . we are not exaggerating if we affirm that the production under notice may compete with any of the modern British School. Duncanson has established high fame in the United States and Canada.[2]

Opening a new studio in Cincinnati, Duncanson joined with other artists in founding the Associated Artists of Cincinnati and participated in several exhibitions to assist in raising funds for the accompanying School of Design.[3] These events coincided with the execution of *Cottage at Pass Opposite Ben Lomond*. His late Scottish paintings, which were an immediate sensation and in great demand, culminated his career. In these works, fantastic landscape had given way to an authentic pastoral vision of nature. Extolling the virtues of rural life had now taken precedence over Romantic allegorically-inspired work. Duncanson embraced landscape as a direct manifestation of God. He now painted what he saw: painting was no longer an exotic exercise in mastering form, color, and pictorial order. This different approach was less dependent on an imagined nirvana.

Painted after Duncanson's return from a tour of the Scottish Highlands in 1866, *Cottage at Pass Opposite Ben Lomond* is derived from sketches made on portable canvases carried during the tour.[4] Duncanson was able to paint convincing depictions of particular places well after he had visited them, as this work attests. The accuracy and profusion of the details of topography are testimony to this capability. A wholly persuasive effect of light and atmosphere is indicative of the maturity evidenced at this juncture. Coming near the end of his life, when his career was at its zenith and his work was motivated by different expressive needs, it showed a conviction and relaxed authority recognized by his peers. The influence of English Romantic authors Alfred Tennyson and Thomas Moore had been seen in earlier works. After reading Sir Walter Scott's *Waverley Novels,* Duncanson's imagination soared.[5] Duncanson produced *Cottage at Pass Opposite Ben Lomond* following a series of larger landscapes inspired by Scott. They depicted a region long sought out for its picturesque, alluring vistas and rich verdure.

A quiet monumentality and reverence for nature helps in promulgating this mythic symbol of mid-nineteenth-century Scotland. Echoing themes represented in larger works, a bucolic scene of a settler's cabin, with cattle and staffage figures nearby, are reminiscent of an American pioneer family living on the fringes of society. Narrative elements are, however, subordinated to the uncultivated, rustic countryside where man appears comfortably at home in the environment. On the far side of a silver-blue lake are several undiscernible figures in front of an expanse of trees, dwarfed by salmon-pink and blue-grey mountains. The central placement of the thatched roof cabin follows a carefully regulated geometric order of diagonals. Its image, carefully reflected in the lake, suggests an increasing interest in literal transcription. In many respects, *Cottage at Pass*

*Opposite Ben Lomond,* with its carefully manipulated light and tranquil presentation of nature as compatible with civilization, reflects a shift in Duncanson's landscape aesthetic. With a measure of respect and recognition in hand, fantastic creative urgency gave way to an increased naturalism. This paralleled a shift in his personal life that longed for official approval and recognition.

—Kenneth G. Rodgers

1. See David C. Driskell, *Hidden Heritage* (Bellevue, Washington: Bellevue Art Museum and The Art Museum Association of America, 1985), pp. 16–17.

2. Cited in Norman E. Pendergraft, *Duncanson: A British American Connection* (Durham: North Carolina University Art Museum, 1984), p. 13.

3. Joseph D. Ketner's exhaustive study of Duncanson indicates that Duncanson was one of the major exhibitors. The goal was to make Cincinnati a mecca for artists by establishing a permanent gallery and art school. See Joseph D. Ketner, *The Emergence of the African-American Artist: Robert S. Duncanson 1821–1872* (Columbia: University of Missouri Press, 1993), p. 157.

4. Ibid., pp. 157–58.

5. Romare Bearden and Harry Henderson, *A History of African American Artists: From 1792 to the Present* (New York: Pantheon Books, 1993), pp. 30–36.

## Minnie Evans
### (1892–1987)
**Painter**

Evans's first drawing was inspired by a dream in 1935. Her work is often called visionary or mystic. This self-taught artist's work is in vivid primary colors, symmetrical in balance, but not in the designs which are filled with eyes, heavenly figures, leaves, birds, animals, flowers, devils, and angels. She created strongly hued, inexplicable dream fantasies incorporating the presence of Caribbean, East Indian, Chinese, and Western ideas. For years her job as attendant at the admission booth of Airlie Gardens (Wilmington, North Carolina) gave her daily contact with botanical specimens.

90. *Jesus Christ,* 1963
Oil, ink, and graphite on paper
16½ x 19¼
Collection of North Carolina Central University Art Museum, gift of Paul and Virginia Clifford

88

# Frederick C. Flemister

## (1917–1976)

**Painter**

Flemister earned a B.A. from Morehouse College in 1939 where he studied under Hale Woodruff. Flemister studied at the John Herron Art Institute before serving in the army and instructing at Atlanta University. Although Flemister's works are eclectic in style, he excelled in portraiture.

91. *Man with a Brush*, 1940
Oil on canvas
26 x 21
Collection of Clark Atlanta University Art Galleries, university purchase

91

When discussing formally trained black artists who lived and worked in the South during the pre-Civil Rights era, Edwin Augustus Harleston and Hale Aspacio Woodruff come to mind. Harleston, a South Carolina artist-teacher who graduated from Atlanta University and rose to prominence as a portrait painter in the 1920s, died suddenly in 1931. This void in Southern aesthetic leadership was filled by Hale Woodruff, who graduated from the John Herron Art Institute and returned from Paris in order to establish an art department in the Atlanta University Center. Students from Spelman and Morehouse Colleges eagerly filled Woodruff's painting and drawing classes. One such student was Frederick C. Flemister.

Flemister entered Morehouse College in 1935 to be a part of the Atlanta University's "regional center for aspiring art students" and to study with Hale Woodruff. In an effort to encourage their creativity, Woodruff formed the Painter's Guild, a group that spent a great deal of time sketching and painting in the run-down neighborhoods near the campus or out in the Georgia countryside.[1] The training that Flemister received as a member of the Painter's Guild and in the art classes and lectures transformed him from a struggling student into a promising artist by the time he graduated in 1939. Woodruff was so confident about Flemister's artistic ability that he secured a scholarship at the John Herron Art Institute for his talented protégée. After graduation in 1941, Flemister returned to Atlanta University to work as an art instructor with his teacher and mentor.[2]

Although the small body of works attributed to Flemister are eclectic in style and wide-ranging in content, he seems to have excelled in the area of portraiture.

Evidence of his skill can be seen in his 1940 self-portrait, *Man with a Brush*. In this smoothly finished mannerist style painting, Flemister presents himself as a sixteenth-century artist who stands before a blank canvas, delicately holding a brush in his left hand. In the background, a partially opened curtain reveals a vast landscape which has been painted in a manner reminiscent of Woodruff's early style. The warm, brown tones used to model the smooth contours of the artist's handsome face convey a feeling of self-confidence. Flemister has replaced the austere, haughty glance seen in a typical mannerist portrait with a calm, inwardly contemplative, yet inviting gaze. In *Man with a Brush*, Flemister has managed to produce the same sophisticated elegance coveted by artists of the sixteenth century.

Flemister's skill as a painter and his unique approach to subject matter captured the attention of the critics. Cedric Dover, author of *American Negro Art*, described Flemister's self-portrait as being one of the most "forceful" works produced in the last twenty-five years.[3] But James A. Porter, a well-known scholar and art historian, was not as generous. In his pioneering art history text, *Modern Negro Art*, Porter described Flemister's work as being extraordinary, "despite [the fact] that he often . . . imitates the forms and textures of bygone styles, and even grossly exaggerates human expression."[4] Although Frederick Flemister's works were criticized and never widely shown, *Man with a Brush* stands out as one of the few works in African American art that successfully integrates techniques and settings from works by old masters with a contemporary subject.

—M. Akua McDaniel, Ph.D.

1. Mary Schmidt Campbell et al., *Hale Woodruff: 50 Years of His Art* (New York: The Studio Museum in Harlem, 1979), p. 19.

2. Harry Polski, ed., *The Negro Almanac: A Reference Work on the Afro-American* (New York: Bellwether, 1976), p. 727.

3. Cedric Dover, *American Negro Art* (New York: New York Graphic Society, 1960), p. 102.

4. James A. Porter, *Modern Negro Art* (New York: Dryden Press, 1943), p. 121.

92

## Allan R. Freelon

**(1895–1960)**

**Painter, printmaker**

Freelon studied at the Pennsylvania Museum School of Industrial Arts, the University of Pennsylvania, and the Tyler School of Art. He later taught art in Philadelphia public schools and became supervisor of the Art Education program. A versatile artist, Freelon was a traditionalist who avoided social commentary. His impressionistic paintings emphasized technique and experimentation.

92. *Number One Broad Street*, n.d.
Aquatint and etching on wove paper
11¹⁵⁄₁₆ x 9¹⁵⁄₁₆ (image); 15³⁄₈ x 11¹³⁄₁₆ (sheet)
Collection of Howard University Gallery of Art

93

## Otis Galbreath

**(1898–1969)**

**Painter**

Little is known about this largely self-taught painter (for a time a chauffeur), whose artistic activities spanned from the 1930s when he first exhibited with the Harmon Foundation in New York until the 1960s when his charming canvases were prominently featured in the Atlanta University Art Annuals.

93. *Let Bygones Be Bygones*, 1964
Oil on cardboard
15¼ x 18¼
First Award in Oil Painting, Atlanta University Art Annual, 1964. Collection of Clark Atlanta University Art Galleries

94

## Sam Gilliam

**(b. 1933)**

**Painter**

Educated at the University of Louisville and Northwestern University, Gilliam, a color-field painter, rose to prominence with his "drape paintings" in the 1960s. In the 1970s his artistic emphasis focused on geometric collages and his technique changed to impasto of acrylic paint layers. His visual surfaces and colliding colors and shapes recall the vitality and spontaneity of jazz. Gilliam is frequently associated with the Washington Color School.

94. *Untitled*, c. 1970
Acrylic on draped canvas
116 x 276
Collection of Clark Atlanta University Art Galleries, gift of the artist

*The Surface is no longer the final plane of the work. It is instead the beginning of an advance into the theater of life.*[1]

Sam Gilliam's monumental draped paintings of the late 1960s marked a radical formal break with the flat surface that had for centuries characterized painting in the Western tradition. Straddling the boundaries between painting and sculpture, Gilliam's works were embraced enthusiastically by critics and artists who held that art should evolve toward greater formal purity characterized by innovative breaks with the past. To the extent Gilliam's graceful draped paintings were three-dimensional and their arrangement was site dependent, they added to discussions, particularly those concerning sculpture, of the importance of the "process" of art-making being reflected in its product.[2] With this truly new work, Gilliam became not only an internationally acclaimed painter but was recognized as a legitimate heir to the tradition of Washington Color School painters Kenneth Noland and Morris Louis, whose styles greatly influenced Gilliam.

When Sam Gilliam arrived in Washington, D.C., in 1962, his painting was characterized by the abstracted figural style practiced by his teachers at the University of Louisville (Kentucky), and by California artist Nathan Oliveira.[3] He did not seek out the established center of African American artists and art criticism at Howard University nor the Washington Color School painters who would influence him later.[4] Although never organized as a "school" in the art historical sense and despite great differences in their work, the Washington Color School artists nevertheless made art that was nonobjective, self-referential, and which derived its meaning from a viewer's sensory responses (elicited primarily through the use of color) rather than from symbolic representation.[5] After exhibitions at the local Adams-Morgan Gallery where Gilliam met Howard Mehring and Paul Reed, and had discussions with other Washington Color School artists such as Thomas Downing, Gilliam quickly abandoned figurative art for a nonobjective style that he has practiced since that time. Gilliam's most important exhibition, "Gilliam-Krebs-McGowin," was held in 1969 at what is now the Corcoran Gallery of Art. The artist installed eight monumental draped canvases in the gallery's atrium that were hung specifically to create a formal interplay with the interior architecture. Gilliam's exploitation of

95

96

the environment in which his work was displayed built upon the Washington Color School concept of de-emphasizing a painting's framing edge, therefore allowing the boundary between pictorial space and the surrounding space to be blurred.[6]

*Untitled* is an example of Gilliam's distinctive style of draped painting and was created during the critical period in the late 1960s and early 1970s that marked the artist's early career. When Gilliam was invited to the Atlanta College of Art as a visiting artist in the early 1970s, he created *Untitled* as a demonstration piece. Executed in the manner established in the 1950s by the abstract expressionist Jackson Pollock, *Untitled* began as an unstretched canvas placed on the floor. Gilliam moved around it, carefully pouring, dripping, and splattering the paint in contrasting, high-keyed colors over the entire canvas.[7] The artist then folded his canvas allowing the paint to run and pool in ways that form the somewhat linear horizontal pattern visible in the finished work.

While each draped work is installed differently in each exhibition space, there is a finite number of possible patterns of display[8] in which the fabric is alternately suspended from the ceiling, gathered together, or crumpled on the floor. The apparent flexibility of the canvas allows the viewer to draw a metaphorical parallel between the "liquid" paint on the canvas and the "fluidity" of the hung work.[9] Gilliam typically installs draped works himself in order to highlight movement and dynamism and the tension created by contrasts, among other things. The bands of color in *Untitled*, for example, cut horizontally across the curvilinear shape the fabric takes when suspended. Contrasts between different colors, between painted patterns and draped form, between art object and architectural environment, underscore the tension between order and chaos and between man-made objects and natural environments.

Sam Gilliam's position as one of the most influential African American artists, his national and international acclaim, and the quality of his work did not leave him immune to controversy. It is precisely the lack of content in his work that made Gilliam and other African American artists who worked in a nonobjective style the object of criticism among some artists even as the mainstream art world embraced Gilliam. As the integrationist ideals of the Civil Rights movement of the sixties gave way to more confrontational approaches to attack racism, some artists, such as those in the black arts movement, advocated the creation of figurative and explicitly race-conscious art. Nonobjective art produced by Sam Gilliam was associated with an elitist and racist white art establishment. Without subject matter, not to mention political content, Gilliam's work was deemed by some black artists as "irrelevant" to African American lives. Gilliam felt such criticism was motivated by conservatism and that artistic style should not be determined by racial identity.[10] As Richard Powell pointed out:

> Gilliam's abstractions articulated the emotional and cerebral musings of an intelligentsia, black and white, as they rebelled against politically prescribed and aesthetically bound art conventions. . . . Gilliam sought a redefinition of blackness that . . . was more evocative than a painted black figure or a cultural slogan.[11]

—David C. Hart

1. Sam Gilliam and Annie Gawlak, "Solids and Veils," *Art Journal* 50 (spring 1991): 10.

2. Jane Addams Allen, "Letting Go," *Art in America* 74 (January 1986): 99.

3. Walter Hopps and Nina Felshin Osnos, "Three Washington Artists: Gilliam, Krebs, McGowin," *Art International* 14 (May 1970): 32.

4. Keith Morrison, *Art in Washington and Its Afro-American Presence: 1940–1970* (Washington, D.C.: Washington Project for the Arts, 1985), p. 53.

5. The term "Washington Color School" is derived from the term "Washington Color Painters" which was first used in 1965 by the Washington Gallery of Modern Art Director Gerald Nordland in his catalogue essay for a traveling exhibition including works by Noland and Louis as well as Thomas Downing, Howard Mehring, Gene Davis, and Paul Reed. LeGrace G. Benson, "The Washington Scene: Some Preliminary Notes on the Evolution of Art in Washington, D.C.," *Art International* 13 (December 1969): 36.

6. Hopps and Osnos, p. 32.

7. Sam Gilliam, interview by David C. Hart, Washington, D.C., 10 July 1998.

8. Hopps and Osnos, p. 34.

9. Gilliam and Gawlak, p. 10.

10. Richard J. Powell, *Black Art and Culture in the 20th Century* (New York and London: Thames and Hudson, 1997), p. 129.

11. Idem

99

## Margaret Taylor Goss-Burroughs

**(b. 1917)**

**Painter, sculptor, author, illustrator**

Goss-Burroughs's formal education took place at Chicago State University, the Art Institute of Chicago, and the Institute of Painting and Sculpture in Mexico. A teacher and organizer, Goss-Burroughs's monument is the DuSable Museum (Chicago) which she founded. Travel and social commentary influenced her figurative work. An accomplished artist, she writes and illustrates children's books that focus on black history and black cultural affirmation.

95. *Friends*, 1942
Lithograph on paper
16 x 9¾
Third Award in Prints, Atlanta University Art Annuals, 1945. Collection of Clark Atlanta University Art Galleries

## George Grosz

**(1893–1959)**

**Painter, caricaturist**

A German-born expressionist painter and graphic artist who immigrated to the United States in 1932, Grosz's first works were caricatures satirizing Germany during and after World War I. He was a founding member of the Berlin Dada group and involved with the Neue Sachlichkeit movement. His art matured under influences of the French graphic tradition and his powerful style of drawing and painting incorporated expressionism and futurism. He returned to Germany after twenty-five years in the United States.

96. *Street Scene*, c. 1933
Watercolor on paper
25⅞ x 18⅝
The Alfred Stieglitz Collection, Fisk University, Nashville, Tennessee, gift of Georgia O'Keeffe

101

## William Harper

**(1873–1910)**

**Painter**

Harper was a transitional figure whose brief life only suggested his potential as a practitioner of evolving French modernist styles. One of the truly significant painters of the late nineteenth-century, this Canadian-born landscape artist studied at the Art Institute of Chicago and apprenticed with Henry O. Tanner in Paris. He was influenced by the Barbizon School of naturalistic painters and his impressionistic style highlighted his outstanding technical skills.

100

97. *Landscape*, c. 1906
Oil on canvas
36⅛ x 36⅛
Collection of Tuskegee University

## Oliver "Ollie" Wendell Harrington

**(1913–1995)**

**Cartoonist, painter, illustrator**

Harrington began his career as a cartoonist during a time when few blacks were entering the profession. A graduate of Yale University, he continued his studies at the National Academy of Design, and later joined the ranks of influential black journalists and expatriates living in France and Germany. A pioneering cartoonist, he is best known for his social commentary cartoons and his cartoon character *Bootsie*, created in the 1930s.

98. *Senator Bilbo Publicity*, c. 1947
Ink with graphite underdrawing on illustration board
11⅛ x 18⅞
Collection of Howard University Gallery of Art

99. *Street Klansman*, c. 1947
Ink with graphite underdrawing on illustration board
9⅛ x 17⅛
Collection of Howard University Gallery of Art

## Marsden Hartley

**(1877–1943)**

**Painter**

Associated with the earliest modern art movement in New York City, Hartley was inspired by Alfred Stieglitz to create his own diverse style—a mixture of European expressionism and his personal interpretations of life and landscape of the northeastern American seaboard. His landscapes reveal intense feelings for nature and evoke a spiritual beauty. He is best remembered for paintings of his native Maine. Extensive travel to Mexico, the West Indies, Germany, and France, influenced many of his paintings.

106

107

109

100. *Movement #6, Provincetown*, 1916
Oil on composition board
20 x 16
The Alfred Stieglitz Collection, Fisk
University, Nashville, Tennessee, gift
of Georgia O'Keeffe

101. *Movement #7, Provincetown*, 1916
Oil on canvas
24 x 20
The Alfred Stieglitz Collection, Fisk
University, Nashville, Tennessee, gift
of Georgia O'Keeffe

102. *New Mexico Landscape*, 1919
Pastel on paper
17¹⁄₈ x 27⁷⁄₈
The Alfred Stieglitz Collection, Fisk
University, Nashville, Tennessee, gift of
Georgia O'Keeffe

103. *New Mexico No. 2*, 1919
Oil on canvas
28 x 36
The Alfred Stieglitz Collection, Fisk
University, Nashville, Tennessee, gift of
Georgia O'Keeffe

104. *Painting #3*, 1913
Oil on canvas
39¹⁄₂ x 32
The Alfred Stieglitz Collection, Fisk
University, Nashville, Tennessee, gift of
Georgia O'Keeffe

## William M. Hayden
### (b. 1916)
**Painter**
William M. Hayden was one of several,
artistically talented Morehouse College
undergraduates who worked closely with
artist Hale Woodruff at Atlanta University
in the 1930s. A teacher for many years in
the Detroit public school system, Hayden
showed his expressive figure paintings in
various museums and galleries at mid-
century, from the Butler Museum of Art
to the Atlanta University Art Annuals.

105. *Saturday Night Function*, c. 1950
Oil on canvas
36 x 48
Second Award in Oil Painting, Atlanta
University Art Annuals, 1950. Collection
of Clark Atlanta University Art Galleries

## Barkley L. Hendricks
### (b. 1945)
**Painter, photographer**
Although Hendricks's early works were in
watercolor, he is best known for his solitary
figures of familiar black life, detailed to
their shoes and sunglasses and realistically
poised to stride away from the canvases.
With a certificate from the Pennsylvania
Academy of the Fine Arts and a M.F.A.
from Yale University, Hendricks has explored and extended his creative talent to
various mediums and materials employing
humor and social documentation.

106. *Dixwell*, 1971
Acrylic on canvas
13 x 16
Collection of North Carolina Central
University Art Museum, gift of Mr. and
Mrs. Clyde de Loache Ryals

## John K. Hillers
### (1843–1925)
**Photographer**
Hillers is best known as the survey photographer for Major John Wesley Powell's
1871–73 survey of the Colorado River. He
worked for the United States Geological
Survey until 1919. Utah's Mt. Hillers is
named for him. He is also known for his
images of southwestern landscapes and
Native Americans.

107. *Big Navajo*, 1879
Albumen print
9 x 7 /14 (sheet); 14 x 11 (mount)
Collection of Hampton University
Museum, 00.4148A

108. *Hibipa Navajo*, c. 1879
Albumen print
12¹⁄₄ x 9¹⁄₂ (image/sheet);
17³⁄₄ x 14¹⁄₂ (mount)
Collection of Hampton University
Museum, 00.4146A

109. *The Ancient Navajo*, 1879
Albumen print
9 x 7 (sheet); 14 x 11 (mount)
Collection of Hampton University
Museum, 00.4145

## Felrath Hines
### (1913–1993)
**Painter, conservator**
Hines's hard-edged geometric paintings
are noted for radiant color and subtle com-
positions. He studied at the Art Institute of
Chicago (1943) and became absorbed in

112

styles such as cubism and abstract expression. In 1972 he was appointed chief conservator for the Hirshhorn Museum and Sculpture Garden, Washington, D.C. An original member of the Spiral Group, he saw himself as an artist who was black, but whose work was outside the context of race. He is responsible for conserving major works of art by black artists as well as by other important American artists.

110. *Facade II*, 1988
Oil on canvas
66½ x 48¾
Collection of Howard University Gallery of Art

## Humbert Howard
### (1906–1990)
**Painter**

Howard's beautifully patterned interpretations of exceptional clarity, force, and elegance are an evolution of personal discovery. Sometimes referred to as "dean of Philadelphia's black artists," he studied fine arts at Howard University under the tutelage of James A. Porter and later transferred to the University of Pennsylvania. Howard regularly participated in the Pennsylvania Academy of Fine Arts Annual Exhibition and exhibited at the Philadelphia Art Alliance.

111. *Portrait of My Wife*, 1950
Oil on canvas
32 x 24¼
Collection of Howard University Gallery of Art

## Clementine Hunter
### (c. 1886–1988)
**Painter**

Hunter first came to public attention with her exhibition of paintings at major galleries and museums in the 1950s when she was in her late sixties. A self-taught artist, Hunter's paintings encompass black life on Melrose Plantation in northern Louisiana. Subjects for her paintings include harvests, weddings, baptisms, funerals, and religious scenes. She worked almost exclusively in oil on cardboard and canvas panels with pure, bright colors.

112. *Crucifixion*, 1965
Oil on canvas
15½ x 8
Collection of North Carolina Central University Art Museum, gift of Mr. Starke Dillard

114

117

## Leonard C. Hyman
### (active 1900s–1930s)
**Photographer**

Hyman moved to Tuskegee from Washington, D.C., where he operated a portrait studio. He was a member of the Tuskegee faculty from 1927–32.

113. *Class in Manuel* [sic] *Training*, c. 1930
Gelatin silver print
8 x 10
Collection of Tuskegee University

114. *Shoemaking Division, Mr. Frank West in charge*, c. 1930
Gelatin silver print
7 x 9 (image); 8 x 10 (sheet)
Collection of Tuskegee University

115. *Untitled (man with cabbage)*, c. 1930
Gelatin silver print
10 x 8
Collection of Tuskegee University

## Wilmer Angier Jennings
### (1910–1990)
**Painter, printmaker, jeweler**

A 1931 graduate of Morehouse College and student of Hale Woodruff, Jennings studied at the Rhode Island School of Design and was a WPA muralist. Best known for his black-and-white prints, Jennings was an innovator who created his own carving tools and incorporated black themes and scenes in his art work. A natural storyteller, he used humor and social commentary in his art which included wood engravings and linocuts. His compositional placement invoked his interest and training in jewelry design (head designer at the Imperial Pearl Company until his death). His paintings varied from portraiture to abstractions.

116. *Hill Top House*, 1939
Wood engraving on thin wove paper
7⁹⁄₁₆ x 7¹⁵⁄₁₆ (image); 9½ x 9¾ (sheet)
Collection of Howard University Gallery of Art

117. *Still Life—#71*, 1937
Wood engraving on light-weight Japanese paper
9⁷⁄₈ x 8 (image); 14⅛ x 10³⁄₁₆ (sheet)
Collection of Howard University Gallery of Art

118. *Truck Farm*, 1938
Woodcut on thin wove paper
8⅝ x 10½ (image); 11 x 15¾ (sheet); Fisk University, Nashville, Tennessee, gift of the Harmon Foundation

# Malvin Gray Johnson
## (1896–1934)
### Painter

Educated at the National Academy of
Design, New York, and employed as a
commercial artist, Johnson found inspiration in Negro spiritual themes and
Harlem life. In addition to his genre paintings, Johnson also pursued abstraction
and African-emboldened cubism.

119. *Harmony*, c. 1934
Oil on canvas
24 x 30
Fisk University, Nashville, Tennessee,
gift of the Harmon Foundation

119

Since the nineteenth century, black musicians and dancers have been oft-chosen
subjects in American visual culture. While
many of these images were made to dis-
parage and ridicule, other representations
of black performance commemorate their
subject. *Harmony* is a provocative contribution to the latter category.

Born in Greensboro, North Carolina,
Johnson migrated to New York City to
enroll in the prestigious School of the
National Academy of Design (NAD) in
1916. His art education was interrupted by
service in World War I, but he returned to
the NAD during the twenties. Art did not
afford him reliable means of support, and
yet, it was his lifelong passion. In a biographical statement of 1933, he declared:
"My aim is to paint, and paint well, using
Negro subject matter mostly."[1] When
Johnson died suddenly in late 1934, the
*New York Times* critic Howard Devree
wrote: "His death is a distinct loss to his
race and to American art."[2]

Best known for his iconic portraits
such as *Meditation* (1930) and *Postman*
(1934), Johnson had more than a passing
interest in the theme of music. From 1928
to 1931, he produced a series of ten oil
paintings and one watercolor interpreting
Negro spirituals. His *Swing Low, Sweet
Chariot* (1928) won the top prize at the
Harmon Foundation's exhibition of Negro
artists's work in 1929. That same year, *Art
Digest* reproduced this altarpiece-like painting on its front page and compared it to
"the masterworks of Albert P. Ryder."[3]
Later, Johnson's *Roll, Jordan, Roll* (1930)
brought praise from influential art historians Alain Locke and James A. Porter.
Locke believed this elegantly concise painting marked a breakthrough for Johnson,
and Porter later selected it as the cover
illustration for his seminal publication,
*Modern Negro Art*.

*Harmony* stands out in Johnson's oeuvre. Its brash hues are not typical of the
artist's chosen palette for oil paintings,
often dominated by lush, dark shades. In
*Harmony*, as in most of Johnson's production, analogous color relationships significantly unify the picture. The velvety red
and the cool grays and blues that describe
the trio's costumes also define the framing
stage environment.

Johnson's goal was not to make a
painting that resembled "life," but rather
to exaggerate color and form for expressive
and decorative effects. Like *Marching Elks*
(c. 1931–33) and *Platform Dance* (1934),
*Harmony* interprets musical performance
as figural abstraction. The banjo-playing
men are dramatically simplified bodies
whose distinctive characteristic is angular-
ity. Their sloped shoulders, bent elbows
and knees, and the negative spaces created
by their gestures rhyme with angles elsewhere in the composition. Overall, these
figures are multiplied, serialized, and generalized into a pattern as uniform as the
floor planks beneath their feet.

*Harmony* is clear evidence of Johnson's
willingness to treat all pictorial elements
democratically. In doing so, he tested the
limits of realism and naturalism. Modernist modes—especially, cubism, expressionism, and abstraction—generally veered
toward distortion, exaggeration, or abbrev-
iation of human figures and space, and
these artistic strategies aroused the ire
and suspicion of the period's art critics
and audiences. Furthermore, as a formally
trained painter, Johnson was not interested
in discarding all Western standards of
figural representation in favor of radical,
non-objective art. Instead, he experimented cautiously to fashion an original,
stylistic compromise.

*Harmony* presents a challenge to easy
interpretation. The faces of its principals
are denuded and mask-like, and their
audience an unpictured mystery. However
culturally symbolic its subject matter,
this painting's ambiguities are deliberate,
arguably meant to subvert racial stereotype, and disturb romantic and nostalgic
readings of black musical performance.

—Jacqueline Francis

1. Malvin Gray Johnson, "Biographical Data,"
Harmon Foundation form, 19 January 1933, in
Johnson folder, Harmon Foundation Papers, box
76 (Washington, D.C.: Library of Congress).

2. H.D. [Howard Devree], "Five Diverse Talents,"
*New York Times*, 25 April 1935, p. 17.

3. *Art Digest* 3 (mid-January 1929): 5.

# William Henry Johnson
## (1901–1970)
### Painter

Considered to be one of the most important artists of his generation, Johnson lived and worked in the United States, Europe, and North Africa and the subject matter and style of his paintings were as wide ranging as his wanderings—from naive to academic, utilizing impressionism, Fauvism, expressionism, and cubism. He studied at the National Academy of Design, the Cape Cod School of Design, and independently in Europe. Before mental deterioration claimed him, he was a prolific favorite of the Harmon Foundation. After 1945 he was best known for his colorful portrayals of the everyday lives of African Americans in a simplified expressionistic manner.

120. *Booker T. Washington Legend,*
c. 1942–43
Gouache, pen and ink on medium-weight wove paper
20 x 16½
Fisk University, Nashville, Tennessee, gift of the Harmon Foundation.

121. *Doug,* 1930
Oil on canvas
28 x 20
Collection of Howard University Gallery of Art

122. *Evening,* c. 1941
Relief print on medium-weight wove paper
17⅞ x 13⅞
Collection of Hampton University Museum, 67.44.29, gift of the Harmon Foundation

123. *Folk Couple,* c. 1941
Opaque watercolor on paper
18¼ x 16¾
Collection of Hampton University Museum, 68.1.9, gift of the Harmon Foundation

124. *"Lame Man,"* c. 1941
Linocut on medium-weight wove paper
19 x 13½
Collection of Hampton University Museum, 67.44.28, gift of the Harmon Foundation

125. *London Bridge,* 1941
Opaque watercolor with pen and ink on wove paper
11¾ x 12⁷⁄₁₆
Collection of Tuskegee University

126. *Mom Alice,* c. 1944
Oil on cardboard
25 x 31
Collection of Howard University Gallery of Art

127. *Quintet,* c. 1941
Opaque watercolor with pen and ink on wove paper
14¹⁄₁₆ x 16 (image); 15⁷⁄₈ x 18 (sheet)
Collection of Howard University Gallery of Art

128. *"Sitting Model,"* c. 1941
Linocut on medium-weight wove paper with graphite sketch on verso
18¾ x 12½
Collection of Hampton University Museum, 67.44.26, gift of the Harmon Foundation

129. *Spring Blossom,* c. 1937
Oil on canvas
28 x 31
Collection of Tuskegee University

130. *String Band/Street Musicians,* c. 1940
Opaque watercolor, pen, and ink on paper
17½ x 14
Collection of Hampton University Museum, 68.14.1, gift of the Harmon Foundation

131. *Three Generations,* c. 1941
Opaque watercolor with pen and ink on medium-weight wove paper with ink and graphite drawing on verso
14⅛ x 17¹³⁄₁₆
Collection of Howard University Gallery of Art

132. *Untitled (farm couple at work),* c. 1941
Oil on plywood
34 x 37¼
Collection of Tuskegee University

133. *Untitled (seated man),* c. 1939–40
Oil on panel
30 x 25½
Collection of Hampton University Museum, 63.188, gift of the Harmon Foundation

134. *Woman in Blue/Ida,* c. 1939
Oil on burlap
32 x 24¼
Collection of Clark Atlanta University Art Galleries

130

131

# Frances Benjamin Johnston
## (1864–1952)
### Photographer

Johnston, the first female press photographer, was given her first camera by family friend George Eastman. She opened a successful studio in Washington, D.C., in 1890 and photographed much of official D.C. She was considered the unofficial White House photographer, having taken the portraits of Presidents Cleveland through Taft. Her series of photographs on Hampton Institute is considered one of the best examples of her pre-World War I work. Johnston also worked at Tuskegee Institute.

135. *The Hampton Albums: Agriculture. Plant Life. Study of plants or a "plant society,"* 1899–1900
Platinum print
7½ x 9⅜ (image); 9½ x 11½ (sheet)
Collection of Hampton University Archives

136. *The Hampton Albums: Arithmetic. Measuring and pacing,* 1899–1900
Platinum print
7½ x 9⅜ (image); 9½ x 11½ (sheet)
Collection of Hampton University Archives

137. *The Hampton Albums: Class in American History,* 1899–1900
Platinum print
7½ x 9⅜ (image); 9½ x 11½ (sheet)
Collection of Hampton University Archives

138. *The Hampton Albums: Class Studying South Africa,* 1899–1900
Platinum print
7½ x 9⅜ (image); 9½ x 11½ (sheet)
Collection of Hampton University Archives

139. *The Hampton Albums: Drawing. Simple work from the object,* 1899–1900
Platinum print
7½ x 9⅜ (image); 9½ x 11½ (sheet)
Collection of Hampton University Archives

140. *The Hampton Albums: Football-Team,* 1899–1900
Platinum print
7½ x 9⅜ (image); 9½ x 11½ (sheet)
Collection of Hampton University Archives

141. *The Hampton Albums: Geography. Studying the Cathedral towns,* 1899–1900
Platinum print
7½ x 9⅜ (image); 9½ x 11½ (sheet)
Collection of Hampton University Archives

142. *The Hampton Albums: Geography. Studying the Seasons,* 1899–1900
Platinum print
7½ x 9⅜ (image); 9½ x 11½ (sheet)
Collection of Hampton University Archives

143. *The Hampton Albums: History. Class in ancient history. Seniors,* 1899–1900
Platinum print
7½ x 9⅜ (image); 9½ x 11½ (sheet)
Collection of Hampton University Archives

144. *The Hampton Albums: Indian Orchestra,* 1899–1900
Platinum print
7½ x 9⅜ (image); 9½ x 11½ (sheet)
Collection of Hampton University Archives

145. *The Hampton Albums: Physics. Estimating the combined draught of horses,* 1899–1900
Platinum print
7½ x 9⅜ (image); 9½ x 11½ (sheet)
Collection of Hampton University Archives

146. *The Hampton Albums: Physics. The Screw as applied to the cheese press,* 1899–1900
Platinum print
7½ x 9⅜ (image); 9½ x 11½ (sheet)
Collection of Hampton University Archives

147. *The Hampton Albums: Stairway of Treasurer's Residence. Students at work,* 1899–1900
Platinum print
7½ x 9⅜ (image); 9½ x 11½ (sheet)
Collection of Hampton University Archives

148. *The Hampton Albums: Trade School. Plastering,* 1899–1900
Platinum print
7½ x 9⅜ (image); 9½ x 11½ (sheet)
Collection of Hampton University Archives

149. *The Hampton Albums: Watercolor. Studying the butterfly,* 1899–1900
Platinum print
7½ x 9⅜ (image); 9½ x 11½ (sheet)
Collection of Hampton University Archives

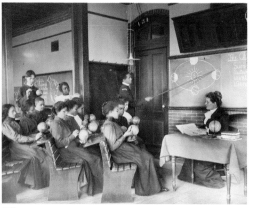

142

Well-educated, strong-willed, and skillful, photographer Frances Benjamin Johnston enjoyed a distinguished career in social documentary and architectural photography, as well as in portraiture. She began her studies at the Nôtre Dame Convent in Govanston, Maryland, then went on to study art both at home and abroad. Johnston completed her artistic training in an apprenticeship with Professor Thomas William Smillie in the Smithsonian Institution's Division of Photography and in 1890 she opened her first professional studio.[1]

From the onset of her career, Johnston capitalized on her technical skills and social connections. She accepted commissions from periodicals to create documentary photographs of the workplace, the first woman to do so, and began photographing Washington dignitaries. Over the years, Johnston's clients included Presidents Harrison, Cleveland, McKinley, Theodore Roosevelt, and Taft as well as numerous senators, cabinet members, and luminaries such as John Philip Sousa, Susan B. Anthony, Booker T. Washington, and Mark Twain. These commissions earned Johnston a reputation as the "photographer of the American court."[2]

In 1909 Johnston undertook her first architectural commission and in 1913 she joined fellow photographer Mattie Edwards Hewitt in opening a business devoted to architecture and interior décor photography. Johnston enjoyed considerable success in this venture as well, working for such renowned architects as Cass Gilbert and McKim, Mead & White. She later catalogued much of the South's beautiful colonial and federal architecture, an undertaking which led to her 1945 appointment as an honorary member of the American Institute of Architects.

Johnston is perhaps best known for a body of photographs collectively known as *The Hampton Albums.* Shot in 1899 and rediscovered by the art world in the 1940s, these images chronicle the educational life of the Hampton Normal and Agricultural Institute, a school founded after the Civil War for the education of freed Negroes. The photographs, platinum prints, are grouped in three albums: two in the holdings of the Hampton University Archives and a third in the holdings of The Museum of Modern Art in New York.[3]

In the waning months of 1899, Dr. Hollis B. Frissell, principal of Hampton Institute, and Thomas J. Calloway, director of the Negro Educational Exhibit for the

Paris Exposition Commission, began collaborations on an exhibit for the Paris Universal Exposition of 1900. The exposition marked the onset of a new century and, as director of the Negro Exhibit, Calloway sought "a well selected and prepared exhibit, representing the Negro's development in . . . his professions and pursuits in general will attract attention . . . and do a great and lasting good in convincing thinking people of the possibilities of the Negro."[4] As principal of Hampton, an institution dedicated to training "selected Negro youth who should go out and teach and lead their people . . . and to these ends, build up an industrial system, for the sake not only of self-support and intelligent labor, but also for the sake of character,"[5] Frissell had a vested interest in seeing Calloway succeed.

Frissell informed Calloway of his preference that the school's achievements be represented not through a manual training exhibition, but "only by its photographs, which I think are going to be extremely good."[6] The photographs to which Frissell referred were a series of 150 images being created by Frances B. Johnston that month. Frissell had commissioned Johnston to take the documentary photographs at Hampton based on the success of the images she shot in the public school system in Washington, D.C. "The general plan of the exhibit revolves about agriculture as the central thought in Hampton's education," the article noted, "and the pictures illustrate the training of the classes in the schoolroom, in the workshop, and in the field."[7]

*The Southern Workman* reported Johnston's successful completion of the project, praising the images as powerful illustrations of Hampton's efforts to effect change in the lifestyles of its Negro and Indian students through educational and vocational training. "The value of such an exhibit lies not only in showing to others but in making clear to the school itself what it is doing," noted the writer.[8]

Examination of one image from *The Hampton Albums* reveals the didactic nature of the photographs as well as Johnston's aesthetic approach. *Physics. The Screw as applied to the cheese press.* depicts a classroom peopled by eight young Hampton students and their teacher. The teacher and four of the youth are gathered around a cheese press, earnestly examining the mechanics of the device, while the other four students huddle around a table, laboring over their calculations. In the background, a partially visible blackboard reveals their assignment: "Make measurement and calculate the force on the cheese in the press." Reference to the physics

143

146

course description in Hampton's catalogue for the 1899–1900 school year reveals the institution's mandate that all physics courses be conducted in the laboratory and notes the inherent value of relating the discipline to the actual situations the student might encounter.[9] Johnston's photograph offers visual confirmation that this mandate is being met.

At the same time, the photograph reveals Johnston's deft touch with a camera. The figures are sharply delineated and the classroom's physical aspects are crisply described, yet the atmosphere is suffused with a soft, silvery light. This latter quality is a result of Johnston's chosen medium of the platinum print. Rendered on paper made light-sensitive with platinum salts, this type of print is characterized by a long tonal scale, delicacy in the grays of the image, a tendency toward soft results, and great permanence.[10] Thus, Johnston's images are as strikingly beautiful today as when she rendered them over a century ago. Like Johnston's other documentary photographs, *Physics* is also distinguished by the photographer's lack of involvement with her subjects. The image communicates the dignity of the young students's labors in clear, concise terms, but does not involve us in their emotional lives. Here and in other images in *The Hampton Albums*, Johnston chose to advocate for societal change dispassionately, rather than making strident appeals to the viewer's emotion like her contemporaries Jacob Riis and Lewis Hine.

—Lori Mirazita

1. In 1883 Johnston moved to Paris, entered the Académie Julian and began studying painting and drawing. Upon returning to the United States, she enrolled at the Art Students League of Washington, D.C. (later the Corcoran Gallery School), focusing on the medium of photography. *The Hampton Album* (New York: The Museum of Modern Art, 1966), p. 53.

2. Naomi Rosenblum, *A History of Women Photographers* (Paris, London, and New York: Abbeville Press, 1994), p. 66–67, 307. Also see Adele Alexander, "At the American Court," *The Washingtonian* (October 1984), p. 173.

3. Photographer Lincoln Kirstein discovered Johnston's photographs in an album of 159 plates when visiting a used bookstore in Washington, D.C. in the 1940s. Twenty years later, he brought them to the attention of The Museum of Modern Art, New York, and in 1966, forty-four of these photographs were selected for exhibition at the museum. The images were subsequently published in a volume entitled *The Hampton Album*. See *The Hampton Album*, pp. 4–5. Two more of Johnston's albums (one containing sixty-three platinum prints and the other sixty platinum prints) are in the collection of the Hampton University Museum. These prints, unlike those owned by The Museum of Modern Art, are not titled.

4. Louis R. Harlan and Raymond W. Smock, eds., *The Booker T. Washington Papers*, 14 vols. (Urbana: University of Illinois Press, 1972) 5: 226–27.

5. S.C. Armstrong, *Twenty-Two Years' Work of the Hampton Normal and Agricultural Institute* (Hampton: Normal School Press, 1893), p. 6.

6. Dr. H.B. Frissell to Mr. Thos. J. Calloway, director of Negro Educational Exhibit, Paris Exposition Commission, Washington, D.C., 14 December 1899, #868 in Dr. Hollis B. Frissell Letterbook, 17 March 1899 to 3 January 1900, Hampton University Archives.

7. *The Southern Workman and Hampton School Record* 28 (December 1899): 498.

8. *The Southern Workman and Hampton School Record* 29 (January 1900): 8. In Dr. Frissell's 32nd annual report to the Trustees of Hampton Institute, he again references the photographs by Johnston, noting that at the completion of the project, 140 photos had been made. Frissell further states that the images serve to illustrate the school's approach to education, whereby, all classes attempt "to dignify the common things of life" and provide students with a mechanism for coping with conditions at home. This approach constituted an attempt, Frissell stated, to foster better relations between the races through education. *The Southern Workman and Hampton School Record* 29 (May 1900): 289. Also of interest—Johnston's photographs appear frequently in the pages of *The Southern Workman* in the ensuing years, as illustrations for articles on teaching at Hampton; a series of 40 images was used by Dr. Albert Shaw in an April 1900 article on teaching at Hampton, "Learning by Doing at Hampton," which appeared in the periodical *Review of Reviews*. *The Southern Workman* (May 1900): 264.

9. *Catalogue of the Hampton Normal and Agricultural Institute, Hampton, Virginia for the Academic Year 1899–1900* (Hampton: Hampton Institute Press, 1900), pp. 40–41.

10. Beaumont Newhall, *The History of Photography from 1839 to the Present* (New York: The Museum of Modern Art, 1982), p. 142.

135

136

## Loïs Mailou Jones
### (1905–1998)
**Painter**

Jones's work has strong influences from both European impressionist painting and African art. She was considered a strong force in teaching and promoting African American artists. She established the art department at the Palmer Memorial Institute in Sedalia, North Carolina, and taught at Howard for forty-seven years. Her pupils included Elizabeth Catlett and David C. Driskell. Her personal artistic style and purpose were enriched by her contact with French, Haitian, African, and American cultures. A textile designer and book illustrator as well as a painter, Jones attended the School of the Museum of Fine Arts, Boston, Boston Normal Art School, Académie Julian (Paris), and Harvard University.

150. *Jennie*, 1943
Oil on canvas
41¾ x 34
Collection of Howard University Gallery of Art

Jennie, one of Loïs Mailou Jones's Saturday morning students at Howard University, served as the model for this warm, domestic portrait of a young woman cleaning fish. Painted with her bravura brush strokes and a palette knife in the manner of the impressionists, the portrait is charming, lively, done with lightness and elegance; the tonal relationships are exact and subtle. Early in her career, Jones became a faithful follower of the American and French impressionists as is evident in this work. Still lifes, landscapes, and street scenes of Paris, as well as portraits, reveal the technique and subject preference of this style. Between 1939 and 1945, Jones created works which focused on the black experience. Alain Locke, the first black Rhodes scholar, philosopher, and professor at Howard University, and self-described "philosophical mid-wife of the Harlem Renaissance"[1] admonished her, as well as other black artists, to re-examine their cultural heritage; he also stressed the importance of the black subject in their works. *Jennie* and other paintings (e.g., *Mob Victim*, *Egyptian Heritage*, and *Dans un Café à Paris/Leigh Whipper*) evolved as a direct result of his challenge.

One of her few genre compositions created in this period, *Jennie* deftly illustrates Jones's knowledge and understanding of color theory. She has combined in the same picture, tonal unity with color contrasts. Warm yellows and varied brown tones are complemented by the crispness of the white cloth and the accented fish in the foreground. Placed in the middle of the composition, Jennie, dressed in a yellow short-sleeved bowed blouse and pleated skirt, with a subtle orange band, stands to the right, holding a fish in her left hand as she scales it with her right hand. Other fish, revealed in their paper wrapping, await her attention. In the left corner, two lemons and a brown water pitcher balance and complement Jennie's stance, who is placed in front of a dish-filled cabinet. Greens, grays, varied brown tones, and patches of red and white, round out the palette of *Jennie*.

150

*Jennie* was exhibited at the National Academy of Design, New York, in 1944. Records are not available to indicate when the work was acquired by the IBM Corporation; however, in March 1961, the IBM Department of Arts and Sciences was given the authority to "deaccession selected works outside the primary emphases of its collections."[2] Four sculptures and seven paintings were donated to the Howard University Gallery of Art and delivered in June 1961. *Jennie* was among those works.

Loïs Mailou Jones's career—painting impressions of such disparate venues as Martha's Vineyard, Haiti, France, and Africa—spanned more than seven decades. Her depictions of light-filled French hillsides are as distinguished as her African paintings; her Haitian watercolors are as captivating as her Parisian cityscapes. One of America's premiere painters, Jones was a rare talent whose work embraced great cultural, social, and geographical variety.

Born in Boston, Jones graduated from the School of the Museum of Fine Arts, Boston as a textile designer in 1927. Aided by a scholarship, she began graduate work at the Designers Art School of Boston, where she studied with Ludwig Frank, an internationally known German textile designer. Jones became an active freelance designer of fabrics and textiles for department stores and textile manufacturers, particularly the F.A. Foster Company in Boston and the Schumacher Company in New York. Not satisfied with anonymity, the standard for textile designers, Jones, the designer, wanted to be known for her artistry and resolved to cultivate the fine arts and become a painter.

In the summer of 1928, Jones was recruited by Charlotte Hawkins Brown, the founder and director of the Palmer Memorial Institute, a junior college with a preparatory school division in Sedalia, North Carolina, to serve as chairperson (and founder of the art department) and instructor. She was persuaded by James V. Herring, chairman of the department of art at Howard University, to join its faculty. As an instructor of design, Jones provided skills and knowledge that augmented the fundamental curriculum and balanced the art department's offerings until her retirement from Howard in 1977. She took a personal interest in the development of her students, urging them to be well grounded in the fundamentals. "Talent is the basis for your career as an artist—but hard work determines your success" was her pithy reminder to students over the years.

In 1937 Jones made her first trip to France to study at the Académie Julian.

She fell in love with the country and the freedom it gave her to be herself. Moreover, the stylistic preference for impressionism was reinforced throughout her stay there and continued after her return to America the following year.

Whether in the subdued tonalities of the early days, when she was fascinated by impressionism or in the bold brilliant colors and decorative patterns that dominate her canvases of Haiti and Africa, Jones's compositions possess a clarion color always hinged on structure and design. Because of her unswerving determination and dedication to her artistry, many of these masterpieces, such as *Jennie*, ensure Loïs Mailou Jones's place in the history of American art.

—Tritobia Hayes Benjamin

1. Richard Barksdale and Kenneth Kinnamon, *Black Writers of America, A Comprehensive Anthology* (New York: Macmillan Publishing Co., 1972), p. 573.

2. J. A. McDonald, director, Civil Program, IBM Corporation, in a letter to Dr. James M. Nabrit, Jr., president of Howard University, 27 March 1961, Howard University Gallery of Art archives, Washington, D.C.

151

# Eddie Jack Jordan, Sr.
## (b. 1927)
**Sculptor, painter**

Jordan received his training in art at Langston University, Oklahoma State University, State University of Iowa, and Indiana University. After teaching for several years in South Carolina and Oklahoma, Jordan moved in 1961 to New Orleans, Louisiana, where he taught for many years at Southern University. In addition to being a sculptor, painter, university art professor, and author, Jordan is one of the founding members of the National Conference of Artists, a consortium of African American artists, art historians, and art educators.

151. *The Old Slave*, c. 1967
Granite
20 x 10½ x 6
Second Award in Sculpture, Atlanta University Art Annual, 1967. Collection of Clark Atlanta University Art Galleries

# Jacob Lawrence
## (b. 1917)
**Painter**

Lawrence has produced stylized, figurative scenes of black life which make him a highly celebrated and popular artist working almost exclusively in gouache (opaque watercolor or tempera). Educated at the Harlem Art Workshop and the American Artists School, Lawrence produced a number of narrative series documenting, in his abstract, colorful style, the history and struggles of people in the African diaspora. He cites Augusta Savage and Henry Bannarn as major players in his early formation.

152. *Brownstones*, 1958
Opaque watercolor on masonite
24 x 30
Collection of Clark Atlanta University Art Galleries, gift of Chauncey and Catherine Waddell

153. *Frederick Douglass Series No. 30*, 1938–39
Casein tempera on gessoed hardboard
17⅞ x 12
Collection of Hampton University Museum, 00.4268.30, gift of the Harmon Foundation

154. *Harriet Tubman Series No. 7*, 1939–40
Casein tempera on gessoed hardboard
17⅞ x 12
Collection of Hampton University Museum, 00.4261.7, gift of the Harmon Foundation

155. *Palm Sunday*, 1956
Opaque watercolor and graphite on medium-weight wove paper
40 x 32
Collection of North Carolina Central University Art Museum, purchased with funds given by Friends of the Museum and a grant from the National Endowment for the Arts

Almost from the beginning Jacob Lawrence's reassertion of the legitimacy of narrative painting placed him in the front ranks of African American artists. In 1941 the style that he called "dynamic cubism" was not only formulated but recognized as one of the most original to develop in America. One of the first black artist to gain national recognition, he was primarily associated with producing a series of works about African American history and culture. Lawrence's penchant for African American history began at the Harlem Community Art Center directed by Augusta Savage. Continuing at the 135th Street Library, under the tutelage

153

154

155

of Charles Alston and Professor Charles Seifert, the steadfast embrace of African and African American aesthetics and philosophic exploration began. Using this newly discovered reservoir, a conceptional focus on the role of historic personages became fertile ground for exploration in serial format.[1] The first, the *Toussaint L'Ouverture* series of 1937–38, dealt with the Haitian military leader who led his country to independence.[2] This series also was a definitive statement about Lawrence's indifference to art movements and academic rules about drawing and perspective.

*Palm Sunday* was painted at a pivotal time in Lawrence's career. During the previous year 1955, he had spent two months at Yaddo Foundation in Saratoga Springs, New York, producing the *Struggle* series, one of the largest historical series ever created by an American artist. It focused on the efforts of the American people to win freedom beginning with the Revolutionary War. Temporarily abandoning black history, American history that included blacks in the struggle of humankind became the focus of his work.

By 1956, the date of the execution of *Palm Sunday*, the stylized serial format chronicling the struggle of black Americans had become synonymous with his work. He did not abandon themes with universal human resonance, however. His visits to Abyssinian Baptist Church, pastored by Adam Clayton Powell, Sr., left an indelible impression on the artist. As he pointed out, "I can remember going to church regularly and being in Sunday school and participating in church plays."[3] Painting directly what he knew and saw in Harlem, using his boyhood absorption with patterns, Lawrence deviated from most foundational elements of Western art.

*Palm Sunday* presents New Testament iconography in a moment commonly seen on the Sunday before Easter. Lawrence focuses on the incidents after the services have ended: the gathering of members of the congregation to exchange pleasantries before leaving the sanctuary. Prominently positioned is the minister, compellingly resplendent in a translucent black robe, who embraces an impressionable child who anchors the composition. In his hands are dramatic, arc-like palms that create an exciting spatial dynamic, which imposes integrity and continuity throughout the composition. The effect is immediate and powerful, and affirms a mastery of compositional design. The universal symbol of Christianity, the cross, prominently clings to his lower robe, whose opaque and transparent textural qualities are repeated elsewhere. Not unlike the

cubists, Lawrence's volume and space is integrated, rendering simplified form in a non-perspectival space. A man and woman carry on a lively dialogue immediately behind the minister. To the right, a mother carries one of her children while holding the hand of the other. While there is a dialogue between the mother and another couple, the more intriguing one appears between the two children, where an underlying innocence is quite evident.

Like Lawrence's other narrative genre pieces of 1956–57, arcs to the left and right, top and bottom, serve to keep the composition away from the corners and edges.[4] Yellow and green stylized palm leafs held by the children and the minister tie the composition together while presenting a realistic setting without naturalistic detail. Significantly, simplified figures are presented through representational images, yet there is a lack of concern for individuality or portraiture. He forcefully presents an accounting of a religious moment and his own reaction to it.

That Lawrence's work was not synthetic, never depending on the latest avant-garde movement for direction, points to a consistent originality. With a reductive style similar to folk painters, technical sophistication can be taken for granted. Ultimately, *Palm Sunday* pays homage to Lawrence's signature narrative element and conveys a complex patterning that continues today.

—Kenneth G. Rodgers

1. Regenia Perry, *Free Within Ourselves* (Washington, D.C.: National Museum of American Art, Smithsonian Institution, 1992), p. 29.

2. Romare Bearden and Harry Henderson, *A History of African-American Artists: From 1792 to the Present* (New York: Pantheon Books, 1993), p. 296.

3. Jacob Lawrence, interview by Carroll Greene, Jr., Washington, D.C.: Archives of American Art, Smithsonian Institution, 26 October 1968.

4. Ellen Harkins Wheat, *Jacob Lawrence: American Painter* (Seattle: University of Washington Press, 1986), p. 28.

156. *Playland*, 1948
Egg tempera on board
24 x 20
First Award in Oil Painting, Atlanta University Art Annuals, 1948. Collection of Clark Atlanta University Art Galleries

The announcement that Jacob Lawrence had won the First Purchase Award for his painting, *Playland*, in Atlanta University's "1948 Exhibition of Paintings, Prints, and Sculptures by Negro Artists of America," did not come as a surprise to anyone.[1] During the 1940s, Lawrence had not only been given a one-man showing of his *Migration of the Negro* series (1940–41) at the Downtown Gallery in New York, but he also received financial support from the Julius Rosenwald Fund. Less than a year later, his critically acclaimed *Migration* paintings were successfully followed by the *John Brown* (1941) and *Harlem* (1942–43) series, making him one of the most important black artists in the country. The outbreak of World War II and being drafted into the United States Coast Guard in 1943 were the only events that slowed his momentum. After the war ended in 1945, Lawrence continued to paint. Instead of focusing exclusively on historic events and everyday life in the black community, he began to seek inspiration beyond the borders of Harlem.

In *Playland*, Lawrence departs from his familiar neighborhood environment and ventures into what appears to be an arcade located in another part of the city. An integrated population of blacks and whites casually wander through several gaming areas with some stopping along the way to observe. In the foreground, a large, brightly colored pinball machine decorated with spades, hearts, diamonds, clubs, and images of playing card royalty dominates much of the picture plane. Two male and one female player stand in front of this machine while a fourth figure on the right casually watches. In the upper right corner, a small crowd has gathered around another card game while others mill about. The two-dimensional style of Lawrence's work and his use of strong vertical and horizontal lines to construct the figures and the pinball machine create the impression that this moment has been frozen in time.

Although the content of Lawrence's *Playland* is still firmly rooted in 1930s Social Realism and the flat, angular treatment of his subjects remains consistent with his earlier paintings, the decorative quality of the pinball machine is a new element in his work. This special emphasis on pattern and design came as a result of his brief association with Josef Albers.[2] In the summer of 1946, Jacob Lawrence was invited to teach at Black Mountain College in North Carolina along with Albers and several other artists. Albers had been a follower of Cézanne and the cubists earlier in his career, but he abandoned this painting approach while studying at the Bauhaus.[3] As a proponent of Bauhaus theory, Albers introduced Lawrence to the idea that mastery of the visual elements and principles of design should take precedence over content when creating a work of art.[4]

The imprint of this association can be seen in *Playland*, for it is in this painting that Lawrence exhibits a heightened sense of design. Among the randomly selected rectangles covering the surface of the pinball machine, he has carefully reproduced the intricate costumes of the playing card royalty. It is this attention to detail and his use of curved diagonal lines to structure their clothing which contrasts with the strong vertical and horizontal organization of the composition that imbues this section of the picture plane with energy. This decorative interest has been extended throughout the picture plane by Lawrence's use of zigzag lines on the playing surface of the pinball machine and vertical stripes in the clothing worn by the foreground and background figures.

*Playland* is one work within a small series of paintings produced between 1946 and 1948 that documents Lawrence's growing interest in complex design. This shift from the simplicity of his earlier works to a more decorative approach also marks Lawrence's transition from his Harlem neighborhood into the world community.

—M. Akua McDaniel, Ph.D.

1. *Atlanta University Exhibitions of Paintings, Prints, and Sculptures by Negro Artists of America* (Atlanta: Atlanta University Press, 1948), Clark Atlanta University Art Gallery Archives, n.p.

2. Ellen Harkins Wheat, *Jacob Lawrence: American Painter* (Seattle: University of Washington Press, 1986), p. 72.

3. Matthew Baigell, "Josef Albers," in *Dictionary of American Art* (New York: Harper & Row Publishers, 1979), p. 6.

4. Wheat, pp. 73–74.

157. *Strike*, 1949
Opaque watercolor on board
19¹⁵⁄₁₆ x 23⁷⁄₈
Collection of Howard University Gallery of Art

156

# Edmonia Lewis
### (1845–c. 1911)
### Sculptor

Although she spent most of her life in Europe, Lewis was the first neoclassical sculptor of color to gain an international reputation. Her sculpture stresses the humanity of her subjects and she is best known for her works that reflect her dual African American and Native American heritage. She created portrait busts of Colonel Robert Shaw, Henry Wadsworth Longfellow, and Abraham Lincoln. The imagery of her sculpture was largely centered on the Bible, mythology, and abolitionist themes.

## Leigh Richmond Miner
### (1864–1935)
**Photographer, painter**

Miner became an instructor at Hampton Institute in 1898 and served as director of the applied arts department. He ran his own New York studio from 1904–07. Miner created a compassionate record of the lives of the black inhabitants of St. Helena Island, South Carolina, and Hampton, Virginia, which offered a corrective to the prevailing photographic record of rural Negroes from the period.

183

184

174. *Candle Lightin' Time*, 1901
Digital reproduction from original cyanotype
7¹⁄₂ x 4¹⁄₂
Collection of Hampton University Archives

175. *Candle Lightin' Time*, 1901
Digital reproduction from original cyanotype
7⁵⁄₁₆ x 4⁷⁄₁₆
Collection of Hampton University Archives

176. *Portia in drawing room*, 1907
Digital reproduction from original cyanotype
6¹⁄₂ x 4⁹⁄₁₆
Collection of Hampton University Archives

177. *Portia ironing*, 1907
Digital reproduction from original cyanotype
6⁹⁄₁₆ x 4⁹⁄₁₆
Collection of Hampton University Archives

178. *Portia Peyton*, 1907
Digital reproduction from original cyanotype
9¹⁵⁄₁₆ x 7³⁄₈
Collection of Hampton University Archives

179. *Portia Peyton teaching school gardening*, 1907
Digital reproduction from original cyanotype
6¹⁄₂ x 4¹⁄₂
Collection of Hampton University Archives

180. *Portia Peyton playing basketball*, 1907
Digital reproduction from original cyanotype
6⁷⁄₁₆ x 4⁹⁄₁₆
Collection of Hampton University Archives

181. *Portia polishing brass*, 1907
Digital reproduction from original cyanotype
6⁹⁄₁₆ x 4³⁄₈
Collection of Hampton University Archives

182. *Study hour*, 1907
Digital reproduction from original cyanotype
6⁵⁄₈ x 4⁵⁄₈
Collection of Hampton University Archives

183. *The Young Chief*, 1902
Oil on canvas
23 x 28
Collection of Hampton University Museum, 00.4317.3

184. *Untitled (man in 6' tall field)*, c. 1907
Gelatin silver print
7¹⁄₂ x 9⁷⁄₁₆
Collection of Hampton University Archives

## Archibald J. Motley, Jr.
### (1891–1981)
**Painter**

Motley, a genre painter of modern black life, studied at the Art Institute of Chicago and was influenced by George Bellows who shared his passion for painting common folk. His paintings, derived from black culture with intensely colored surfaces, did not attempt to glorify or idealize activities of his subjects, but rather depicted them as he often saw them in urban settings of the 1920s and 1930s. He is known for his street scenes and sensuous portrayals of people, seemingly caressed by jazz and a distinct perceptual softness.

185. *Barbecue*, 1937
Oil on canvas
39 x 44
Collection of Howard University Gallery of Art

186. *Black Belt*, 1934
Oil on canvas
31⁷⁄₈ x 39 4/2
Collection of Hampton University Museum, 67.371, gift of the Harmon Foundation

187. *Carnival*, 1937
Oil on canvas
30 x 40
Collection of Howard University Gallery of Art

188. *The Liar*, 1936
Oil on canvas
32 x 36
Collection of Howard University Gallery of Art

Howard University's Gallery of Art is the home for six very important paintings by the Chicago artist Archibald J. Motley, Jr. Thanks to a dispersal during the late 1940s of WPA/FAP art works from Fort Huachuca (a segregated, all-Negro, United States Army post), Howard University received six paintings by Motley, five of which (*Barbeque, Saturday Night, The Liar, The Picnic,* and *Carnival*) are part of his fabled *Bronzeville* series. This series (for which Motley created approximately twenty paintings between 1930 and 1937) documents and takes visual license with the lives and activities of Chicagoans residing in the largely African American neighborhood that, c. 1930, was roughly bordered by 26th Street to the north, Cottage Grove Avenue to the east, 47th Street to the south, and Wentworth Avenue to the west. In their book *Black Metropolis: A Study of Negro Life in a Northern City,* authors St. Clair Drake and Horace R. Cayton write that the term "Bronzeville" (a euphemism for this predominately black section of Chicago) was coined in 1930 by an African American newspaper editor who had organized a mock-election among black Chicagoans for the "Mayor of Bronzeville." Interestingly the term "Black Belt" (another early-twentieth-century colloquialism for this predominately African American, South Side Chicago neighborhood) is also the title of one of these legendary *Bronzeville* paintings by Motley (owned by the Hampton University Art Museum).[1]

185

187

Motley's *Bronzeville* paintings usually depict one of three kinds of exterior scenes or indoor settings in black Chicago: 1) pedestrian-clogged streets and other public gatherings (such as carnival side shows and picnics in the park); 2) nightclubs and cabarets (featuring the typical habitués in these places, like dancing couples, hovering waiters, and jazz bands); and 3) pool-rooms and gambling dens. *The Liar* fits into this last category and, as typical of so much of Motley's work during this period, revels in the more gritty, seamy side of black urban life. Motley shows us the interior of a pool-room, where six black men play billiards, drink, smoke, and converse amongst themselves with a casual, yet attentive demeanor. Prominently displayed in this scene is a large drinking goblet, a whiskey bottle, a matchbox holder, a lit cigar, and two partially filled shot glasses, all resting on a round table covered with a pristine white tablecloth. Barely discernible in the lower left corner of the composition is a cartoonish-looking brown dog, sound asleep.

Although the title of Motley's painting ostensibly refers to just one of the six men (probably the large one on the left, gesturing and leaning back on his chair), all of them exude (through their sly glances, adverted heads, or contrapposto poses) an unpredictable, furtive quality. This enigmatic element is further conveyed in the anti-naturalistic colors and brushy painting technique that Motley has employed. From the greasepaint-like reds, magentas, and purples of their complexions, to the almost blurry, impressionistic quality of their faces and hands, Motley's braggarts and listeners seem almost illusory: more suggestive of black urban types than substantive portrayals of real black men. The densely packed interior and busy composition (along with the conscious juxtaposition of disparate shapes, color opposites, and contradictory perspectives) add to Motley's theme of the deceitful narrator and, perhaps subliminally, also hint at the more troubling issue in much of Motley's work: the conundrum, illusion, and unreliability of racial perceptions.[2]

Like so many of his artistic contemporaries in the 1920s and 1930s, Motley excavated the black underclass, in search of artistic and emotional truths, as well as racial and class-based ones. His *Bronzeville* investigations also uncovered aspects of the Negro experience that, in addition to showing what Alain Locke called the "new psychology" and "spirit" of contemporary Negro life, revealed something else that, at times, was unseemly, absurdist, outrageous, and, as evinced in the many accolades that he received for this new work, tantalizing. Like author and anthropologist Zora Neale Hurston and her celebrations of common, everyday Negro speech, performance, and aesthetics, Motley's *The Liar* and the other paintings from his *Bronzeville* series made an artistic centerpiece out of Chicago's black community. Washington Park picnics and Bud Billiken parades, the streetlight-lit nightlife and vibrant music scene on Chicago's South Side, and the glamorous but often dangerous criminal elements in the community were all prime subjects for Motley to paint. Comparisons with independent black films of the 1930s (that also made antiheroes out of Negro bootleggers, gamblers, and roustabouts) suggest that Motley's mixed message in *The Liar*—*exaltation* of culture and community, and *exploitation* of criminality and "the blues"—revises a one-dimensional perspective on Harlem Renaissance arts and aesthetics: a modification that, despite the call for a new, more racially sensitive realism, acknowledges the emotional power and expressive contours of an art informed by the unlettered yet artistically nascent Negro masses.[3]

—Richard J. Powell

1. St. Clair Drake and Horace R. Cayton, *Black Metropolis: A Study of Negro Life in a Northern City*, vol. II (1945; reprint, New York: Harper Torchbooks, 1962), pp. 383–85. For a monograph on Motley's life and work, see Jontyle Theresa Robinson and Wendy Greenhouse, *The Art of Archibald J. Motley, Jr.* (Chicago: Chicago Historical Society, 1991).

2. For Motley's own thoughts on the question of racial identity in art, see Archibald J. Motley, "The Negro in Art," n.d., Archibald J. Motley Papers, Archives and Manuscript Collection, Chicago Historical Society.

3. Richard J. Powell, "Re/Birth of a Nation," in Richard J. Powell, ed., *Rhapsodies in Black: Art of the Harlem Renaissance* (Berkeley: University of California Press, 1997), pp. 23–28.

189

## Richard Bruce Nugent
### (1906–1987)
**Author, illustrator, poet, playwright**
Nugent used his talents to address the joys and problems of being part of the gay world during the Harlem Renaissance. He was a prolific author of poems, plays, and short stories. Nugent composed a ballet and designed costumes for the theater.

189. *Smoke, Lilies, and Jade*, c. 1925
Black ink and watercolor with graphite underdrawing on paperboard
11½ x 9
Collection of Howard University Gallery of Art

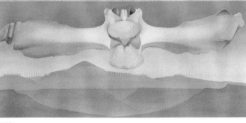

190

## Georgia O'Keeffe
### (1887–1986)
**Painter**
Painter and wife of Alfred Stieglitz, O'Keeffe's early abstract paintings explored formal and modern concerns through imaginative, breathtaking colors and scale. Her paintings are endowed with surrealistic tones and fierce emotional energy. An Art Institute of Chicago graduate, O'Keeffe is popularly associated with the Southwest, particularly New Mexico.

190. *Flying Backbone*, 1944
Oil on canvas
12 x 26
The Alfred Stieglitz Collection, Fisk University, Nashville, Tennessee, gift of the artist

191. *Radiator Building—Night, New York*, 1927
Oil on canvas
48 x 30
The Alfred Stieglitz Collection, Fisk University, Nashville, Tennessee, gift of the artist

## Suzanna Ogunjami
### (active 1920s–1930s)
**Painter**
Suzanna Ogunjami was active in New York City from 1928–34 after which she returned to West Africa to live. Her work evokes powerful connections between ancient African art forms and modern Western themes.

192. *Full Blown Magnolia*, c. 1935
Oil on burlap
20 x 24
Collection of Hampton University Museum, 67.275, gift of the Harmon Foundation

The out-takes of *A Study of Negro Artists*, the 1930s film produced by the Harmon Foundation, includes footage of Suzanna Ogunjami discussing her painting *Nupe Princess* at the opening of her one-woman exhibition at Delphic Studios in New York in 1934.[1] According to the 1935 "Directory of Negro Artists,"[2] and correspondence from Mary Beattie Brady (director of the Harmon Foundation) to Dr. E. George Payne in the department of education at New York University,[3] Ogunjami was the first African woman to have an exhibit— not to mention a one-woman show—in a commercial gallery in the United States. The exhibition, on view December 1934, featured her metalwork, jewelry, and twenty-seven paintings.[4] The two-minute film clip on Ogunjami did not allude to all of the media in which she worked but focused on her painting. This footage is intriguing for two reasons. First, in contrast with the artists in the film who are easily recognized such as Richmond Barthé, Palmer Hayden, Loïs Mailou Jones, and Augusta Savage, Ogunjami is not familiar. Her presence in this film invites questions about this unknown artist who gained such acclaim that, by the 1930s, she had a one-woman exhibition under the auspices of a distinguished foundation. Secondly, because Ogunjami's paintings feature women braiding each other's hair in idealized African settings and portraits of African people, her art stands out from other artists's work featured in this film. Ogunjami's past acclaim contrasted with her current anonymity suggest that her life and art warrant further analysis.

Suzanna Ogunjami, born of Igbo (Nigeria) ancestry, left West Africa for Jamaica at a young age.[5] In 1921 after completing her primary education in the West Indies, Ogunjami (occasionally referred to by her married name Suzanna Wilson) moved to New York and began taking classes in fine arts and textiles at Teachers College, Columbia University, earning a bachelor of science degree in 1927. The following year, she was awarded a master's degree in fine arts and a diploma certifying her to teach fine arts. While still a student at Teachers College, Ogunjami experienced considerable success when *Sunflower*, one of her earliest oil paintings, was included in the 1928 Harmon Foundation exhibition at International House in New York. Shortly thereafter, the Harmon Foundation arranged for her to have her first (and only) one-woman exhibition. In 1935 her paintings were featured in an exhibition at the New Jersey State Museum. Considering her artistic achievements, it is indeed intriguing that, with the exception of a brief mention in *Against the Odds: African American Artists and the Harmon Foundation*, information on her life and art is absent from published documents on the Harmon Foundation as well as other sources.

192

The subjects of Ogunjami's personal correspondence and the majority of her paintings suggest that although she painted a variety of subjects, she was primarily interested in religious education and creating images that countered the idea that African peoples were uncivilized. Her paintings suggest that she wanted to depict the sophistication of African peoples and their preoccupation with adornment and physical beauty. Because she left Nigeria at an early age, the subjects of her paintings were based on what she recalled of Africa and what she had read.

The considerable amount of acclaim that Ogunjami received in New York art circles in 1928 was short lived. In early 1935 when her husband, Rev. M.N.O. Wilson, was called to Freetown, Sierra Leone to fulfill religious duties, the couple left New York permanently. There she pursued printmaking; however, most of her time and energies were dedicated to religious service. She founded the West African Normal and Industrial Institute, a school in Freetown that aimed to "build strong character and to train our girls and boys not only how to use their brains but their hands also; and to fit them for future useful service."[6]

*Nupe Princess* (c. 1935), an oil on canvas, is in the permanent collection of The Carl Van Vechten Gallery of Fine Arts at Fisk University. The current whereabouts of most of her paintings, however, are unknown and exist only through reproductions. It is interesting that in 1935 when *Full Blown Magnolia* was first exhibited, it was described as mirroring the "wild landscape, the exotic foliage and the unusual people of her native land."[7] This description ignored the fact that magnolias are indigenous to the southern United States and that *Full Blown Magnolia* had more in common with still life painting by artists such as Martin Johnson Heade (1819–1904) whose still life paintings of flowers represented women in the manner of Victorian tastes and aesthetics. Moreover, *Full Blown Magnolia* was subjected to scrutiny that was informed by stereotypical perceptions of Africa. The painting, given to the Hampton University Museum when the Harmon Foundation's activities ceased in 1967, consists of a single flower in a bulging vase with purple undertones that sits on a table. The dark velvety drape behind the lone flower creates a theatrical tone, removing it further from its natural setting and placing it in isolation. Magnolia trees, are common symbols of perseverance, sensuousness, love, beauty, and refinement. Considering Ogunjami's personal and aesthetic interests, it is understandable why she depicted the attractive flower. Magnolias are enormous trees that bear large creamy-white flowers, glossy leathery leaves, and conspicuous egg-shaped fruit that are often used as decorative ornamentation. Since information on *Full Blown Magnolia* and Ogunjami are omitted from Harmon Foundation publications on African and African American art, it is especially significant that *Full Blown Magnolia* is resurrected in this exhibition.

—Andrea D. Barnwell

1. *A Study of Negro Artists* (outtakes) (New York: Harmon Foundation, 1937) National Archives, #200-HF-214x reel 6.

2. Harmon Foundation, "Directory of Negro Artists," *Negro Artists and Their Achievements* (New York: Harmon Foundation, 1935), pp. 41–59.

3. Letter from Mary Beattie Brady to Dr. E. George Payne, 12 December 1934, Papers of the Harmon Foundation, Library of Congress, Container #79.

4. Announcement for Suzanna Ogunjami's exhibition at Delphic Studios, December 1934, Papers of the Harmon Foundation, Library of Congress, Container #79.

5. The following discussion is based on an unpublished interview with Suzanna Ogunjami, 20 December 1934, Papers of the Harmon Foundation, Library of Congress, Container #79.

6. Prospectus/Announcement for The West African Normal and Industrial Institute, 2 April 1935, Papers of the Harmon Foundation, Library of Congress, Container #79.

7. Harmon Foundation, "Directory of Negro Artists," p. 34.

## Nicholas Panesis
### (b. 1913)
### Illustrator

An artist and illustrator active at mid-century, Panesis is well known for his illustrations in children's books. Examples of his work can be found in *Journey Cake* (1942) and *Nuba's New Moon* (1944).

193. *George Washington Carver*, c. 1940
Lithograph on medium-weight wove paper
10½ x 8¾ (image); 19¼ x 12½ (sheet)
Collection of Howard University Gallery
of Art

## Rose Piper
### (b. 1917)
### Painter

Rose Piper emerged in the 1940s New York art world as a promising and formidable talent, making her mark with a series of semi-abstract paintings (c. 1947) based on the blues and Negro life in the southern United States. Educated at Hunter College and closely associated with fellow painters Charles Alston, Yasuo Kuniyoshi, and Vaclav Vytlacil, Piper was the recipient of Rosenwald Fellowships and has work in several museums and galleries nationwide, including the Ackland Museum of Art at the University of North Carolina, Chapel Hill.

194. *Grievin' Hearted*, 1947
Oil on canvas
30 x 36
Best Portrait-Figure Award, Atlanta
University Art Annuals, 1948. Collection
of Clark Atlanta University Art Galleries

Early in her career Rose Piper won acclaim with a series of paintings, which were inspired by her engagement with themes expressed in Negro musical traditions. Poet Myron O'Higgins suggested she contact Sterling Brown, then at Howard University, who became a source for slave songs and recordings and race records of every type.[1] Through the years Piper would employ this process of mining a body of music, conceiving a series of paintings that meditated upon and transcended the wrenching experiences shared by the legions of rural blacks who tied their fortunes to the North.

In 1940 she graduated from Hunter College with a major in art and a minor in mathematics, determined that she would never become a teacher.[2] The 1940s were a prodigiously creative and productive period for Piper, culminating in a trip to Paris at the end of World War II and the birth of her two children. For much of the decade

193

she, Romare Bearden, Jacob Lawrence, and Charles "Spinky"Alston formed a nucleus of artists who came together frequently to critique and support each other's work. Says Piper, "Spinky was just marvelous. He introduced me to a lot of people who were very helpful."[3] In 1943 she joined the Art Students League where she trained under Yasuo Kuniyoshi for three years; later in the decade she studied with Vaclav Vytlacil and the illustrator Arthur Lidov. She received successive fellowships from the Rosenwald Fellowship Fund in 1946 and 1947 which she used to support her travels across the American South in search of "the folk Negro."[4] This type of ethnographically based project was typical of the period. Whether Piper conceived the journey as a necessary part of her own education or whether the Rosenwald Fund announced its own interest in discovering "the folk," the process itself was filled with irony. Why was it necessary for Piper, whose father and mother hailed from Georgia and Virginia, respectively, to have to investigate these roots, and who was this folk Negro, this authentic Negro from the South? At the time, James Baldwin had said the South was "the old country" to blacks who migrated to the North, so perhaps this pilgrimage was an inevitable step for an artist whose work expands the meaning of black experience in America.

Still, Piper did not romanticize the folk and she avoided the clichés that have come to represent the black experience. When her first show opened at New York's RoKo Gallery in 1947 with the fourteen oil paintings in her *Negro Work Songs and Blues* series, Rose Piper was lionized by the art world. Her work was exalted by local artists, critics, gallery owners, and collectors and it sold quickly.[5] "Outstanding as usual are the simple, strong designs and controlled expression of Rose Piper . . . ," an *Art Digest* critic wrote of the show, which included *Grievin' Hearted*. While her work was widely touted as "strong, affirmative, sound in composition and moodily emotional in color," critics rarely failed to note that her paintings also succeeded as "social statements . . . because of their emotional impact, [and were] effective because they escape[d] the shrillness that mars so much 'social' painting."[6] Piper was heartened by the work's phenomenal success and reveled in the knowledge that she was one of few artists of any race who could make a living from her painting. Two years later the RoKo Gallery invited her to participate in an exhibition of Negro artists.[7]

*Grievin' Hearted* fetched first prize at Atlanta University's Seventh Art Annual (1948), in a competition that included Alston, Bearden, Robert Blackburn, Richmond Barthé, and Jacob Lawrence. Her "moving primitive" was hailed as the best portrait or figure painting in the show.[8]

An excellent example of what Piper has termed her "semi-abstract expressionism," the composition captures the artist's transition between modes of representation and abstraction. Her approach is stark, not idealized; her subject is not the community, but dignified and lonely individuals yearning and in despair. "I was very unhappy when I painted *Grievin' Hearted*," said Piper. "It was me being broken hearted, grievin' hearted. I had been jilted. I was that man."[9]

The male figure in *Grievin' Hearted* evokes immediate comparisons to Picasso with his stylized pose, impossibly curved spine and a general heaviness which seems to root him to the ground. "He *is* rooted to the spot, immobile, a statue. He's done in," Piper said.[10] Her articulation of body parts is most unusual: references to musculature, particularly the delicate hand resting on the shoulder in a state of lassitude; the strong, almost sculptural toes; and tree trunk-like right arm set Piper's work apart from the realistic figure painting of her peers.

Like her more widely known *Slow Down Freight Train* (1948)[11] that also takes the consequences of one's actions as its subject matter, Piper plays with light and dark and with shadows, but in a less abstract manner. Here we have a realistic background with a partially denuded tree and an expanse of fields. The expression on the woman's face provides minimal information. Is she the cause of the man's grief? Is he crushed under the weight of a burden she has recently shed?

Piper's ascendancy in the competitive and volatile art world was short lived. She could not afford single-minded dedication to her art but had to pursue another vocation while deferring her art career. When her husband and her parents became ill, she chose to become the primary income-earner for her extended family, gave up her studio, and found full-time employment, and for nearly three decades she shelved her painting and worked in the textile industry. Her dilemma was all too familiar. Piper's own sense of survival and obligation took priority over the advancement of her career as a painter.

In 1978 after raising two children, establishing a greeting card company, and retiring from a career as a textile designer

and executive, Piper began to create images again. She returned to some familiar themes, yet her style had changed dramatically as she worked on smaller canvases and in greater detail with effects that approach trompe l'oeil. The abstraction of her early work is supplanted by a new, exacting realism that, nevertheless, encompasses the hopes, dreams, and nightmares of the human psyche.

—Kirsten Mullen

1. Rose Piper, interview by Kirsten Mullen, New York, 18 July 1993.

2. Rose Piper, interview by Kirsten Mullen, New York, 15 August 1994. Although she received a scholarship to Pratt Institute, her father forbade her to attend because it was not an accredited college, nor was she able to attend her second college choice, the University of Chicago. Her father had invested heavily in property, stocks, and bonds, and lost everything when the market crashed; consequently, he could not afford to send her to Chicago. Piper resigned herself to attend Hunter College, which did not charge tuition.

3. Alston and Bearden were associates of Piper's, but it was Alston, known affectionately as "Spinky" who took a special interest in Piper and introduced her to fellow artists and gallery owners.

4. Ann Eden Gibson, *Abstract Expressionism: Other Politics* (New Haven and London: Yale University Press, 1997), p. 110 and Richard J. Powell, *Black Art and Culture in the 20th Century* (London: Thames and Hudson, 1997), p. 100.

5. "Art by Villagers Placed on Display: Downtown Artists Open Show at Center—RoKo Extends Exhibition by Rose Piper," *New York Times*, 25 October 1947.

6. A.L., "Rose Piper's Debut," *Art Digest*, 1 October 1947.

7. "Honoring Negro History," *Art Digest*, 15 February 1949, n.p. Piper's *Empty Bed Blues* and *Conjur* were featured. She was one of seven artists to show two pictures. A total of eighteen African American artists were represented in the RoKo Gallery exhibition in February 1949.

8. Ackland Art Museum, University of North Carolina at Chapel Hill, Curatorial File. N. A., "Rose Piper Wins Top Award at Atlanta University," *Art Students League News* 1, 15 May 1948: 2:11.

9. Rose Piper, interview by Kirsten Mullen, 24 September 1998.

10. Ibid.

11. Ackland Art Museum. Permanent Collection. In a 1990 letter to the museum's director, Charles Millard, Piper indicated that the painting was inspired by the Trixie Smith recording, "Freight Train Blues," a "woman's plea for the train to slow down so that she might go along with her man."

194

## Horace Pippin
### (1888–1946)
**Painter**

An entirely self-taught artist, Pippin completed his first painting at forty-three years of age and is known for drawings done by applying a hot poker to wood panels. A World War I injury immobilized his right hand which he manipulated across the canvas with his left. He imaginatively interpreted religious and military subjects as well as domestic scenes of his own experiences and added scenes from the lives of black people which were dominated by reality and filled with dignity as well as vigor and continuity of life.

195. *Christ Crowned with Thorns*, 1938
Oil on canvas
16 x 18⅞
Collection of Howard University Gallery of Art

195

## Prentiss H. "P.H." Polk
### (1898–1984)
**Photographer**

Polk learned photography from two older photographers, Cornelius M. Battey at Tuskegee Institute and Fred Jensen. In 1927 he opened his own photography studio in Tuskegee. He was appointed to the Tuskegee University faculty in 1928, and served for fifty years.

196

196. *"Bill Pipes" and his Melody Barons*, c. 1935
Gelatin silver print
3¹⁵⁄₁₆ x 8¹³⁄₁₆
Collection of Tuskegee University

197. *George Washington Carver*, before 1943
Gelatin silver print
9½ x 7⅛ (image); 10 x 8⅛ (sheet)
Collection of Tuskegee University

198. *George Washington Carver's Laboratory in the Ag building*, before 1943
Gelatin silver print
4¹¹⁄₁₆ x 6½
Collection of Tuskegee University

P.H. Polk was always on the go, oftentimes in a hurry. As "the picture man" in Tuskegee, Alabama, he was in much demand. Tuskegee University administration and the student newspaper and yearbook staff vied for his time as did his many community clients who wanted him to make their portraits.

197

Mr. Polk was a magician with images; he recognized the presence of the spirit as well as the physical. With his camera, he was able to capture the true essence of his subjects—to bring out their heroic qualities. He simply liked people and let them know it. He possessed dignity and projected an uncluttered openness. Mr. Polk and his subjects as viewed through his lens shared the same human qualities—the same air of dignity and self-knowledge. In some way, he seemed to enter into the hearts of the people he photographed. Perhaps his most outstanding attribute was that he was never afraid of being personal.

As a student at Tuskegee in the 1960s, I found great pleasure and much enlightenment listening to Mr. Polk reflect on his style of working. He was most fond of the photographs he made outside of his university work and paying clients. His personal pursuit of true art would begin when he got into his car and drove the back roads of Macon County in search of images of rural, often uneducated people. To him these simple folk possessed something truly noteworthy: character and dignity. He embraced the humanity of those whose life responsibilities put his kind of advanced education beyond their reach. He was the living embodiment of the philosophy of Tuskegee University—never to separate ourselves from those who are less fortunate and to admire and encourage dignity in all of us.

The gains from his professional obligations at Tuskegee afforded Mr. Polk the opportunity to document the lives of the rural elderly poor. He struck a balance between these two worlds, and he achieved it so well. He documented the well-to-do with all the pride of possibility. And he documented the less-than-well-off with the love of a brother, bringing us all into his heart, into his house of pictures. With his camera he would put both on proud display.

Some weekends when he did not have the time to travel the rural farm roads, he would keep an eye peeled on the street outside his home for passing farmers. On one such day, a woman walked by with a corn cob pipe. On another day, he spotted a woman with a sash over her breast. The moment he saw passersby who appealed to his artistic eye, he would drop whatever he was doing and run outside. He would then plead with them to let him make a photograph, at the same time assuring them that it would not cost them anything. Inviting them back into his studio, he would position his big format camera mounted on a movable stand, duck his head under the black focusing cloth, and

199

200

202

squeeze the shutter release; thereby, making another picture that warmed his heart.

In life many of us succeed because we stand on the broad shoulders of those who encouraged our success. Mr. Polk credited Tuskegee with providing him opportunity. It was here in 1925 that he came after taking a correspondence course in photography from the Art Institute of Chicago. Under the guidance of Cornelius Marion Battey, the head of photography and personal photographer to Booker T. Washington, Mr. Polk discovered a personal philosophy that would serve him well for the rest of his life.

—Chester Higgins, Jr.

## James A. Porter
**(1905–1971)**
**Painter, art historian**
Author of the classic work *Modern Negro Art*, Porter was the chronicler of achievements of black artists. He earned a B.A. at Howard in 1927, an M.A. at New York University's Institute of the Fine Arts in 1937, and taught at Howard from 1927 to 1971. As head of the art department and director of Howard's art gallery, he was responsible for many one-person shows of black artists.

199. *Woman with Jug*, 1930
Oil on canvas
21 x 19½
Fisk University, Nashville, Tennessee

## Richard Riley
**(active 1900s)**
**Photographer**
Riley was active in the Hampton Camera Club (1897–1904) and involved with the photography for several poetry books by the renowned author Paul Lawrence Dunbar.

200. *On Butler Farm*, c. 1900
Digital reproduction from original cyanotype
4½ x 6¹⁵⁄₁₆
Collection of Hampton University Archives

## C.D. Robinson
**(active 1910s)**
**Photographer**
One of many photographers hired to capture for posterity the people, landscape, and activities of Tuskegee Institute, Robinson leaves a rich photographic legacy that awaits further identification, documentation, and research.

201. *Bethel Grove Public School, Macon County, AL*, c. 1915
Gelatin silver print
7 x 9 (image); 8 x 9¹⁵⁄₁₆ (sheet)
Collection of Tuskegee University

202. *Dorsey Public School, Lee County, AL*, c. 1915
Gelatin silver print
7¾ x 9¾ (image); 8 x 9¹⁵⁄₁₆ (sheet)
Collection of Tuskegee University

203. *Greensboro Public School, Hale County, AL Old Building*, c. 1915
Gelatin silver print
7¹¹⁄₁₆ x 9¹¹⁄₁₆ (image); 8 x 9¹⁵⁄₁₆ (sheet)
Collection of Tuskegee University

204. *State Road Public School—Perry Co., Ala. Old building*, c. 1915
Gelatin silver print
9¾ x 7¾ (image); 10 x 8 (sheet)
Collection of Tuskegee University

205. *Trustee Board*, c. 1915
Gelatin silver print
10 x 8
Collection of Tuskegee University

## John N. Robinson
**(1912–1994)**
**Painter**
From the mid-1930s—while working full-time as a cook and supporting his family—John Robinson painted crisp, realistic urban landscapes, church murals, and portraits of his family and friends. Although he was primarily self-taught, Robinson studied briefly with Howard University art professor James A. Porter and, as a result, figured significantly among artistic and cultural circles in Washington, D.C., for many years.

206. *Anacostia Hills*, 1944
Oil on canvas
23¾ x 29⅞
Collection of Howard University Gallery of Art

206

207

207. *Mr. & Mrs. Barton*, 1942
Oil on canvas
39 x 31
Second Award in Oil Painting, Atlanta
University Art Annual, 1945. Collection of
Clark Atlanta University Art Galleries

*Mr. & Mrs. Barton* is a double portrait
of John Robinson's grandparents who
raised him since his early adolescence.
Robinson's grandparents were his first
subjects when he realized his serious commitment to art in the 1930s. The portrait
reflects the respect Robinson had for his
grandparents who are represented as icons
of perseverance and dignity in this painting, the last of three portraits of them. The
contentment of home surrounds the couple, who are formally posed in their brightly lit family dining room. The universal
themes of Robinson's portraiture—love
and reverence of family, dignity and hard-
work—elevate his paintings from a personal visual journal to a tribute to the values
of living that carried families through the
troubled times of the Depression and
World War II.

Robinson's detail, which comple-
ments his ability to visualize his subject's
emotion in this painting, communicates
important messages about the personal
character of the Bartons. In the catalogue
of John Robinson's first retrospective and
the bicentennial collaborative exhibition
of the Anacostia Neighborhood Museum
and the Corcoran Gallery of Art, Robinson
reminisces that Ignatius Barton was a
stern and gruff working-class man who
served with the Ninth and Tenth Cavalries
during the Spanish American War.
Robinson also recalls his "warm, lovely"
grandmother, Anna Barton, a laundress
in segregated Georgetown during his
upbringing.[1] Visually, Robinson evokes
a dimension of character through the
hands of Mr. and Mrs. Barton which allude
to his grandparents's work ethic. Their
hands have done a lifetime of work and
show wear; however, the straightforward
gaze of the elder Bartons conveys comfort
rather than weariness. The portraits of
the Bartons's grandchildren on the wall
behind them, Robinson's daughters
Roberta, on the left, and Blanche, on
the right, enrich the pride sensed of the
Bartons in their humble shotgun house.

Robinson's association with the established art world proved beneficial to his
artistic advancement, though his technical
development came from dedicated independent study. His formal training began
and ended in 1929 with one enlightening
semester of composition and design study
with Howard University's art professor
and historian James Porter. Robinson

continued honing his talents in the 1930s
while raising a family of six. In 1945
Robinson entered *Mr & Mrs. Barton* in the
Atlanta University Art Annual and won
second prize in painting in the national
Negro art competition. Later Robinson
was recognized by James V. Herring and
Alonzo Aden of the Barnett-Aden Gallery.
The Barnett-Aden Gallery was the harvest-
ing ground for Negro artists who received
support, guidance, and exposure through
its integrated art exhibitions. Through the
Barnett-Aden Gallery, he met artists Loïs
Mailou Jones and Alma Thomas. In 1947
Robinson exhibited with Jacob Kainen and
Jack Perlmutter, whose acquaintances led
to their assistance with entering his art in
"whites-only" competitions.

Robinson mainly pursued avenues that
gave the local public direct exposure to his
art work and remained virtually unaffected
by surrounding stylistic influences. He
participated in outdoor art fairs in Lafayette
Park, Washington, D.C., in the 1940s, winning seven cash prizes and earning extra
income by creating "minute paintings" of
passersby. The aspect of his work that has
received the least scholarly investigation is
the church murals Robinson produced in
his early career. Robinson's most ambitious
stylistic development was the rendering
of reflecting mirrors in painted interiors
which created vistas that revealed physical
surroundings or psychological terrains.
With his mastery of perception and composition, Robinson's reflections extend
an invitation to viewers into his personal
world to digest the universal values attendant in his imagination.

Art critic Paul Richard dubbed *Mr. &
Mrs. Barton* "Anacostia Gothic"[2] because
it exalts a typical Negro folk scene to the
point of reverence through a keen realist
eye. Robinson's artistic success hinges on
the fact that he paints a picture for everyone by painting a picture for himself.
Robinson's reputation remains relatively
obscure in the art world outside of Washington. Still, his influence within the
Washington art scene has been minor,
and his artistic legacy is only superficially
exposed in recent art publications and
exhibitions. The focus and dedication that
John Robinson yielded to produce his art
work during dire times should be fuel for
the next generations of ambitious artists.

—Brett A. Crenshaw

1. Anacostia Neighborhood Museum, *John
Robinson: A Retrospective* (Washington, D.C.:
Smithsonian Institution Press, 1976), pp. 13–25.

2. Paul Richard, "Mr. Robinson's Neighborhood," *Washington Post*, 17 September 1993.

208

## Charles Sallee
**(b. 1913)**
**Printmaker**
After studies at Western Reserve University, John Huntington Polytechnic Institute, and the Cleveland Museum of Art School, Sallee taught art for a brief period at Cleveland's Karamu Settlement House. While employed by Cleveland's WPA/FAP during the late 1930s and early 1940s, Sallee was one of the city's most productive printmakers, as evidenced in numerous examples of his work at the Cleveland Museum of Art and Howard University.

208. *Swingtime*, 1937
Aquatint and etching on wove paper
5½ x 6¹⁵/₁₆ (image); 9⅞ x 13 (sheet)
Collection of Howard University Gallery of Art

209

## Augusta Savage
**(1892–1962)**
**Sculptor**
After being educated at Tallahasee State Normal School and Cooper Union (New York) and years of studying, exhibiting, and traveling in Europe, Savage opened community art schools and renounced the artist's life for more altruistic roles of arts educator and community activist. Her sculpture career blossomed from the 1920s to the 1940s. Dignity and faithfulness to her subjects became hallmarks of her heroic portrayals in bronze, plaster, and clay.

209. *Gamin'*, c. 1929
Bronze
9 x 4 x 4½
Collection of Howard University Gallery of Art

210

## William Edouard Scott
**(1884–1964)**
**Painter**
Best known for his portraits and murals, Scott studied at the Art Institute of Chicago and at the Académie Julian in Paris. A protégé of the renowned artist Henry Ossawa Tanner, Scott also painted in Haiti in the 1930s, fusing his academic approach with an exploration of black folkways and racial portraiture.

210. *Grandma Collie (Old Age)*, c. 1933
Oil on canvas
22 x 18
Collection of Tuskegee University

211. *Woman at Rest by Candlelight*, c. 1912
Oil on canvas
18 x 22
Collection of Clark Atlanta University Art Galleries, gift of Judge Irvin C. Mollison

## Addison Scurlock
**(1883–1964)**
**Photographer**
Scurlock is best known for portraits of businessmen, political leaders, writers, artists, and celebrities. He photographed his black clientele with a keen awareness of their respective styles and preserving their sense of self-worth. He owned his own successful photographic studio in Washington, D.C., from 1911 to 1964 and for a period was the official photographer for Howard University. During the 1930s, Scurlock created weekly newsreels featuring Washington events that were screened in local theaters nightly.

212. *Moton as President of Tuskegee Institute*, c. 1920
Gelatin silver print
9¹⁵/₁₆ x 7½
Collection of Tuskegee University

213. *William Artis, Sculptor with Model Miss Coleman, Giving Demonstration, (Portrait Sculpture Class: "Bust of Miss Coleman")*, 1946
Gelatin silver print
8⅛ x 10 (image); 9¼ x 11¼ (sheet)
Collection of Howard University Gallery of Art

214. *William Artis, Giving a Demonstration, (Portrait Sculpture Class: "Bust of Miss Coleman")*, 1946
Gelatin silver print
8⅛ x 10 (image); 9¼ x 11¼ (sheet)
Collection of Howard University Gallery of Art

## Charles Sebree
**(1914–1985)**
**Painter, illustrator**
A member of the art scene that developed on Chicago's South Side in the 1930s and a graduate of the Art Institute of Chicago, Sebree utilized the visual and humanitarian legacy of Chicago's black culture to produce paintings with a myriad artistic statements. Influenced by his vast number of friends in other creative mediums, Sebree designed costumes and stage sets. Toward the end of his life he lived and worked in Washington, D.C.

215

215. *War Worker*, 1949
Paint on paperboard
10¹/₁₆ x 8
Collection of Howard University Gallery
of Art

## Alvin Smith
### (b. 1933)
**Painter, illustrator**
Smith's training in art and art education is
broad, having transpired at the University
of Illinois, State University of Iowa, Kansas
City Art Institute, New York University, and
Columbia Teachers College. A recipient of
the Pollock-Krasner Award for lifetime
achievements in art, Smith has taught at
both the high school and university levels,
and has also served as an illustrator of
children's books. One of his books, Maia
Wojciechowska's *Shadow of the Bull* (1965),
received the prestigious Newberry Award.
In addition to Clark Atlanta University's
art collection, Smith's works are in the
collections of the Dayton Art Museum,
the National Museum of American Art,
Smithsonian Institution, and Tougaloo
University.

216. *Neshoba Specter*, 1966
Oil on canvas with collage
60 x 35¹/₂
First Award in Oil Painting, Atlanta
University Art Annual, 1966. Collection of
Clark Atlanta University Art Galleries

## Alfred Stieglitz
### (1864–1946)
**Photographer**
One of the most important art influences
on American cultural life before World War
II, he was among the first to introduce the
art of the European and American avant-
garde to the American public while simultaneously championing, publishing, and
exhibiting much of the best photography of
the period. His career spanned more than
fifty years and bridged nineteenth- and
twentieth-century styles in photography.
His photographs are deeply personal and
steeped in both natural landscapes and the
romance of modern cities.

217

217. *Apples*, 1921
Gelatin silver print
5 x 4
The Alfred Stieglitz Collection, Fisk
University, Nashville, Tennessee, gift of
Georgia O'Keeffe

218. *Equivalent*, 1925
Gelatin silver print
5 x 4
The Alfred Stieglitz Collection, Fisk
University, Nashville, Tennessee, gift of
Georgia O'Keeffe

219. *Equivalent*, 1925
Gelatin silver print
4 x 5
The Alfred Stieglitz Collection, Fisk
University, Nashville, Tennessee, gift of
Georgia O'Keeffe

220. *Equivalent*, 1926
Gelatin silver print
5 x 4
The Alfred Stieglitz Collection, Fisk
University, Nashville, Tennessee, gift of
Georgia O'Keeffe

221. *Equivalent*, c. 1924
Gelatin silver print
5 x 4
The Alfred Stieglitz Collection, Fisk
University, Nashville, Tennessee, gift of
Georgia O'Keeffe

222. *North from an American Place*, c. 1931
Gelatin silver print
10 x 8
The Alfred Stieglitz Collection, Fisk
University, Nashville, Tennessee, gift of
Georgia O'Keeffe

223. *Poplars Beside Porch, Lake George*,
c. 1932
Gelatin silver print
10 x 8
The Alfred Stieglitz Collection, Fisk
University, Nashville, Tennessee, gift of
Georgia O'Keeffe

224. *Poplars Beside Porch, Lake George*,
c. 1932
Gelatin silver print
10 x 8
The Alfred Stieglitz Collection, Fisk
University, Nashville, Tennessee, gift of
Georgia O'Keeffe

225. *Radio City from Shelton Hotel*, 1930
Gelatin silver print
8 x 10
The Alfred Stieglitz Collection, Fisk
University, Nashville, Tennessee, gift of
Georgia O'Keeffe

## Henry Ossawa Tanner
### (1859–1937)
**Painter**

Tanner is the most acclaimed black painter of the late nineteenth-century. Although Tanner believed that his work should be considered without regard to race, he became a model for many young black artists especially during the Harlem Renaissance. His paintings evoke intense emotional depth and rich sentiments and are marked with religious expression. He taught briefly at Clark College, (Atlanta, Georgia, c. 1888), and in 1909 he was the first black artist nominated to the National Academy of Design. From 1893 until his death, he lived and worked in Paris and the surrounding French environs.

226. *Disciples Healing the Sick*, c. 1930
Oil on board
40 x 52
Collection of Clark Atlanta University Art Galleries, university purchase

227. *Poplars*, c. 1930
Oil on cardboard
9³/₈ x 13
Collection of North Carolina Central University Art Museum, purchased with funds given by Friends of the Museum, Hillside High School Class of 1932, and Treasures Auction

228. *Return at Night from Market*, n.d.
Oil on canvas
25¹/₂ x 20¹/₂
Collection of Clark Atlanta University Art Galleries, university purchase.

229. *The Three Marys*, 1910
Oil on canvas
42 x 50
Fisk University, Nashville, Tennessee, gift of the Art Institute of Chicago

## Prentiss Hottel Taylor
### (b. 1907–1991)
**Painter, lithographer**

Taylor, an art therapist at St. Elizabeth's Hospital in Washington, D.C., was a pioneer in the use of art in psychotherapy. His research examined how art could reintegrate the disordered mind. He studied at the Art Students League, the Corcoran School of Art, the George Miller Workshop in New York, and he taught at American University. His work illuminated landscapes and architecture rather than people and showed the influence of cubism and primitivism. He worked with Langston Hughes on pamphlet publications with historic black themes and created the cover for Hughes's *Scottsboro Limited*. Although Taylor was best known for his lithographs, his watercolors are testimony to his wit and wide-ranging humanist concerns.

230. *Macedonia, A.M.E., April 1934*, 1934
Lithograph on wove paper
9⁹/₁₆ x 13³/₈ (image); 13¹/₄ x 17 (sheet)
Collection of Howard University Gallery of Art

## Alma Woodsey Thomas
### (1891–1978)
**Painter**

Thomas was the first student to enter and graduate from Howard University's art department (1924). Beginning her career as an art teacher, she did not devote full time to her painting until her early sixties. Her work is characterized by the use of flat colors and uniform strokes. She used the application of color as a metaphor for the natural order of the environment.

231. *Orange Glow*, 1968
Acrylic on canvas
30 x 48
Collection of Howard University Gallery of Art

232. *Spring Flowers Near Jefferson Memorial*, 1963
Acrylic on canvas
50 x 60
Fisk University, Nashville, Tennessee

From work on the "Projects" of the New Deal, to the receipt of individual grants from the National Endowment for the Arts in more recent times, American art and artists have benefitted greatly from United States government patronage in many forms. Alma Thomas may be the only American artist to have benefitted mostly from the work of the United States Park Service. In the nation's capitol, the Park Service operates one of the great gardening displays of the world, supplying seasonal blooms in the odds and ends of triangles, rhomboids, and circles brought into being by Pierre L'Enfant's layout of the city, a grid of alphabetical and numbered streets overlaid by the avenues of the states, which sometimes seems designed almost in the manner of Pick-Up-Sticks. The floral bounty of the Park Service provided Alma Thomas with her models and inspiration for a long productive life in art.

229

230

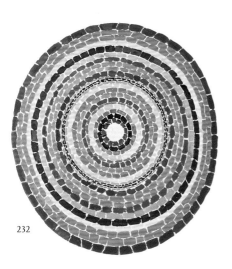

232

Thomas came to Washington as a child with her parents in 1907, moving into the house on 15th Street in which she lived and worked until her death. She prepared herself for a life in art deliberately and intelligently.

The first graduate of Howard University's art department (1924), Alma Thomas enrolled in painting classes at American and Columbia Universities when she was in her fifties. She received a travel fellowship to European art centers, and she was the first black woman artist to be given a solo exhibition at the Whitney Museum of American Art in New York. Like many artists, she found she could make a living teaching art, which she did at Shaw Junior High School.

Since color plays a large part in her work and since she lived most of her life in Washington, she is often thought of as representing the Washington Color School. There are significant differences. Even in coloring large areas—rectangles, or as in *Spring Flowers Near Jefferson Memorial*, circles—Ms. Thomas always presented her colors almost as atomic particles rather than as large, solid areas, in the manner of Kenneth Noland and Morris Louis, the two leading practitioners of the Washington Color School.

By both her own account and the evidence of her work, she seems, more than anything else, to be an abstract nature painter. She wrote in a catalogue statement for a 1971 exhibition at Fisk University:

*Man's highest inspirations come from nature. A world without color would seem dead. Color is life. Light is the mother of color . . . Spring delivers her dynamic message to the world each year, drenching one's thoughts with its magnificent outburst of light hues of color to darker ones as the weather grows warmer. Autumn, with the aid of Jack Frost, gives overwhelming, luscious strong colors to the earth to enrich man's soul, seemingly relieving him of the hardships he encounters in daily life.*[1]

She classified *Spring Flowers Near Jefferson Memorial* as one of her "earth paintings," of which she wrote:

*My earth paintings are inspired by the display of azaleas at the Arboretum, the cherry blossoms, circular flower beds, the nurseries as seen from planes that are airborne, and by the foliage of trees in the autumn.*[2]

—Frank Getlein

1. David C. Driskell, *Recent Paintings by Alma W. Thomas: Earth and Space Series, 1961–1971* (Nashville: Carl Van Vechten Gallery of Fine Arts, Fisk University, 1971), p. 4.

2. Idem

235

237

## Dox Thrash

### (1892–1965)
### Printmaker, painter

Thrash studied art through correspondence school, at the Art Institute of Chicago, and under Earl Hortor of the Graphic Sketch Club in Philadelphia. He is the co-inventor of the carborundum print process. His earliest work featured portraits executed in carborundum print, aquatint, lithography, watercolor, ink wash, and graphite, showing introspective qualities and subtle ranges of tonal variations. Dark, smoky atmospheres dominate his landscapes.

233. *Alice*, c. 1933
Aquatint on wove paper
7 1/8 x 5 3/4 (image); 9 5/8 x 7 3/8 (sheet)
Collection of Howard University Gallery of Art

234. *Blue Monday*, c. 1930
Aquatint on wove paper
8 7/16 x 6 15/16 (image); 9 15/16 x 8 1/16 (sheet)
Collection of Howard University Gallery of Art

235. *Boats At Night*, 1937
Aquatint and etching on wove paper
7 3/8 x 11 3/8 (image); 11 3/8 x 14 3/8 (sheet)
Collection of Howard University Gallery of Art

236. *Cabin Days*, c. 1930
Aquatint and etching on wove paper
10 x 9 1/8 (image); 13 1/16 x 10 13/16 (sheet)
Collection of Howard University Gallery of Art

237. *Catfishin'*, c. 1930
Aquatint and etching on wove paper
8 1/16 x 10 1/4 (image); 9 15/16 x 12 1/2 (sheet)
Collection of Howard University Gallery of Art

238. *Surface Mining*, c. 1930
Aquatint and etching on wove paper
6 11/16 x 9 7/8 (image); 9 x 11 1/4 (sheet)
Collection of Howard University Gallery of Art

## Herbert Pinney Tresslar

### (active early 1900s)
### Photographer

In 1892 Tresslar took over the photography studio founded by his father in 1885 in Montgomery, Alabama.

239. *William J. Edwards and the teachers at Snow Hill Institute*, n.d.
Gelatin silver print
6 5/16 x 8 1/4 (image); 8 5/8 x 11 1/2 (sheet)
Collection of Tuskegee University

# Doris Ulmann

## (1882–1934)

**Photographer**

This internationally known portrait photographer is best remembered for her pictorial documentation of rural life of the poor in Appalachia and the Deep South. She spent six to eight months a year traveling through the South. Her photographs of black Southerners from the Lang Syne Plantation in South Carolina accompanied Julia Peterkin's text in the period piece *Roll, Jordan, Roll* (1933).

240. *The Mourner's Bench*, c. 1929–30
Coated platinotype
8 x 6⅛
Collection of Howard University Gallery of Art

240

The end of the Great War marked America's ascendance to the position of leading world power, inspiring a wave of intense Americanism. There was also the suspicion that America had been so irrevocably altered that traditions and ethics had been lost forever. Cultural leaders called for a new American art that identified the nation's authentic characteristics and values. Two divergent subjects emerged in American arts and letters in response: one focused on the triumphantly modern American city and the other rediscovered traditional, rural folk culture. The first celebrated America's modernization and success in creating a civilization free of the afflictions plaguing European society. The second highlighted the roots and distinctiveness of American culture which provided a bulwark against the disorienting transformations to everyday life engendered by modernity.

The oeuvre of Doris Ulmann reflects the tension between these two impulses in American art. Ulmann was an affluent New York photographer of German-Jewish descent who began her career making portraits of "moderns," figures who were at the vanguard of the changes sweeping the nation.[1] In the late twenties, Ulmann shifted her attention to folk subcultures such as the Mennonites, Shakers, and the Appalachian mountain people who retained historically American customs. The author, Julia Peterkin, invited Ulmann to photograph the Negro workers of Lang Syne, her South Carolina plantation, in 1929.[2] These people were Gullah, the descendants of slaves who had developed a distinctive blend of African and European cultures living in virtual isolation along the coast of Georgia and South Carolina. Seventy-two photographs by Ulmann were published in the 1933 book, *Roll, Jordan,*

*Roll*, along with text by Peterkin.[3] This collaboration yielded an ethnographic account of everyday life for rural Negroes.

*The Mourner's Bench* is one of a suite of images depicting the religious practices of the Gullah who had been required to adopt Christianity during slavery. The scene shows several women kneeling before a minister and his attendants. While the photographs are not meant to be illustrations, the text explains that the "mourners" are not bereaved but repentant sinners who come to kneel before the "mourner's bench . . . in front of the pulpit" to be guided towards righteousness.[4] The church is a modest building made of rough-hewn boards reflecting the poverty of the congregation. The worshippers are still carefully dressed in their best clothes attesting to the significance of religious ritual in their lives and the seriousness of their faith. The title, an appropriation from the well-known spiritual, indicates that the book was intended to be a recognition of black cultural traditions and an acknowledgement of their contribution to American culture.[5]

Ulmann's celebration of black folk culture was noticeable because how Negroes were conceived affected the credibility of theories underpinning the white racial hegemony so fundamental to American society. Caricature and stereotypes were used to designate the roles that Negroes were expected to play in society. In the twenties, Negroes forged a modern urban culture, challenged the identity imposed upon them, and agitated for the full rights and privileges of citizenship.[6] White artists who represented this "New Negro" as an aspect of city life ignored the social agenda of Negroes. They caricatured them as exotics or primitives and fixated on the entertaining spectacle of jazz music and dance.[7] *Roll, Jordan, Roll* employs a similar strategy by creating an atavistic world that bore little resemblance to actual black experience and deflects attention from racial dilemmas. Ulmann conjures up a pastorale of a simple, agrarian people undisturbed by the advent of modernity. Recasting old stereotypes with a new veneer, the photographs echo Peterkin's overt allusion to postbellum Southern literature and its revisionist account of plantation life with "Old Negroes" who were happy to eschew modernity and freedom for their quaint folkways and devoted service to whites.[8]

Ulmann's aesthetic reflects her oscillation between a sincere interest in black culture and the desire to neutralize any threat that Negroes might pose to the social order. Ulmann utilized an old-fashioned view camera that used glass negatives instead of the newly invented

241

35mm cameras and roll films.[9] Her choice afforded her more selective focus, a broader, subtler tonal range, and softer delineation ensuring that Ulmann controlled the mise-en-scene and the direction of the viewer's attention. The careful elision of traces of modernity confines the subjects to Ulmann's contrived world, robbing them of agency and the ability to effect change.[10] Ulmann employed the pictorialist mode rather than the prevalent "straight" style lending a nostalgic, glamorous aura to the photographs which suggested that her vision of black life was the most attractive social formation.[11] At once a step forward and a longing look backward, Ulmann's Gullah photographs are located at the crossroads of conflicts over race, nation, and modernity that Americans grappled with during the interwar years.

—Camara Dia Holloway

1. David Featherstone, *Doris Ulmann, American Portraits* (Albuquerque: University of New Mexico Press, 1985).

2. Ulmann's connection to Peterkin and the genesis of this trip is described in Michelle Laumunière, "*Roll, Jordan, Roll* and the Gullah photographs of Doris Ulmann," in *History of Photography*, 21 (winter 1997): 4: 294–302.

3. Julia Peterkin and Doris Ulmann, *Roll, Jordan, Roll* (New York: Robert O. Ballou, 1933). A second limited edition containing eighteen additional photographs was published in 1934.

4. Peterkin and Ulmann, p. 84.

5. Spirituals and later black musical styles, like the blues and jazz, were widely considered to be the only original, authentic American music. "Roll, Jordan, Roll" was so well known that it was the first entry in the first compilation of spirituals, see William Francis Allen, *Slave Songs of the United States* (New York: A. Simpson & Co., 1867). This fact is noted in Richard Newman, *Go Down Moses: Celebrating the African-American Spiritual* (New York: Clarkson Potter, 1998), pp. 190–91.

6. Extensive scholarship on this period exists, see David Levering Lewis, *When Harlem Was in Vogue* (New York: Alfred A. Knopf, 1981). The cultural and social agenda of Negroes during this era was articulated in an anthology edited by Alain Locke, see *The New Negro: An Interpretation* (New York: Albert and Charles Boni, Inc., 1925).

7. This is true of the following selection of popular works of the era: Carl Van Vechten, *Nigger Heaven* (New York: Alfred A. Knopf, 1926), Miguel Covarrubias, *Negro Drawings* (New York: Alfred A. Knopf, 1927), and *The Jazz Singer* (Warner Brothers, 1927).

8. Julia Peterkin's oeuvre, especially her Pulitzer Prize-winning novel, *Scarlet Sister Mary* (Indianapolis: The Bobbs-Merrill Company, 1928), were part of the Southern Renaissance, a literary movement in the early twentieth century that supposedly challenged older representations of Negroes. As with my argument regarding Ulmann, such efforts still fell prey to the demands of racial ideology. Despite Peterkin's intimacy with and simpatico for Negroes, her works do not deviate far from long-held stereotypes. For further information, see her biography, Susan Millar Williams, *A Devil and a Good Woman, Too: The Lives of Julia Peterkin* (Athens: University of Georgia Press, 1997). From the end of the Civil War, reminiscences about the glorious old South were a hugely successful literary genre throughout the nation and became a recurring theme in popular media, especially in advertising, see Jo-Ann Morgan, "Mammy the Huckster: Selling the Old South for a New Century," in *American Art*, 9 (spring 1995): 1: 86–109.

9. Ulmann had the financial resources to procure the newer equipment. She chose not to avail herself of it even though she had several physical limitations that made it difficult for her to wield the heavy view camera and she needed to employ an assistant to help her.

10. There is a significantly disruptive sign of modernity in the book: a sequence of photographs of a chain gang. Its presence alludes to the measures whites took to ensure that Negroes would continue to provide labor necessary to the American enterprise after the Civil War. The chain gang sentence was only one tactic of a larger system designed to extract Negro labor. With the sanction of state and local policy, Negroes could be jailed on the barest of pretenses or otherwise compelled to work, see Willam Cohen, "Negro Involuntary Servitude in the South, 1865–1940: A Preliminary Analysis," in *The Journal of Southern History* XLII (February 1976): 1: 31–60, reprinted in *The Age of Jim Crow: Segregation from the End of Reconstruction to the Great Depression,* edited by Paul Finkleman, *Race, Law and American History, 1700–1900. The African-American Experience,* vol. 4 (New York: Garland Publishing, Inc., 1992), pp. 13–42.

11. Ulmann was trained at the Clarence H. White School of Photography, whose curricula provided ample training in the latest developments in modernism, such as "straight" photography, see *Pictorialism into Modernism: The Clarence H. White School of Photography,* edited by Marianne Fulton, with texts by Bonnie Yochelson and Kathleen A. Erwin (New York: Rizzoli, 1996).

# Carl Van Vechten
## (1880–1964)
### Photographer, author

In 1932 Van Vechten became a portrait photographer after a successful career as a journalist and music critic. Van Vechten used the camera to handsomely capture black celebrities in the arts, theater, music, and literary worlds. He contributed his extensive photography collections to Fisk, Howard, and Yale Universities, among other educational institutions.

241. *Aaron Douglas,* 1933
Gelatin silver print
10 x 8
Fisk University, Nashville, Tennessee, gift of the artist

242. *Cab Calloway*, 1933
Gelatin silver print
10 x 7
The George Gershwin Memorial
Collection, Fisk University, Nashville,
Tennessee, gift of the artist

243. *Georgia O'Keeffe*, 1935
Gelatin silver print
10 x 8
Fisk University, Nashville, Tennessee, gift
of the artist

244. *Horace Pippin*, 1940
Gelatin silver print
10 x 8
Fisk University, Nashville, Tennessee, gift
of the artist

242

245. *Lena Horne*, 1940
Gelatin silver print
9⁷/₈ x 7⁷/₈
The George Gershwin Memorial
Collection, Fisk University, Nashville,
Tennessee, gift of the artist

246. *Man Ray*, 1934
Gelatin silver print
9¹/₂ x 6¹/₂
Fisk University, Nashville, Tennessee, gift
of the artist

247. *Marcel Duchamp*, 1933
Gelatin silver print
10 x 6³/₄
Fisk University, Nashville, Tennessee, gift
of the artist

248. *Richmond Barthé*, 1934
Gelatin silver print
10 x 8
Fisk University, Nashville, Tennessee, gift
of the artist

In 1941 the American writer and photographer Carl Van Vechten began a crusade—as quiet as it was unique—to construct a program of racial intellectual integration, reasoning that good black collections in white universities would draw black scholars there; that good white collections in black universities would similarly draw white scholars; that color-blind collections could even begin to break down prejudice. His own photographs led him to establish collections in a dozen institutions, two of which—Yale University and Fisk University—are now of major dimension and of inestimable value.

He founded the "James Weldon Johnson Memorial Collection of Negro Arts and Letters" at Yale, based on holdings he had amassed since the turn of the century, developed through his growing interest in black literary and artistic matters as well as popular entertainments—from which his sympathetic 1926 novel *Nigger Heaven* grew—and expanded through the rest of his long life with his own photographs of African Americans who were widely recognized in various fields. Subsequently, the collection was enhanced with the papers of Langston Hughes, James Weldon Johnson, Claude McKay, Wallace Thurman, and others identified with the New Negro movement of the twenties, as well as with the papers of later figures like Chester Himes and Richard Wright. Also, it included Van Vechten's extensive letters from these figures and from many other black artists and writers; rare, historical photographs, sheet music, and programs; an extensive library of books by and about African Americans; and nearly complete sets of recordings by several popular singers.

Carl Van Vechten had been a music critic early in his career, so at Fisk he founded the "George Gershwin Memorial Collection of Music and Musical Literature" to hold his similarly large collections of related materials. It included rare music manuscripts and autographed letters from a broad range of composers, opera singers, and musicians; a library of opera and orchestral scores, biographies, novels, and books of musical criticism; and rare, original photographs of musical luminaries, all primarily white. Also, he established the "Florine Stettheimer Memorial Collection of Books About The Fine Arts," and he arranged for Stettheimer's estate to give Fisk one of her more important paintings, *Asbury Park*. To these two collections Van Vechten then added large selections of his photographs of artists and musicians of all races.

Then he persuaded his friend, Georgia O'Keeffe, to donate to Fisk substantial holdings from the estate of her husband, the photographer Alfred Stieglitz. The remarkable archive—now housed in the Carl Van Vechten Gallery of Fine Arts—includes work by Charles Demuth, Arthur Dove, Marsden Hartley, and John Marin, as well as by O'Keeffe and Stieglitz—all of whom are represented in *To Conserve a Legacy: American Art from Historically Black Colleges and Universities*.

Van Vechten would feel himself honored to be included. His commitment to Fisk University, which awarded him an honorary doctorate in 1955, was long-standing, and his photographs there—from which those in the exhibition have been drawn—offer a good introduction to his work in this medium.[1]

After two decades as a subsequently influential critic, and another decade as a popular novelist, Carl Van Vechten turned to photography in 1932. His major interest was in portraits, and documenting celebrated people connected with the arts became his passion. His literary connections gave him many subjects, and his wife, the actress Fania Marinoff, knew plenty of people in the theater. He began with Eugene O'Neill and Henri Matisse, and over thirty years later he ended with Lincoln Kirstein and Gloria Vanderbilt. In between, his early interests—ballet and dance, black arts and letters—gave him his most frequent subjects, and these, together with the best of his portraits of figures in other fields, give ample evidence of an impressive achievement.

Unlike most photographers, Van Vechten made finished prints of nearly every picture he took. In recalling the Yousuf Karsh portrait of Albert Einstein, or the Nickolas Muray portrait of D. H. Lawrence, or indeed the Berenice Abbott portrait of Carl Van Vechten himself, one knows of a single image in each case. Contrarily, there are many portraits of some of Van Vechten's subjects: over a dozen each of Edward Albee, Alvin Ailey, Isak Dinesen, William Faulkner, Ella Fitzgerald, Martha Graham, Billie Holiday, Langston Hughes, H. L. Mencken, Leontyne Price, Paul Robeson, and Bessie Smith, for example; nearly a hundred of Gertrude Stein; several hundred of Alicia Markova. The complete Van Vechten archive numbers about fifteen thousand photographs.

This plenitude leads to a good deal of unevenness because Van Vechten was inconsistent in his judgment of his work. He always claimed, "I throw out anything that isn't perfection," but he could be his own worst enemy in the darkroom. He printed up almost everything, and sometimes his prints have faded because he failed to wash them thoroughly in his eagerness to share them, or to establish other archives, notably in the Berg Collection and Lincoln Center and Schomburg branches of the New York Public Library; in Harlem's Wadleigh School (now at the University of New Mexico); in Howard University; in the Piney Woods School in Mississippi.

In the beginning, Van Vechten's photographs were characterized by a strong *chiaroscuro* and later by a more documentary quality. As Van Vechten neither cropped nor retouched his work, it is sometimes disappointing. At their best, however, his photographs are memorable. Those in this exhibition, however, are atypical and largely unfamiliar. Horace Pippin

at the Barnes Foundation, Man Ray on a Paris street corner, Lena Horne at Joe Louis's training camp, and Georgia O'Keeffe on the roof of the Sheraton Hotel, are all *al fresco* shots, as happy as they are candid. Richmond Barthé, a surprisingly pensive Cab Calloway minus his usual white tux and black ringlets, Aaron Douglas, and Marcel Duchamp, are masterful studio portraits.

It was all a labor of love: he gave the prints away to their subjects and to friends; he never accepted commissions; he never photographed anybody he did not want to; he never sold his photographs. He sent the fee for an occasional permission for reproduction to the endowment fund of the Johnson Collection at Yale, and he specified in his will that any future income from his work go there as well.

His interests and intentions were always historical as well as aesthetic, and he liked to say about that, "My photographs are intended primarily as documents, but I believe that is no reason they should not be beautiful."

—Bruce Kellner

# James Weeks
## (1922–1998)
### Painter
An Oakland, California-born painter, Weeks studied at the California School of Fine Arts with several prominent Bay Area figurative artists, including David Park and Marian Hartwell. Years later Weeks taught at the California School of Fine Arts, as well as the California College of Arts and Crafts, University of California at Los Angeles, and Boston University. A painter and a musician, he is well known for his c. 1960s paintings of solitary figures, especially jazz musicians.

249

249. *Jazz Musician,* 1960
Oil on canvas
58 x 42
Collection of Howard University Gallery of Art

James Weeks was a contemporary of Richard Diebenkorn, Elmer Bischoff, and other Bay Area artists who came to prominence during the 1950s. The Bay Area figurative artists, as they came to be known, rejected abstraction, choosing to paint the figure instead.[1] Unlike his colleagues, Weeks did not work in abstraction.[2] Throughout his long career, Weeks painted the figure and, occasionally, landscapes, and still lifes.

James David Northrup Weeks's father was Anson Weeks, the famed hotel dance band leader of the 1930s. His mother Ruth Daly was an accomplished classical pianist. As a youth in the 1920s and 1930s, James spent much of his time in the company of musicians and through these experiences developed a lifelong passion for piano playing. The musical Weekses were highly regarded in the Bay area and especially in Nob Hill where, in the 1930s, Anson's nightly radio broadcast was heard coast to coast. Weeks became close friends with several members of the famed Dave Brubeck octet, of which his brother Jack Weeks was a member.[3]

As a teenager in the late 1930s, Weeks not only demonstrated a clear penchant for music but also proved to be a talented visual artist as well, aspiring to illustration and comic strip art. After Weeks graduated in 1940 from Oakland's Lowell High School, he enrolled in evening courses at the California School of Fine Arts (CSFA), which later became the San Francisco Art Institute. Following a stint in the Air Force, from 1944 to 1945, Weeks resumed his studies as a day student at the CSFA, where he was influenced by the figurative artists David Park and Hassel Smith.[4] In 1946 Weeks enrolled in the Marion Hartwell School of Design to study design and illustration. After teaching there in 1947, he joined the faculty at the CSFA.

In the years following World War II, the CSFA faculty's impressive line-up of painters included Elmer Bischoff, David Park, Mark Rothko, Clyfford Still, and Weeks's longtime friend, Richard Diebenkorn. Firmly associated with this group, Weeks was included in a faculty exhibition (1950) at the M. H. de Young Memorial Art Museum in San Francisco; his first major exhibition. Ten years later, he gained national attention with a solo exhibition at New York's Poindexter Gallery. Having destroyed a number of his earlier works, Weeks, by this time, had begun to paint exceptionally assured compositions with bold colors, gestural brushwork, and sophisticated formal arrangements.[5] For subjects Weeks often looked to music. Jazz musicians and comedians were sources of inspiration for the artist.

Much of the energy in Weeks's work stems from the tension between the spatial ambiguity of the foreground and background. He manipulated shapes by suppressing lines, in favor of large sections of color. Except in the case of portraits, Weeks's figures are usually anonymous, a quality he attained by simplifying and distorting the linear geometry in the faces. Aggressive, almost violent, emotions are suggested by his use of bold colors and gestural paint application. *Jazz Musician* (1960) is characteristic of the artist at the peak of his career.

The painting became part of the Howard University collection (1961) when it was included in "New Vistas in American Art," the ambitious inaugural exhibition of the school's new art gallery.[6] James A. Porter, chair of the department of art and director of the gallery, assisted by the gallery's curator Albert J. Carter, organized the exhibition.[7] Consistent with the philosophy of Porter, who aspired to provide the widest possible experiences for Howard students and the community, a variety of artists was selected; Selma Burke, Jacob Lawrence, Loïs Mailou Jones, Alma Thomas, Charles White, Phillip Evergood, and Robert Gwathmey were among the many artists. A grant from the Eugene and Agnes Meyer Foundation allowed the university to acquire several significant works by black and white artists of various media that depicted themes from black life. Weeks's *Jazz Musician,* an important acquisition, won first place in painting.

The carefully planned arrangement of shapes and colors reveals a typical motif of Weeks's paintings of the 1960s, musicians at rest. A lone male sits casually, frontally posed with legs crossed, on an oversized formal chair. The unidentified man, who is black, seems tall and larger than life. Wearing a business suit and tie, he appears collected, bringing to mind images of musicians in those timeless, archival black and white stills associated with the period. For this painting Weeks employed cool tones, treating red as a cool color in his palette, and emphasizing the musician's landscape of simplicity and comfort. The manipulation of color in this manner, with sections of white paint on the shoulder and the upper chair, suggest that the musician is simply "chilling out," perhaps resting between sets.

Following the Howard exhibition, Weeks continued to gain in artistic stature and receive national acclaim. His work was exhibited in the "Corcoran Biennial" (1961) at the Corcoran Gallery of Art and three years later he was given a major solo exhibition at the San Francisco Museum of Art. With his painting career more visible, and after teaching stints at the College of Arts and Crafts, Oakland and the University of California at Los Angeles (1967), Weeks moved to Boston to accept an associate professorship at Boston University, where he taught until his retirement in 1987.

250

In 1990 Weeks was included in "Bay Area Figurative Art, 1950–1965," organized by the San Francisco Museum of Modern Art, which had venues at the Hirshhorn Museum and Sculpture Garden and the Pennsylvania Academy of Fine Arts.

—Teresia Bush

1. Caroline Jones, *Bay Area Figurative Art, 1950–1960* (San Francisco: San Francisco Museum of Modern Art; University of California Press, Berkeley, Los Angeles, Oxford, 1989), p. 71.

2. Bonny B. Saulnier, *James Weeks* (Waltham, MA: Rose Art Museum; Brandeis University, 1978), p. 13.

3. Ibid, p. 7. R. Cook and B. Morton, *The Penguin Guide to Jazz on CD*, 3d. ed. (London, 1996), pp. 194, 348. Thomas Albright, *Art in the San Francisco Bay Area: An Illustrated History* (Berkeley: University of California Press), p. 68.

4. Joan Bossart, *James Weeks, Paintings 1950–1992* (San Fransciso: Campbell-Thiebaud Gallery, 1994), p. 1.

5. Thomas Albright, *Art in the San Francisco Bay Area: An Illustrated History* (Berkeley: University of California Press), p. 70. Jones, *Bay Area Figurative Art, 1950–1960*, p. 43.

6. Leslie Judd Ahlander, "Howard U. Opens New Art Gallery," *The Washington Post*, 2 April 1962, p. G7.

7. James A. Porter, *New Vistas in American Art* (Washington, D.C.: Howard University, 1962), p. 2.

251

## James Lesesne Wells
### (1902–1993)
**Printmaker, painter**
Educated at Lincoln University, the National Academy of Design, and Teachers College (Columbia University), Wells developed fame as a printmaker of predominantly religious, mythical, and natural subjects. His works meshed the influence of African sculptors and German Expressionists and early in his career he was a prize-winning painter. Wells became a pioneer in the use of color in printmaking. Founder of Howard University's graphics art department, he taught printmaking from 1929 until his retirement in 1968.

250. *African Fantasy*, c. 1932
Linocut on Japanese paper
11 x 8¹⁵⁄₁₆ (image); 13¹⁄₂ x 12¹⁄₁₆ (sheet)
Collection of Howard University Gallery of Art

251. *Bookplate Design from Dr. Alain Locke Library*, n.d.
Linoleum cut on Japanese paper
9¹⁵⁄₁₆ x 5¾ (image); 11 x 8¹⁄₂ (sheet)
Collection of Howard University Gallery of Art

252. *Negro Worker*, c. 1940
Lithograph on wove paper
14⁵⁄₈ x 9¹³⁄₁₆ (image); 19¹⁄₈ x 12⁵⁄₁₆ (sheet)
Collection of Howard University Gallery of Art

253. *Song of the Nile*, c. 1928
Linocut on Japanese paper
15¹⁄₂ x 12¹⁄₂ (image); 19¹⁄₄ x 14¾
Fisk University, Nashville, Tennessee, 1991.283

## Nat Werner
### (1910–1991)
**Sculptor**
Werner studied at the Art Students League and had his first exhibition in 1937. Throughout this sculptor's career, he worked in both figurative and abstract styles and with nearly every sculptural medium including terra-cotta, carved wood and stone, welded steel, and found object assemblage.

254. *Lynching*, c. 1936
Wood
48 x 20 x 24
Collection of Howard University Gallery of Art

## Pheoris West
### (b. 1950)
**Painter, graphic artist**
During the late 1970s, West constructed a visual language that embodied his concept of blackness. Contemporary, urban genre scenes were infused with varied painting techniques, metaphysical compositions, and symbols of African cultures. Multiple layers of paint and modeling of muted tones with bright colors became West's mantra.

255. *Mystified*, 1977
Oil on canvas
18 x 24
Collection of North Carolina Central University Art Museum

255

# Charles White

## (1918–1979)

**Painter, draftsman, printmaker**

White's drawings of black people were large scale, moderately expressionistic, minutely executed, and resonating with emotion, vulnerability, and dignity. His works drew attention to inequality, triumphs over adversity, and white-on-black violence. His educational background included the Art Institute of Chicago, Art Students League, and Taller de Grafica Popular in Mexico where he was impressed by Mexican muralists and their social messages. In his mural painting, White brought black history to the public's consciousness.

256

256. *Progress of the American Negro*, 1939–40
[*Five Great American Negroes*]
Oil on canvas
5' x 12' 11"
Collection of Howard University Gallery of Art

Around 1932, when he was fourteen years old, Charles White read Alain Locke's *The New Negro*, a pivotal work of the so-called Negro Renaissance. The first African American Rhodes scholar and head of the philosophy department at Howard University, Dr. Locke was among the most prominent authorities on Negro culture at the time. Of his work, White later exclaimed: "Man, it blew my mind . . . I discovered that Folks wrote books! That Folks wrote fiction; they wrote poetry; that they were sociologists, anthropologists . . . I didn't know black people did these things!"[1] White's *Progress of the American Negro* emerges against this background of the New Negro movement, reflecting his abiding interest in Negro history and its legacy of political, social, and artistic achievement.

Begun in 1939 after he had graduated from the School of the Art Institute of Chicago and qualified for employment under the WPA/FAP, White's mural-scale painting celebrates in five dramatic portraits the escaped slave and women's rights advocate Sojourner Truth, the educator and reformer Booker T. Washington, the abolitionist and statesman Frederick Douglass, the agricultural chemist George Washington Carver, and the famous contralto Marian Anderson. In its composition, the mural presents a historical movement from left to right, from slavery and the abolitionist movement to modernity and the achievements of Negroes in the arts, sciences, and letters. The facial expressions of the figures, ranging from sorrow to defiance, and the visual structure of the painting, however, maintain the pervasive memory of slavery. To the far right, a teacher discusses with a student a volume of Negro history. Unifying the composition and bringing together past and present, the curve of the teacher's arm echoes and draws the eye back to the sweeping line of spirited slaves led by Truth on the far left. Fittingly, the work would be exhibited in 1940 at the Library of Congress as part of a show organized by Howard University marking the seventy-fifth anniversary of the Thirteenth Amendment to the Constitution, which had abolished slavery. The painting's success would lead to other mural projects for White, culminating in his monumental *Contribution of the Negro to Democracy in America* at Hampton University (1943).

Despite White's singular focus on Negro history, it would be misguided to discuss his early work simply in terms of a tradition of "Negro Art." Indeed, the possibilities of such a category were strongly contested in the 1930s and early 1940s. Although Locke had earlier advocated a racially based art that drew inspiration from Southern Negro folk culture and from African art, such prominent art historians as James A. Porter increasingly criticized this view. A lifelong supporter of White's art, Porter argued that artists engage the mainstream of American culture and produce an art of social criticism that reflected modern Negro experience more directly.[2] As social realism came to outweigh the "Africanist" or "neo-primitive," the aesthetic and political issues White addressed also informed the work of many contemporary American artists, whether Negro or not.

In its emphatic rhetoric, bulky, stylized figures, strong contours and bold colors, condensed spaces and flowing compositional lines, White's mural is readily aligned with the work of such influential American scene muralists as Thomas Hart Benton and, more closely, with that of such revolutionary Mexican muralists as Diego Rivera, José Clemente Orozco, and David Siqueiros.[3] Not merely stylistic, these ties were ideological. Through his formative contact with Chicago-based WPA artists who had worked in Mexico, White conceived of the mural in the current Marxist terms—as a popular and politicized art instrumental in resisting oppression and raising race- and class-consciousness. As White would assert in a 1940 interview with Willard Motley, "I am interested in the total, even propaganda, angle of painting. . . . Painting is the only weapon I have with which to fight what I resent."[4] Discussing the importance of the mural, White would further say, "My main concern is to get my work before common, ordinary people . . . A work of art was meant to belong to people . . . Art should take its place as one of the necessities of life, like food, clothing, and shelter."[5] With the rise of progressive liberalism, socialism, and communism in the United States during the Depression, the WPA became for many artists an important vehicle for such ideas.

In its polemical mural format and emphasis on American history, *Progress of the American Negro* also advances the government mandate for public art. As envisioned under the New Deal, art would serve a didactic purpose helping to promote a harmonious and enlightened citizenry, and as the most monumental of art project forms, the mural would help forge this new national identity along progressive, democratic lines. The integration of Negro communities into this projected unity became a government priority by the late 1930s so that "artist," "citizen," and "Negro" effectively became equivalents in project discourse."[6] Charles White's *Progress of the American Negro* becomes in turn a powerful testimony to this pre-war period of newfound opportunity and hope within the Negro artistic community.

—Scott Allan

1. M.J. Hewitt, "A Tribute to Charles White," *Black Art: an international quarterly* 4, pt. 1 (1980): 32.

2. For a thorough account of this changing critical climate, see David C. Driskell, "The Evolution of a Black Aesthetic, 1920–50," *Two Centuries of Black American Art* (New York: Knopf, 1976), pp. 59–67.

3. Lizetta LeFalle-Collins, "African American Modernists and the Mexican Muralist School," *In the Spirit of Resistance* (New York: The Studio Museum in Harlem, 1996), pp. 27–67, 84–89.

4. Romare Bearden and Harry Henderson, *A History of African-American Artists: From 1792 to the Present* (New York: Pantheon, 1993), p. 408.

5. Lizetta LeFalle-Collins, "Contribution of the American Negro to Democracy: a History Painting by Charles White," *The International Review of African-American Art* 12, no. 4 (1995): 51. For a discussion of the importance of the mural to African American artists more generally, see Edmund Barry Gaither, "The Mural Tradition," *A Shared Heritage: Art by Four African Americans* (Indianapolis: Indianapolis Museum of Art, 1996), pp. 124–46.

6. Jonathan Harris, *Federal Art and National Culture* (Cambridge: Cambridge University Press, 1995), p. 51.

257

# William T. Williams
## (b. 1942)
### Printmaker

Williams's early work reflects Bauhaus theories of design and composition. Broadly painted, geometric displays of dueling colors were his signature. By the 1970s Williams's paintings had lost some of their mechanical look and his focus had changed to an investigation of common symbols in densely worked surfaces. His formal education includes a B.F.A. from Pratt Institute and an M.F.A. from Yale University. Formerly an art teacher at Pratt Institute and the School of the Visual Arts, he has been a professor of art at Brooklyn College, City University of New York for the past twenty-eight years.

257. *Do You Think A is B?*, 1969
Acrylic on canvas
85 1/8 x 61
Fisk University, Nashville, Tennessee, gift of Leonard Bocour

*Do You Think A is B?*, is one of three paintings created in 1969 by William T. Williams indicating his reintroduction of recessional space into his paintings for the purpose of asserting his expressionist tendencies.[1] While Williams's art up to this time had demonstrated his interest in the then prevalent minimal formalist aesthetic, familiarly referred to as minimalism, it also revealed his mounting desire to replace its static and frontal qualities with an infused dynamism.[2] To achieve this, he no longer attempted to keep the elements parallel to the surface plane, but began to allow them to compete with recessional space. The result was that the elements appeared to be simultaneously sharing the same space, and denying such a reading of their location.

Williams's art talent was recognized early in his life, and led to his attendance at the High School of Industrial Arts in Manhattan (now the High School of Art and Design). In 1962 he entered Pratt Institute to study painting. While in his junior year there, he won a summer scholarship to the Skowhegan School of Painting and Sculpture in Maine. During his stay at Skowhegan, he decided to become a professional artist. After graduating from Pratt he earned an M.F.A. degree at Yale University where his mentor was Al Held, who at the time, specialized in minimalist painting.

During the 1960s minimalism dominated American abstract painting, and was made apparent through its practitioners's preference for simple, mechanically drawn forms and shapes that were painted in intense, flat colors. These characteristics were intended to convey the tenets of minimalism, such as the emphasis on reducing visual stimuli to the essentials, the insistence that painting avoid reference to an object or event beyond the painting itself, and the elimination of traces of the artist's brushwork. Besides recessional space, another important feature of Williams's 1969 paintings was the curve, often functioning as concentric circles, in various scales and colors, to enhance the sense of complex movement within the various dimensions. The source for his adoption of the curve was African sculpture, in particular, the abstract representation of the antelope with an arc for the headdresses of the Tyi Wara association of the Bamana in Mali.[3]

The dual-colored diamond dominating the center of *Do You Think A is B?* is energized by the numerous concentric circles overlapping it. The diamond is a frequently recurring motif in Williams's paintings executed between 1968 and 1973, due to his appreciation of its inherent ability to stabilize the composition and to balance the underlying structure.[4] In addition, he was aware of the diamond's historical use in art by portraitists and modernists, as well as its cosmological and spiritual significance within the tradition of African American art of the deep South.[5] Finally, a counter-movement to the curve has been created within the painting by diagonals strategically inclined toward diverse directions.

In contrast to the high-key color that is characteristic of Williams's paintings of the period, much of the color in *Do You Think A is B?* has been toned down to balance with the value of the light gray ground, except for the vivid red and yellow. The artist had recently returned from a trip to France and attributes his more subdued palette in this painting to the influence of an exhibition he saw there of Henri Matisse's art and his understanding of how impressionist painters used gray as a foil for the bright colors of nature.[6]

By the 1970s Williams's expressionist tendencies became more overt as he began to convey his personal and artistic histories in his art. Over the past twenty-eight years, he has created several series of paintings that reveal his success in this endeavor. His memories of places and events, along with his knowledge of non-western cultures continue to inspire his experimentations with innovative techniques, the effects of color, and mark-making systems to prove the viability of the modernist aesthetic.[7]

—Valerie J. Mercer

1. The two other paintings were *Elbert Jackson L.A.M.F., Part II* in the collection of The Museum of Modern Art, and *Sophie Jackson, L.A.M.F.* in the collection of the artist.

2. Valerie J. Mercer, "Behind Closed Doors," *American Visions Magazine 6* (April 1991): 14–19.

3. William T. Williams, interview by Valerie J. Mercer, 8 August 1998.

4. Valerie J. Mercer, *William T. Williams: Works on Paper* (New York: The Studio Museum in Harlem, 1992), p. 6.

5. Ibid.

6. William T. Williams, interview by Valerie J. Mercer, 8 August 1998.

7. Valerie J. Mercer, *William T. Williams: Fourteen Paintings* (Montclair, New Jersey: The Montclair Art Museum, 1992).

# John Wilson
### (b. 1922)
**Draftsman, sculptor, printmaker**

Impressed with Mexican muralists and frescoes documenting struggles of poverty and despair, Wilson made drawings and prints of similar United States themes— racism and oppression of black people. Later Wilson created sculptural pieces signifying lyricism and hope. The power of African and Asian sculpture influenced his subsequent art work as he moved from two-dimensional to three-dimensional pieces. Wilson created a series of drawings based on Richard Wright's poignant short stories. He is known for his sculpted bronze memorial to Martin Luther King, Jr., created for the United States Capitol. Wilson studied at the School of the Museum of Fine Arts, Boston, Tufts University, and the Fernand Léger School of Paris.

258. *Negro Woman*, 1952
Oil on fiberboard
22 x 18½
Best Portrait/Figure Award, Atlanta University Art Annual, 1955. Collection of Clark Atlanta University Art Galleries

# Thomas Waterman Wood
### (1823–1903)
**Painter, etcher**

Portraitist, etcher, and revered art teacher, Wood's art celebrated the social and economic realities of the average American in the 1850s. He achieved both "likeness" and a genre quality in his portraits; skills he aquired studying in the studio of Chester Harding and at the Dusseldorf School.

258

259

259. *Charles Wilson Fleetwood Jr.*, 1858
Oil on canvas
24 x 16
Collection of Howard University Gallery
of Art, gift of Dr. Annette Hawkins Eaton,
1954.1

Portraitist, etcher, and revered art school
administrator during the Gilded Age of
American painting (1870–1900), Thomas
Waterman Wood, became a major factor
during the anthesis of American art
through his descriptive recordings of
late-nineteenth-century, middle-class life.
These contributions are evident in nearly
every stage of his career, paralleling historic events in American art, and bringing
it from under the followings and shadows
of European styles and schools. His works
celebrated the morals, values, social conditions, and realities of the average American by exploring and exhibiting themes of
common everyday life. He was known for
his meticulous study and detail in object
shape and placement, and by defining
varied textures with an uncanny ability to
render the inherent differences in subject
materials. His precise and exacting detail
and keen insight to character studies,
enabled his portraiture to achieve both a
"likeness" and a genre quality as illustrated in the portrait of Charles Wilson
Fleetwood, Jr. The son of a cabinetmaker,
Thomas Waterman Wood was apprenticed
after elementary school in his father's
shop. In addition to making drawings for
furniture orders, he taught himself free-
hand drawing through the art-instruction
booklets of John Burnet. Upon learning of
his son's natural gift, Wood's father sent
him to Boston to live with an uncle, where
he studied in the studio of the celebrated
portrait painter Chester Harding in 1846.
He returned home and made his living
doing portraits and signs for local residents.
After his marriage to Minerva Robinson
in 1850, they moved to New York where
he opened a "figure"painting studio. He
received commissions from prominent
business and congressional people in
Washington, D.C., Baltimore, and Canada,
commanding sitting fees up to $200.1

It was in 1858 that he gravitated
toward genre-type portraiture in Baltimore,
Maryland, portraying many free Negroes
as single-figure images. At that time
Maryland had the largest number of "free
persons of color" and "Negro household-
ers," 84,000; many of them living in the
city.2 John C. Brune (1814–1864), Wood's
chief patron, commissioned him in 1858
to do several paintings with Negroes as
subjects, which included *Charles Wilson
Fleetwood Jr.*, *Market Woman*, *Hindoo John*
and *Old Moses*, *The Baltimore News-Vendor*

which were exhibited at the National
Academy of Design bringing him national
acclaim. All four were sold that year with
the Fleetwood portrait accounting for $75
of the $260 sale.3 Of the nineteen paint-
ings commissioned, many were portraits
of his family, including the domestic staff
of which the subject of this essay was the
senior member. According to the subject's
granddaughter, Edith Fleetwood, Charles
Fleetwood was the "Chief Steward" of the
Brune household.

Wood's hallmarks of a successful
genre work are exemplified in his use
of gesture—the act of filling the glasses,
while the bowing pose of the subject
indicates that a "good evening" has been
offered. The color composition of the
murky background of greys and greens
creates an unclutteredness that highlights
the subject's face, which is further enhanced by the three-centered style arched
frame, which accentuates the subject's
authority in his own working environment.
A rhythmical flow to the composition is
achieved by the pouring action of the large
ewer-shaped cruet, which simultaneously
serves six glasses on a silver salver as the
subject greets the viewer. Completing the
composition is the detailed elegancy of
the cassoulette-style corner oil lamp sur-
mounting the fluted marble pedestal that
projects outward to the viewer, while the
flowing drapes and plush, flowered carpet
create a warm and welcoming interior.

This is heightened by the well-
groomed subject's elegant evening livery,
replete with fluted white tie, vest, gloves,
and gold pocket watch. Indeed, what we
see here is not a mere portrayal of a common butler, batman or footman, but an
amazing image of a secure, free, and most
importantly, *literate* man of color who has
worked very hard to establish his status
and is proud of it. Viewers have remarked
that he resembles someone they know,
perhaps it is because his direct, engaging
smile makes his gestured greeting almost
audible. Charles Fleetwood was born a
free Negro in Baltimore on September 12,
1812 and he died September 29, 1884. In
1842–46 he was listed in the Baltimore
City Directories as a "bay trader," "barber
of hair," "waiter," "confidential servant,"
and as a "Negro Householder." His
son, Sergeant-Major Christian Abraham
Fleetwood, was a Civil War Congressional
Medal of Honor recipient as a "standard
bearer" at the Battle of Chapin's Farm,
Virginia.4

Following his Brune commissions, Thomas Waterman Wood's first recorded venture into genre painting brought him instant acclaim from the public and his fellow artists. Upon returning from Europe, that was a combination of the Grand Tour and study at the Dusseldorf School, he moved to Nashville, Tennessee, producing *Cornfield* in 1861. This was followed by his *War Episodes* in 1866 which was a triad series based on a crippled Louisville Negro Civil War veteran's destitute condition, and whose features bear a striking resemblance to Charles Fleetwood's. Not only was he acclaimed nationally because of these works, but was elected to the National Academy of Design with future works selling for as much as $2,000.[5] This marked the beginning of his thirty-year scholarly association with the academy, the Century Club, the New York Etching Club, and the American Watercolor Society.[6]

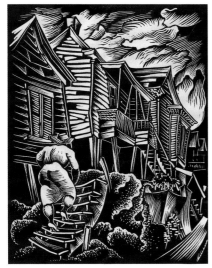

264

260

Although his energies were spent administering to the academy and creating portraits of prominent New Yorkers, he still produced *racial* masterpieces such as: *The Serving Maid* and *His First Vote* (1868), *Crossing the Ferry* (1878), and *The Faithful Nurse* (1893). With the untimely death of his wife in 1889, Wood turned his full energies to the school resulting in his election as president in 1891. His greatest achievement was to bring the academy into the twentieth century addressing such things as: student unrest concerning art supplies, tuition, exhibit prizes, usurpment practices by foreign-owned New York galleries, sales at the annual shows, admission of women to the life drawing classes with nude male models, membership integrity, (which became an issue critical for the "Americanization" of American artists), and securing funds for a new building in 1899.[7] Thomas Waterman Wood had the distinct honor of creating his own art museum while still teaching, painting, and collecting. In 1895 he donated forty-two of his paintings to the city of Montpelier, creating the initial collection for today's Wood Art Gallery. He spent his retirement cataloguing his remarkable collection of paintings and by the time of his death, he had inventoried over 1,500 canvases and well over 1,000 portraits.

At the turn of the century all of the Academy goals had been met and the very essence of American genre painting had survived the challenges of time and taste. American genre painting shed the sentiments of the past and established a distinct American style in the international arena, as evidenced by the controversial but highly acclaimed Armory Show of 1913. This was reinforced by the works of Norman Rockwell who, since 1913, revived and strengthened the genre painting style. Although he considered himself an illustrator, he was, in fact, a genre easel painter. His works, like Thomas Waterman Wood's, vividly told stories about distinctly American things, making them so familiar that they were no longer noticed, but became chroniclers of their own times.[8]

—Scott W. Baker

1. Leslie A. Hasker and J. Kevin Graffagnino, "Thomas Waterman Wood and the Image of Nineteenth-Century America," *Antiques Magazine* (November 1980), pp. 1032–38. The 1866 *War Episodes* were individually titled: *The Contraband, The Volunteer,* and *The Veteran* illustrated on p. 1037.

2. Lesley C. Wright, "Men Making Meaning in Nineteenth-Century American Genre Painting, 1869–1900" (Ph.D. diss., Stanford University, 1993), p. 164. This is an extensive study on Wood, Seymor Guy, and John George Brown.

3. Paul W. Worman, who is currently gathering material for a catalogue on Wood for the Wood Art Gallery, sent me written information on Brune Fleetwood for this essay.

4. Charles Wilson Fleetwood, Jr., to Christian Abraham Fleetwood, 17 June 1867. Letter to his son describing a back injury, and an inquiry about his army maneuvers with the 4th United States Colored Troops. Additionally, there is a photograph of Charles Fleetwood at the age of 72. See the Christian Fleetwood Papers, Library of Congress.

5. Maria Naylor, *The National Academy of Design Exhibition Record 1861–1900* (New York: Kennedy Galleries, 1973). Information on the fifty-seven paintings exhibited by Wood, from 1861 to 1899. It also includes sale prices with the names and addresses of all buyers and owners.

6. William C. Lipke, *Thomas Waterman Wood, P.N.A. 1823–1903* (Montpelier: Wood Art Gallery, 1972). Definitive work on Wood including boyhood years, artistic development, marriage, travels, and a detailed study on his national prominence.

7. Eliot Clark, N.A., *History of the National Academy of Design* (New York: Columbia University Press, 1954).

8. Laurie N. Moffatt, *Norman Rockwell: A Definitive Catalogue* (Stockbridge: The Norman Rockwell Museum, 1988).

# Hale Aspacio Woodruff
## (1900–1980)
### Painter, muralist, printmaker

Woodruff studied at the John Herron Art Institute in Indiana and years later, independently with Diego Rivera in Mexico City. His 1938 commission—for the *Amistad Murals* for the Savery Library at Talladega College—is one of his best known works. He also painted a series of murals entitled *Art of the Negro* (1950–51) for Atlanta University's Trevor Arnett Library. In the 1930s he painted realistic scenes of life in the rural black South portraying the poverty and the few joys of life in a depressed and segregated society, but in the 1950s abstraction and free invention replaced social commentary in his work. Toward the end of his tenure at Atlanta University (1931–45), Woodruff initiated the Atlanta University annual art exhibitions which provided African American artists nationwide with exhibition opportunities and patronage.

260. *Country Church*, c. 1935
Woodcut on paper
7½ x 10
Collection of Clark Atlanta University Art Galleries, gift of Judge Irvin C. Mollison

261. *Erosion in Mississippi*, n.d.
Pastel on wove paper
17¾ x 22¼
Collection of North Carolina Central University Art Museum, gift of Mrs Alfonso Elder

262. *Galaxy*, c. 1959
Oil on canvas
47½ x 35½
Collection of Clark Atlanta University Art Galleries, gift of Chauncey and Catherine Waddell

263. *Georgia Woodland*, c. 1934
Linocut on wove paper
12¾ x 8½ (image); 17¾ x 12 (sheet)
Fisk University, Nashville, Tennessee, 1991.527

264. *Returning Home*, c. 1935–39
Linocut on wove paper
Edition 3/10
10 x 8 (image); 11¹³⁄₁₆ x 8⅞ (sheet)
Collection of Howard University Gallery of Art

263

# Photo Credits

Photographs of works of art reproduced in this volume have been provided in some cases by the owners or custodians of the works identified in the captions and checklist. Individual works of art appearing herein may be protected by copyright in the United States of American or elsewhere, and may thus not be reproduced in any form without the permission of the copyright owners. The following and/or other photograph credits appear at the request of the artist's representatives and/or the owners of the individual works.

©Romare Bearden Foundation/Licensed by VAGA, New York, NY: pp. 30, 82, 176

©Elizabeth Catlett/Licensed by VAGA, New York, NY: pp. 144–45, 181–82

©Clark Atlanta University Art Galleries: pp. 18, 101, 122, 138, 144 left, 174, 188 checklist 68

Christopher Ethelbert Cheyne: p. 22

©Fisk University, Nashville, Tennessee: pp. 51, 202

Frank Graham: pp. 73, 76, 84, 87 checklist 66, 161, 163, 222 checklist 200

Jarvis Grant: p. 32

©George Grosz/Licensed by VAGA, New York, NY: p. 198

©Hampton University Museum: pp. 23, 64, 80, 170–71, 173, 178 checklist 39, 189 checklist 74, 209

Greg Heins, Boston: pp. 15–17, 35, 42, 48–50, 53, 57 right, 62, 70, 78–81, 85–86, 87 checklist 60, 90–91, 96–97, 99, 102, 104, 107, 109, 113, 115–16, 124, 127, 129–131, 142, 159–160, 169, 175, 177, 180–81, 184–87, 188 checklist 73, 190, 191 checklist 80, 192, 193 checklist 86, 195, 197 checklist 94, 198–201, 203–206, 209, 212 checklist nos. 164 and 65, 207, 213 checklist 165, 214 checklist nos. 167 and 68, 215 checklist 184, 216, 217 checklist 189, 219, 221 checklist nos. 196 and 197, 222 checklist 202, 223, 224 checklist 228, 225 checklist 217, 226, 227 checklist nos. 235 and 237, 228–30, 232 checklist nos. 233 and 239, 238 checklist 264, back cover

©Howard University Gallery of Art: pp. 24–25, 106, 207

©Timothy Hursley: p. 19

BJ Larson: p. 37

Barbara Lemmen: p. 14

©North Carolina Central University Art Museum: p. 27

Quarles Studio: p. 29

Jock Reynolds: pp. 40–41, 52, 54, 58, 61, 71, 74

Vando L. Rogers, Jr.: pp. 20–21

Ezra Stoller: p. 128

Tuskegee University: p. 112

Williamstown Art Conservation Center: front cover, frontispiece, pp. 30, 43–44, 46, 55–56, 57 left, 59–60, 63–67, 69, 72, 75, 77, 82–84, 88–89, 92–95, 98, 100, 106–7, 117–19, 125–26, 133–35, 141, 144 right, 145, 146–158, 166, 168, 172, 173, 176, 178 checklist 42, 179, 186, 189, 191 checklist 78, 193 checklist 87, 194, 196, 197 checklist nos. 92 and 93, 208, 210–11, 213 checklist 166, 214 checklist 173, 215 checklist 183, 218, 220, 221 checklist 195, 222 checklist 199, 224 checklist nos. 209 and 210, 225 checklist 215, 227 checklist 231, 231, 234–37, 238 checklist 260

©John Wilson/Licensed by VAGA, New York, NY: pp. 117, 236

John Woolf: pp. 48–49, 116, 230